Development Models in Muslim Contexts

EXPLORING MUSLIM CONTEXTS

Series Editor: Abdou Filali-Ansary

Books in the series include

Development Models in Muslim Contexts:
Chinese, "Islamic" and Neo-Liberal Alternatives
Edited by Robert Springborg

The Challenge of Pluralism:
Paradigms from Muslim Contexts
Edited by Abdou Filali-Ansary
and Sikeena Karmali Ahmed

The Possibility of Pluralism
Edited by A. C. Grayling

DEVELOPMENT MODELS IN MUSLIM CONTEXTS

Chinese, "Islamic" and Neo-Liberal Alternatives

EDITED BY ROBERT SPRINGBORG

EDINBURGH UNIVERSITY PRESS
IN ASSOCIATION WITH

THE AGA KHAN UNIVERSITY
INSTITUTE FOR THE STUDY OF MUSLIM CIVILISATIONS

The opinions expressed in this volume are those of
the authors and do not necessarily reflect those of
the Aga Khan University, Institute for the Study of
Muslim Civilisations.

© Editorial matter and organisation Robert
Springborg, 2009
© The chapters, their several authors, 2009

Edinburgh University Press Ltd
22 George Square, Edinburgh
www.euppublishing.com

Typeset in Goudy Oldstyle by
Koinonia, Manchester and
printed and bound in Great Britain by
CPI Antony Rowe, Chippenham and Eastbourne

A CIP record for this book is available
from the British Library

ISBN 978 0 7486 3968 7 (hardback)

The right of the contributors to be identified
as authors of this work has been asserted in
accordance with the Copyright, Designs and
Patents Act 1988.

Contents

Contents

Introduction:
The Lure of Development Models

ROBERT SPRINGBORG

The appeal and impact of development models track broader movements in world politics. For more than half a century the United States and the Soviet Union provided the political economy models of choice for much of the developing world. As the colonial era was brought to a close by rising nationalism and the Cold War intensified, the superpowers became locked into a competition to demonstrate the superiority of their own political economy, and hence its suitability for export. America's democratic capitalist model was packaged as the "First New Nation", and a wealthy one at that. Having risen in revolt against its British masters, having established the world's first constitutional republic, having welcomed millions of migrants to its shores, having not become a colonial power in quite the same mould as the European Great Powers, and having the world's dominant economy and richest citizens, the United States presented its history and contemporary achievements to make it as appealing as possible to the Third World. So, too, did the Soviet Union, whose communist model of planned, egalitarian development under a vanguard political party enjoyed widespread support at the levels of both state and street in much of the Third World. However, in the end, Washington triumphed and the Soviet model was relegated – remarkably quickly, in fact, – to the dustbins of history.

Although much of the bloom had faded from the American rose during the Cold War, the commencement of a new era of globalisation in the late 1980s rejuvenated America's appeal as a model in much of the Third World. The "Washington Consensus" formulated in the early 1990s in the form of World Bank economist John Williamson's ten commandments for economic reform, was established in the minds of many elites in developing countries as being the right and true path to development.[1]

Widespread adoption of the Washington Consensus may have contributed to increased global economic growth rates since the late 1990s. Its appeal, and that of its country of origin have not, however, been commensurate with its apparent economic success. The downsides of neo-liberalism, especially increased inequality, are only part of the story. For incumbent political elites, the inherent logic of free markets requiring free polities is disquieting. For the politically marginal, the further concentration of wealth and power associated with implementation of the Washington Consensus discredits the model and its progenitor.

Even if the Washington Consensus had been an unmixed economic blessing, it would nevertheless have been an uphill struggle to convince even those adopting the Consensus of the broader relevance and appeal of the American model. The Consensus itself may seem to Westerners to be culturally neutral, as it is an economic prescription. Nevertheless, many in the developing world, and especially Muslims, do not perceive it as such. They view it as emblematic of the secular, amoral Western approach to economic matters; an approach that ignores the question of ethics, which, in their view, should be an inherent aspect of any economic system and, indeed, according to some Muslims, lies at the heart of their preferred "Islamic economics". For many non-Muslims, the alleged cultural ethno-centrism of the model is less of a deterrent than the sheer fact that it is seen to be an American model when America embodies so much of what is seen to be antithetical to their own interests.

The purveyor of the American model for most of the first decade of the twenty-first century, the Bush administration, weakened rather than strengthened its appeal. Its Middle East policies imposed a particularly heavy cost on American popularity. The occupation of Iraq, one-sided support for Israel, stop–start democratisation–promotion, and various other blunders, all underscored Washington's insensitivity and incompetence. And while it misbehaved politically, the Bush administration also presided over a steep decline in US economic performance and, in the autumn of 2008, a credit crisis that shook the global financial system. As a result, the moral, material and political foundations of the appeal of the American model have eroded whatever economic success adherents of the Washington Consensus can claim for it.

Paradoxically, the globalisation that both resulted from and contributed to the spread of the Washington Consensus also undermined its hegemony in the developing world. Enhanced global communications and interactions have stimulated increased awareness. The existence of alternative models of governance and development has become widely known, even if their exact natures remain somewhat obscure to potential emulators. Latin America's current wave of populism, for example, is probably as much written about and discussed in, say, South Asia, as is the European Union's model of continental economic and political integration, East Asia's developmental state approach, or the Muslim world's increasing engagement with Islamic finance.

Moreover, it is known at least at a subliminal level that each of these potential political economy models defines governance and development differently, and evaluates the relationship between them idiosyncratically. The Washington Consensus explicitly emphasises neo-liberal economic reforms, along with implicit support for political liberalisation, if not democratisation. The populism in vogue in Latin America espouses a quasi-autarkic model for national economies, coupled with mass mobilisation and de-institutionalisation of governance. The Asian developmental state approach emphasises the need to build state governance capacities and to reinforce the centrality of the state within the economy and polity. To the extent that one can speak about what some wish to call a Muslim moral economy model based on an emerging financial sector that aspires to be Islamic, it prioritises individual behaviour guided by what are held to be "Islamic" precepts as interpreted by the self-appointed "rightly guided", for whom economics and politics are one.

Globalisation has thus witnessed the proliferation of models for governance and development, and spread awareness about them. It has also stimulated the market for these models, as experts, articulate publics and decision-makers shop around for alternative solutions to what are increasingly perceived as common problems. The very fact that the acronym BRIC (Brazil, Russia, India and China) has come into global parlance as a term that signifies rapid economic growth and, implicitly, the emergence of a new global economic order, is a signal that the era for one hegemonic model of governance and development, to the extent there ever was one, has come to a close.

However, the choice of which development model should prevail in any given setting is not a benign, academic matter, decided by experts who have dispassionately and disinterestedly evaluated all the alternatives. This choice is the result of a political contest between competitive local political actors and the progenitors of the models themselves.

Possibly the most interesting such competition at present, both because of the profound difference of the two models and because its champions are the respective leaders of the developed and developing world, pits America's neo-liberal approach against China's version of the developmental state, or, as one observer has dubbed the competition, the Washington-versus-Beijing Consensus.[2] As the development gap between the two closes at remarkable speed, China is rapidly accumulating the material foundations upon which to project soft power, presumably including the appeal of the Beijing Consensus, whose lustre is enhanced by the very fact of its profound difference from the Washington Consensus.

As America becomes less attractive in the eyes of the world, China's popularity is growing. Awareness of the world's largest country has increased due to rapidly growing economic relations, based on the movement of hydrocarbons, goods, capital and, increasingly, people. Chinese trade and investment have had appreciable economic impacts on developing economies in Asia, the Middle East, Africa and Latin America. Most of these impacts are viewed favourably in these countries, although a backlash against China's dogged commercial pursuit of raw materials, and its "dumping" of consumer goods, is also developing.

The appeal of the Beijing Consensus is not just based on economic power. It enjoys comparative advantage vis-à-vis its Washington competitor precisely because it can be used as a counterbalance to American and Western influence more generally, including that of international financial institutions. That China has not been an imperial or neo-imperial power, at least outside of East Asia, reinforces that appeal. So, too, in governmental circles at least, does Beijing's elevation of respect for sovereignty and territorial integrity over human rights, democratisation, or other transnational, "do-gooding" concerns. China's adroit diplomacy in even such tricky areas as relations with Iran, especially when compared to Washington's heavy-handedness, underscores its appearance of judiciousness, non-interference and respect for other nations and traditions. Indeed, as Ramo argues, part of the appeal of the Beijing Consensus is that it valorises the contribution of indigenous cultures to development, rather than insisting, as the Washington Consensus can be interpreted to be doing, that "native" culture must be supplanted by a homogenised, globalised and, in effect, Westernised one, if development is to be achieved.

China's own accomplishments are also strong selling points for the Beijing Consensus. Rapid economic growth is obvious and so, too, is the headlong, modernist physical transformation of coastal China. Home-grown billionaires are sprouting up, and wealth is also trickling down, albeit not universally or evenly.[3] Although some public services are struggling to keep pace with the rush to develop, by and large the delivery of public services is equal to and in some vital areas, such as education, superior to that found in analogous developing economies. Since 1989 hardly a ripple has disturbed the national political surface calm, despite considerable local turbulence.

Intrinsic features of the Beijing Consensus, to the extent they are known in potential emulating countries, are also attractive. Good governance and democratisation are clearly separable concepts in the Chinese model. This may be its most endearing feature to authoritarian emulators. The former can be achieved through a state-fostered elite – in China's case the Communist Party (CCP) – while the latter is deemed, officially at least, to be irrelevant. While single party-regimes are increasingly uncommon, authoritarian ones in need of improved service-delivery to shore up their acceptance, if not their legitimacy, can imagine ready substitutes for the CCP, such as, for example, the ruling

National Democratic Party in Egypt. Beijing's orchestrated, top-down anti-corruption drive is precisely how most autocrats prefer to deal with this nagging issue, as opposed to the alternative method of democratic accountability. So while ruling elites see that the Chinese model enables them to have their cake and eat it too, in that they do not need to surrender power to achieve rapid development with at least somewhat improved governance, their populace is attracted by the promised outputs of the model. When the choice is structured as bread versus democracy, it is the former that has greater appeal in most lower-, lower-middle and middle-income developing countries.

In summary, increasingly we live not only in a multi-polar world, but in a multi-model one as well. The bi-polar, bi-model era of the Cold War has passed, as has the "American moment" which immediately ensued. The Washington Consensus is no longer in vogue, even in the capital from which it takes its name, as Western and even neo-liberal development theoreticians have come to see its weaknesses and search elsewhere for means to repair the model or replace it altogether.[4] Simultaneously the overwhelming success of Asian developmental states, especially of China, and the rapid economic ascents of Brazil, Russia, India and a host of other developing countries, many of which are disdainful of the Washington Consensus, have not only undermined that model's centrality and appeal, but have put tempting new alternatives before potential emulators.

Of these new models, the Chinese one is the most prominent because of the magnitude of the country and its success, coupled with its growing capacity to project itself and its governance model before the world. It is by no means the only alternative to the Washington Consensus, however, so it would be misleading to ignore others in an overview of choices confronting development champions, wherever in the world they happen to be. Moreover, the Beijing Consensus is a more amorphous concept than its Washington predecessor, as a quick read of Ramo's piece in which he coins the term suggests. It has not been boiled down to the banker's checklist of ten commandments that John Williamson managed to do for the neo-liberal model.

Indeed, it is unlikely it ever will be, because while the Chinese political economy may not be opaque, it is certainly translucent in many areas, and a far cry from the comparative transparency of Western political and economic systems. The progenitors of the Beijing Consensus might want to extol its virtues to others, but that task will become increasingly difficult unless they remove the veils that obscure its functioning. An even greater impediment to its generalisation, though, is its lack of institutionalisation in China itself. Unlike the Washington Consensus, which embodies the practice of neo-liberal orthodoxy that has become firmly established throughout the Organisation for Economic Co-operation and Development, the Beijing Consensus remains vague because China itself is not politically static. Serious questions surround its future trajectory. Most important of all, can the 93 million-strong CCP continue to occupy all of the country's political space, or will growing calls for governmental decentralisation, improvement of the legal-judicial system and greater freedom for the media ultimately undermine its political monopoly? Do intermittent rural protests presage more general discontent, or are they the dying gasps of a peasantry in transition to proletariats? Even China's relationship to the global order is open to question. Is it seeking to integrate into the Western-created architecture, including international financial institutions, or does it hold out the hope of creating a parallel global rival? In sum, not only is there considerable ambiguity about China's existing political economy, but its future is shrouded in mystery. Given these uncertainties, the will and capacity to project a model are doubtful, as is the ultimate success of such a venture; for the progenitor of the model is itself undergoing profound change and hence is unstable.

Taking stock of the attraction and utility of development models, with particular attention to the Chinese variant, is an important intellectual undertaking. As alternatives to the Washington Consensus proliferate, with the Chinese one apparently in the lead, it is important to know more about them and their prospects for success outside their countries of origin. Competition between development models is not just a struggle between ideas; it also reflects competition for economic and political power. The models themselves may well play a major role in shaping the objective outcomes of that competition.

The assessment of development models in this book will focus on Muslim-majority countries, which, despite their diversity, share some common characteristics, including what may be interpreted as the prevalent domination of authoritarian governments. Most of them are also pulled towards various development models, including the more or less home-grown one based on the revitalisation of medieval Islamic financial practices. In the past decade or so, the appeal to Muslim decision-makers of alternatives to the Washington Consensus, especially those arising in the developing world, has grown apace. The predominance of authoritarian governments, especially in the Muslim heartlands of West Asia and North Africa, has contributed to the particular appeal of the Chinese model, the attraction of which has been further underpinned by burgeoning trade and investment between most Muslim-majority countries and China.

In order to gain perspective on the relative attractiveness and impacts of development models in the Muslim world, and especially of the Chinese model, it is appropriate to compare receptivity to that model in other regions. To this end, the book includes separate chapters on the Chinese model in Latin America and Africa, both of which indicate that concerns particular to those regions shape perceptions of the model and the likelihood of it playing a significant role in the formulation and implementation of development strategies. By doing so they highlight the particularities of Muslim states where, unlike in Latin America, the authoritarianism of China is less of a concern and there is, as yet, less apprehension than there is in Africa about the "plundering" of raw materials.

The book does not take up discussion of the role of the Washington Consensus in the Muslim world precisely because that subject has already been extensively covered, not least by the World Bank itself in its voluminous publications on the Middle East and North Africa.[5] This volume does consider the principal indigenous competitor, which is that of putative allegedly Islamic models of development, and addresses the vital issue of the importance of governance to development, whatever the model structuring that development. The Washington Consensus emphasises that good governance is vital to rapid, effective development. Paradoxically, it might be argued that the authoritarian Chinese Communist Party provides at least some of the components of good governance, such as accountability, that the Washington Consensus at least by implication associates with representative government. Whatever the structural means for providing governance, however, the issue remains as to how central it is to economic development. If it is indeed of vital significance, then any model that fails to deliver it will ultimately fail in other regards as well. If it is more marginal, then weaknesses of governance may not have fatal consequences for economic development.

The book commences with an investigation of the Chinese model itself, organised around several key questions. How was the transition engineered from a communist system focused on import-substitution to an export-led development strategy under a tutelary state? What is the nature of existing relations between the economy and polity? What roles have been played by the Communist Party and specific social forces and political actors? What long-term political impacts are phenomenal economic growth rates likely to have? What plans do the Chinese have to expand trade and investment in the countries and regions under consideration? Will the Chinese seek to make the adoption of their model by developing countries a foreign policy objective?

The role of the Chinese model in Latin America and Africa is then evaluated in terms of both the ideational and material bases for its existing and potential attractiveness. How much is known about the model? To what extent do incumbent elites have a conscious strategy to learn more about it and to adopt it? Which political actors within states considering the model support and oppose it? What has been the pattern of trade, investment and human movement between China and the regions and countries in question? What linkages exist, and are likely to evolve, between this movement and political influence, including implementation of the Chinese model? The "fit" between the Chinese model, Latin American and African economies can then be assessed by asking if these adopters possess the key elements, governmental and non-governmental, human and physical, that have contributed to the success of the Chinese model. If they don't, can they be developed with sufficient haste and thoroughness to enable the model to function in new settings? What are the likely key obstacles to successful implementation?

The second part of the book is devoted to Muslim-majority countries and the role played within them of the Chinese as opposed to other (including what are assumed to be Islamic) models of development. The initial chapter investigates the same sets of questions listed above with regard to the Arab world as a whole. The subsequent chapter does so with regard to Algeria. It also discusses the appeal and degree of adoption in Algeria, and in North Africa more generally, of "Islamic" financial models. The next two chapters provide a comparative evaluation of putative models with Islamist leanings as they have developed under two Islamist governments – Iran and Turkey – followed by an assessment of the lack of success of Malaysia's fledgling developmental state and of Pakistan's quasi-democratic model of development.

The book's final part is devoted to the centrality of governance to development, whatever the model guiding it. The first chapter in this section argues that governance is key to economic growth, illustrating the argument with the case of Pakistan. The second chapter then contests the relationship, arguing that the Washington Consensus has stretched the concept of governance too far, overstated its importance for development and failed to appreciate that it is more likely to be the product than the cause of economic development.

The conclusion focuses on the likely choices of Muslim-majority countries from among the development models available to them. It addresses different perspectives, including the impact of their appreciation of the importance of governance, within and between countries and regions, as well as the implications from evidence provided about Latin America and Africa. The book, in sum, seeks to address in a comparative framework how and in what ways alternative models of development, and especially the Chinese one, are likely to affect choices about development strategies in the Muslim world.

Notes

1. John Williamson (ed.), *Latin American Adjustment: How Much has Happened?* Washington, DC: Institute for International Economics, 1990, see especially Chapter 2. The ten commandments are fiscal discipline, proper public expenditure priorities, tax reform to broaden the revenue base, liberalising interest rates, a market-determined exchange rate, trade liberalisation, FDI liberalisation, privatisation, deregulation and property rights.
2. Joshua Cooper Ramo, *The Beijing Consensus*, London: The Foreign Policy Centre, May 2004.
3. According to a 2007 World Bank report, the number of poor in China fell by almost

407 million from 1990 to 2004, more than 150 million more than had previously been thought to have been the case. "China is Poorer than we thought, but no less successful in the fight against poverty", World Bank Working Paper 4621, cited in *The Economist*, 22 May 2008.

4. The author of the original Washington Consensus is among those who have worked on refining it. See Pedro-Pablo Kuczynski and John Williamson, *After the Washington Consensus: Restarting Growth and Reform in Latin America*, Washington, DC: Institute for International Economics, 2003. See also the chapter by Clement Henry in this volume.

5. See, for example, *Better Governance for Development in the Middle East and North Africa* and *Claiming the Future: Choosing Prosperity for the Middle East and North Africa*, Washington, DC: World Bank, 2003 and 1995, respectively.

PART ONE

The Chinese Model and its Global Reception

CHAPTER 1

A China Model or Just a Broken Mould?

WILLIAM HURST

INTRODUCTION: A NEW EAST ASIAN MODEL?

It has become fashionable in recent years to argue that China is following a "unique model" of rapid development – one that eschews democratisation or meaningful political opening while racking up world-beating economic growth rates. Leaving aside obvious parallels with the debates between Samuel Huntington and the modernisation theorists of the 1960s, it is useful to review the more recent East Asian developmental state paradigm before assessing specific arguments about the China model. Ideas about alternative Asian development paths that do not hue closely to European or North American experience have long enjoyed a ready audience in academic and policy circles. The current talk of a "China model" largely mirrors the discussion of Japan, Korea, and Taiwan twenty years ago.

During the 1980s, scholars such as Chalmers Johnson and Alice Amsden popularised the concept of an "East Asian model".[1] These early proponents contended that states such as Japan and South Korea exercised guidance and discipline over private firms organised into powerful industrial groups through a set of institutional arrangements that these authors came to characterise as the "developmental state". By investing heavily both in infrastructure and education, as well as protecting sunset and sunrise sectors, the state provided the foundation for economic development alongside window guidance on the precise contours of trade and growth.

Later observers, such as Robert Wade and Stephen Haggard, advanced similar arguments regarding the cases of Taiwan, Hong Kong and Singapore.[2] Eventually, the World Bank codified what had become the conventional wisdom, placing its imprimatur on an official explanation of the "East Asian miracle" and taking in three more Southeast Asian cases – Indonesia, Malaysia and Thailand. Specifically, successful late industrialisers were seen as doing ten things well:

- adhering to some principle of "shared growth" (that is, benefiting a wide segment of society)
- providing stable regulatory institutions to promote business
- relying on deliberative policy co-ordination councils
- investing heavily in human capital development (especially primary and secondary education)
- providing incentives for savings and investment
- ensuring the flexibility of labour markets
- selectively intervening in capital markets
- aggressively importing foreign technology
- promoting and protecting specific industries
- mixing market-friendly and interventionist policies to boost exports[3]

Each of the ten desiderata was thought to bring specific benefits. For example, the provision of stable regulatory institutions and continued flexibility of labour markets were each believed to help promote the development of new domestic firms and even an entrepreneurial sector. The package of policies was also thought to work best when all ten goals could be achieved at once, since many were mutually supportive of one another – human capital investment was necessary to use and improve upon imported foreign technology, for example, just as well-functioning policy co-ordination councils were needed to direct effective intervention in capital markets. By creating and exploiting the "virtuous circles" believed to sprout from these policy combinations, states could break out of the trap of underdevelopment and into the community of advanced industrial nations.

Often left aside, however, was any explicit mention of the authoritarian nature of the states involved. During their periods of high growth, Japan was ruled by a dominant Liberal Democratic Party under a non-competitive electoral system; Malaysia and Singapore were governed by soft authoritarian (or "electoral authoritarian") governments headed respectively by the People's Action Party (PAP) and the United Malay National Organization (UMNO); Taiwan, Korea, and Indonesia were military regimes; and Thailand toggled between civilian authoritarian rulers (elected and non-elected) and military juntas, all reliant for legitimacy and ideological direction upon a powerful monarchy. Backers of the East Asian model frequently spoke of the need for state autonomy or bureaucratic independence. This was necessary to prevent societal interests from hijacking powerful states and steering them off course in their development and investment policies. Such independence, however, does not seem to have been particularly compatible with democratic pluralism. Strong, non-democratic states pursued the mix of policies identified by the World Bank and successfully piloted their societies to very high rates of economic growth, reductions in social inequality and vastly improving competitive positions in the world market.

However, over the last ten or fifteen years, the world has gradually begun to hear a lot less about the East Asian model. This undoubtedly, is related to Japan's economic slowdown that began around 1992, and to the debacle of the Asian financial crisis that unfolded in 1997–1998, engulfing nearly all the other economies that had been held up as paragons of the model's virtues. Nevertheless, like a phoenix from the ashes of that crisis, frenzied talk of a China model began even before markets in Seoul or Bangkok had returned to normal. Such talk was based, in part, on China's steady resolve not to devalue its currency during the crisis, but it also betrayed a deeper conviction among some that China was indeed a new regional economic and political power with a distinctive development model ready for export.

What is the China Model?

First, it is worth mentioning that few, if any, analysts or policy-makers in China would agree that there is such a thing as a "Chinese model" of economic development. Since 1978, the focus in China has always been on short-term fixes to pressing problems and ad hoc experimentation by necessity, in the interests of finding workable solutions to intractable issues while advancing a broad, if often vague, agenda of economic reform and growth. To the extent that there has been any overriding "model", it has been to abide by Deng Xiaoping's famous dictum of "groping for stones to cross the river" (*mo shitou guo he*) – that is, proceeding cautiously in small increments designed to address immediate needs while avoiding bold leaps or comprehensive policy packages.[4]

Nonetheless, many foreign observers have felt emboldened to ascribe to China that which Chinese advocates and planners have been unable or unwilling to see in themselves. Talk of a new "Beijing Consensus" and a "China model" of development has recently reached fever pitch in many quarters.[5] This writer, for one, is sceptical of the veracity of such arguments. Indeed, most who claim a powerful role for a China model or Beijing Consensus are hard pressed to specify precisely what the contents of such a framework might be. The clearest statement to date ends up retreating to platitudes taken almost verbatim from the platform announced at the 16th Chinese Communist Party Congress in 2002.[6]

I believe it is still possible, though, to pin down what a Chinese model might look like. That is, what features of Chinese policies and institutions have promoted sustained aggregate economic growth in the neighbourhood of 8 per cent to 10 per cent per annum over the past twenty years. I maintain that the China model is basically the East Asian model "plus two". The first additional feature is an explicit rejection of democratisation or pluralist politics as incompatible with the aims of economic growth and state consolidation in the developing world. The second is a very heavy reliance on a special kind of capital flow – foreign direct investment (FDI) – used largely for a special purpose: export production.[7] Rejection of democracy is self-explanatory and directly in line with what was likely always present but often left unspoken in the East Asian developmental experience. Reliance on FDI requires a bit more explanation.

In 2002, China became the world's leading destination for FDI.[8] Ultimately, these capital inflows have allowed the Chinese government to pursue reforms it sees as valuable, staving off those that might be destabilising or painful, all the while building an ever-larger cushion of foreign exchange reserves.[9] This flexibility has proved crucial in allowing China to, for example, retain its dollar peg and avoid devaluation of the Renminbi throughout the East Asian financial crisis, spend lavishly on protecting the last remnants of its ailing state sector and developing the infrastructure of its weakest and poorest regions, and refrain from substantial liberalisation of either its capital account or its market in financial services, to say nothing of political reform. Piloting this course between the Scylla of unbridled globalisation and the Charybdis of ossified autarky in a command economy has never been easy for the captains of any ship of state. But China's leaders have made skilful use of FDI and capital inflows to ease their passage through this treacherous strait.

This ability to rely on a particular type of FDI, while building significant foreign reserves and selectively pursuing reform policies, differentiates China from the earlier model of newly industrialising countries (NICs) in Southeast Asia in three main ways. First, unlike the Southeast Asian NICs, China's capital account has remained heavily restricted and largely insulated from the rapid, often speculative, movement of large amounts of investment into and out of the country. Second, though China has found many niches of specialisation in the manufacture of labour-intensive goods and industrial components, most Chinese component producers and sub-contractors are domestically owned, managed and controlled, unlike in many Southeast Asian contexts where many were owned by foreign investors only too happy to move production to a new locale if conditions in the host country became less than ideal. Third and finally, China, unlike most of the Southeast Asian NICs, has exploited foreign companies to help transfer not just technology but also institutions and governance structures to its moribund, and yet possibly reviving, state-owned enterprises. These three special characteristics of China's use of FDI help protect it from many of the risks Southeast Asian industrialisers faced in the 1980s and 1990s that ultimately led to the financial crisis of 1998. The next section explores these and related differences between Chinese and Southeast Asian models, as well as the more general question of the degree to which other countries might hope to emulate China's success.

HOW EXPORTABLE IS CHINA'S SUCCESS?

FDI of the kind China benefits from is a new kind of capital flow that came into its own during the 1990s era of globalisation. Eichengreen and Fishlow astutely differentiated capital flows between bond finance that dominated in the 1920s, bank lending that became a leading force in the 1960s, and equity investments that overtook all other types of capital flows in the 1990s.[10] But the FDI that has made such an impact on China did not, until very recently, flow principally or even significantly into equity markets. Rather, it came largely in the form of foreign companies establishing production operations in China, frequently through sub-contracting agents based in third countries or some combination of joint-ventures and sub-contractors within China itself.

But how distinct was China's model of FDI inflows from that experienced by Southeast Asian countries in their heyday as spokes of globalised production networks in the early 1990s?[11] These countries exploited newly available niches as component producers in cross-national production networks with hubs in Japan and critical intermediary nodes in South Korea, Hong Kong, and Taiwan. In many ways, China has become integrated into a similar web of production networks, with two important differences: (1) the production networks into which China has been incorporated are not based so heavily in a single country as those that Southeast Asian states so often became part of (very often based firmly in Japan); and (2) the specific type of FDI is different in the ways discussed above. This has offered a hedge against economic downturns in any single core country (as unfolded in Japan in the 1990s), insulating China from the worst follow-on risks that a US recession might bring, for example. It also helped reduce the degree to which globalised production took place in enclaves, walled off from the rest of the domestic economy, but vulnerable to the whims of international capital flows and markets.

But, like Southeast Asia, China's success in attracting its special brand of FDI was predicated on conditions in the international economy that came into being around the mid-1990s and will likely not remain in place for ever. Not only is FDI time-specific, attracting it depends on comparative advantage. States looking to rely on large inflows of FDI related to export production are best equipped to do so if they have reasonably efficient infrastructure and a plentiful supply of low-wage labour. Infrastructure helps convey comparative advantage in attracting FDI, in that firms seeking to export goods must rely on local infrastructure for getting these goods to port and shipped abroad. A large, low-cost labour pool is needed to ensure that the wage savings to firms of producing in the host state outweigh any start-up or shipping costs in addition to risks of disruption or instability. Thus, many states are ill-placed to compete for these kinds of FDI flows either because of insufficiently large labour pools to guarantee low wages or because of deficiencies of infrastructure.

China also benefits because even when it does not have a comparative advantage for FDI, it can often attract investors with the promise of a large domestic market. Whether justified or not, many foreign investors maintain hopes of one day penetrating China's domestic market. Though many tend to overestimate both the size and openness of China's market for foreign goods, the lure of "one billion customers" can help keep companies invested in China even when Vietnam might offer lower wages, India might provide workers with higher skills and better institutions of governance, and a number of other countries might match China's physical infrastructure.

Most other countries, then, could not easily benefit from the same kind of FDI flows as China does. Few are of anywhere near comparable size, and those that are (such as India, Indonesia and Brazil, for instance) usually offer far inferior physical infrastructure and a less reliably cheap and acquiescent pool of low-end labour. It appears likely, therefore, that China can maintain its global lead in attracting this sort of FDI, and in building correspondingly large reserves of foreign exchange, for some time into the future, at least so long as conditions in the international economy remain conducive to this sort of capital flow. In this way, China is likely to outshine the economic development successes of other countries with which it is often compared (especially Brazil, Russia, and India) for at least most of the next decade.

Beyond this, though, how many other countries can fulfil the other aspects of the East Asian model? Most governments likely agree that investment in the human capital of their populations is desirable, but not many can deliver it effectively. Likewise, what state would not want access to foreign technology or the achievement of growth that benefits a wide segment of society? That most developing country governments fail to promote or achieve these key goals speaks to the overall institutional weakness many must overcome before they can consider adopting a model with so many prerequisites. Before they are capable of this, there is little point in discussing the diffusion of a model from China that carries additional requirements for the state, beyond even what the basic East Asian model demanded.

Yet, this is not to say that Chinese developmental dominance or ascendency will last for ever. On the contrary, myriad domestic factors conspire to tarnish and undercut, or possibly even de-rail, China's continued success. The following section examines some of the most salient threats to the enduring sustainability of the China model.

HOW SUSTAINABLE IS THE MODEL IN CHINA?

Even the casual observer is tempted to conclude that the China model may not even remain viable in China itself for ever. Factors such as rapidly rising wages for low- and medium-skilled labour in the Pearl River Delta export manufacturing enclave, massive unemployment in the ailing state sector, an over-reliance on the sale of land-use rights in providing local revenues, crises of environmental protection and public health, an increasing vulnerability to the very same problems that brought down the East Asian model in 1998, and an erosion of China's comparative advantage in drawing in FDI together chip away at the sustainability of the model.

China today is faced with two sets of labour issues. First, there is a crisis of rising wages for migrant labour, particularly in export manufacturing zones, that threatens to erode China's comparative advantage in the production of low-cost industrial products. Concerns have percolated among industrialists, investors and bureaucrats since the early 2000s, when factories in the Pearl River Delta began to encounter labour shortages and rapidly rising wage demands from the workers they were able to recruit. Many observers and Chinese policy-makers now realise that China's market dominance of many labour-intensive industries is probably not sustainable. This has even recently become a major topic of debate in the Chinese academic and popular press.[12] If China is unable either to create more opportunities for employment in the countryside or to improve access to more advanced education and training for rural residents, the country risks being left with a gigantic pool of largely unemployable labour coming off the land.

At the same time, more than 60 million jobs in the urban state and collective sectors have disappeared since 1993.[13] The loss of what had been the backbone of urban employment has placed substantial pressure on social services and other functions of local governments. Chinese cities thus already have been forced to manage what forecasters of a worst-case scenario fear could arise in the rural areas – a significant population excluded from the gains and opportunities of reform. This has already sparked waves of protest and open crisis in some cities.[14] It also threatens to destabilise the basic institutions of urban governance and social control. So far, the Chinese government's response on this score, creating a new institutional framework of "community" organisation and control, has yet to achieve the sought-after results, though it is still too early to judge.[15]

Another set of issues has come to prominence in recent years surrounding local fiscal resources. After a significant centralising reform of China's fiscal system in 1994, many cities became increasingly dependent on transfers from above in order to meet spending needs. As pressures from worker lay-offs, infrastructure construction, and other areas have mounted, city governments have frequently found themselves coming up short of funds. While the central government has radically increased transfers to key regions – notably the west and the north-east – since 1999, long-term fiscal problems in cities appear likely.[16]

Rural areas have endured, and continue to struggle with, much more severe fiscal issues. In the late 1980s and early 1990s, while still operating under the grain procurement system that originated in the early days after 1949, rural governments were in such dire straits that they were forced to pay farmers in promissory notes (known as IOUs).[17] Many of these were not repaid for several years, triggering many outbreaks of civil disorder in the early 1990s. After fiscal reform in 1994, many villages and townships were forced to rely on levying extra-budgetary revenues and illicit fees to meet increasing mandates and make up for declining revenues through the formal budget.[18] Since 2002, when the central government began a crackdown against illicit local fees, many local governments in rural areas have come to rely on the sale of land-use rights to win much-needed revenue.[19] This has fuelled great social upheaval as villagers have resisted, sometimes violently, what they often see as the illegitimate confiscation of the land on which their livelihood depends.

Local revenue problems have been compounded by the proliferation of unfunded mandates from Beijing. Most recently, prime minister Wen Jiabao announced in 2005 that school fees would be waived for rural pupils. But the funds supplied to county governments to supplement their education budgets have not made up for the lost fees. At least in some counties, governments have resorted to charging fees under another name that are then used to pay for school budgets.[20] Similar unfunded mandates have plagued attempts to establish more comprehensive urban social service networks.[21] Ultimately, another round of fiscal reform appears likely, in which Beijing will either have to devolve some revenue collection powers back down to the local level or enact new mechanisms to ensure substantial increases in central government transfers to meet localities' social spending responsibilities.

Another set of issues that are beginning to draw attention both within China and abroad, are worsening problems of environmental protection and public health. Environmental crises ranging from the turning to desert of much of northern China to sharp increases in birth defects and certain types of cancer in areas of severe water contamination have raised alarm in Beijing, just as acid rain from eastern China falling in Japan and Mongolian sand blowing ashore in California and Oregon have caused concerns in Tokyo and Washington and elsewhere.[22] The SARS outbreak of 2003 received much attention from the world's media, but much more serious is China's festering epidemic of HIV and AIDS. Though the government has begun seriously to address the problem in the past five years, it may already be too late to prevent HIV from significantly diluting China's future growth prospects. Even more important, the rollback and near-demise of the public health system covering rural residents and several urban workers has led many to suffer from diseases that had been controlled or nearly eradicated in China. Ailments such as tuberculosis, hepatitis B, heart disease and various cancers may yet overwhelm the creaking medical system that covers much of China's population – to say nothing of a major new outbreak of SARS or avian influenza.

Finally, what has looked like a strength of the China model may yet become a major liability. The Chinese banking and financial system has appeared weak, insolvent and incapable of regulating equity markets effectively. Banks have been through a roller-coaster of reform from the mono-bank model in place before 1978, to the dominance of the "Big Four" state banks, to a more thoroughly liberalised and internationally open system under terms agreed to when China joined the WTO in 2001.[23] While it seems that the worst threatened effects of the non-performing loan debacle of the 1990s (which pushed Chinese banks into technical insolvency) may be fading from the scene, Chinese banks are far from safe, as they are starting to have to compete with more savvy and better-run foreign rivals for domestic business.

China's stock markets are perhaps even less stable than its banks. With foreign investments and domestic ones segregated into separate and non-convertible classes of shares, markets have fluctuated wildly. Domestic investors, often with little knowledge or experience of investing in stocks, sometimes risked their life savings on purchases of various rickety state companies (which make up the bulk of those allowed to list on either the Shanghai or Shenzhen exchange), driving up A share prices only to provoke declines and corrections later when they defected by the millions to the next "hot" stock. Foreign investors, lacking detailed knowledge of the true situation of many Chinese state firms, often made bets that were nearly as bad as their Chinese counterparts. Excitement abroad about investing in Chinese equities also has tended to wax and wane, leading foreigners to enter and exit the market in waves that can destabilise B shares.

China's restricted capital account and continuing rigid segregation of domestic and internationalised components of its economy lead to a broader threat – that of domestic asset price bubbles that may prove vulnerable when and if additional rounds of liberalisation are pursued. Currently, Chinese investors have few outlets for their famously large savings. Bank deposits, Chinese government bonds, domestic stocks (A shares) and real estate remain their only real options. Money has flowed into all of these assets, even as banks have paid negative real interest on deposits, bonds have offered returns that are little better, stock markets have endured wild gyrations over the past fifteen years or so, and the real estate market has recently acquired all the signs of a rather over-inflated bubble. If Chinese investors were to be enabled to place their money in other investments abroad or at home, however, it seems the rush to buy houses, bonds and equities or deposit savings in the bank would likely ebb or even reverse, possibly with severe consequences.

The China model, therefore, is not necessarily all it is sometime purported to be. Though it has brought success for China in many areas, it is not easily exportable to most national contexts. Furthermore, it is quite likely limited in its reach by the particular constellation of forces in the international economy during the 1990s and early 2000s that combined to enable China to pursue its specific blend of reliance on FDI, maintenance of a vast state sector and rejection of significant political reform. Finally, the model even in China is under substantial strain, to the point that the sustainability of China's success in the medium to long term must be questioned. While it is certainly possible that China will emerge from its various current crises stronger and more ascendant than ever before, it is not impossible that one or more of the issues just discussed could undermine China's growth and development to the point of bringing the "China miracle" to an end.

To assess China's prospects for sustaining its model, we must look both at what the government and CCP are trying to do and what it is they could ideally do but have not attempted. So far, three main policy initiatives have been adopted to help resolve the problems just discussed: 1) massive investment in rural infrastructure and services; 2) significant investment in elite higher education and other elements seen as necessary for nurturing high-tech sectors; and 3) increasingly comprehensive attempts to reassert Party and government control over key areas of (mainly urban) social and political life. Each of these is both helped and hindered by key elements of the Chinese development model. In addition, the first two measures undermine the third in important ways.

Though necessary for restoring confidence in state and Party legitimacy, the revitalisation of rural infrastructure and social services also promotes two processes that undermine CCP authority: the spread of information and migration. The more integrated into the broader society and polity isolated Chinese villages become, the more glaring the vast gulf of development and living standards between them and the rest of the country appears. The more people move about the country, the harder they are to control or even keep track of. Also, as has happened elsewhere around the world, if subsistence concerns are alleviated but affluence not yet obtained, such a condition of secure poverty can be a catalyst for social contention and resistance. Similarly, an expansion of the educated elite and an upgrading of information technology and communications networks will likely create a new crop of dissidents alongside a new, creative entrepreneurial class, providing both groups with increased means to network and co-ordinate with each other.

In an ideal world, the Chinese state and Party would also undertake certain other reform measures to help cement long-term gains and spread social and economic benefits more widely. Chief among these would be the significant liberalisation of the education system and cultural life, along with significant new programs to help build a comprehensive and universal healthcare system and reform of the household registration (*hukou*) system so as to promote much greater labour mobility. Liberalising the education system and loosening controls on cultural life might finally allow China's investments in education to bear fruit in producing more innovation and the growth of high-technology industries. A universal healthcare system would provide for and protect laid-off workers, farmers remaining in the countryside and people suffering from infectious diseases such as SARS and HIV. Easing restrictive policies to promote labour mobility would help integrate rural and urban labour markets as well as facilitate laid-off workers in de-industrialising areas moving to where new jobs are located. Several factors make it highly unlikely that any of these measures could be adopted in the short to medium term.

The main obstacles to implementing such measures are a lack of fiscal resources and an overriding urgency in the minds of the CCP leadership to maintain social and political control in an era when the regime feels under threat. Education and cultural life must thus be kept under strict oversight to prevent any repeat of anything like what happened in 1989. Similarly, when people are mobile they are less susceptible to surveillance and repression. Allowing workers to move about the country more freely would undermine the Party's initiatives to reinvigorate village governments through limited democracies and enhance local urban state capacity and legitimacy through the expanded community system. Finally, establishing and maintaining a universal healthcare system would be prohibitively expensive, particularly in light of other competing spending priorities, for the Chinese government. In the absence of these three initiatives, however, the CCP's ability to address any of the major problems it faces is compromised.

Conclusion

Though China has never sought to offer any explicit model for economic development, and talk of a "Beijing Consensus" is almost certainly overblown, it is possible to impute a rough sketch of a China model from the policies that have produced Chinese success in key areas. What emerges is a picture striking in its similarity to the by now passé East Asian model. China's critical new additions to this basic model are an explicit rejection of pluralist politics, or democratisation, and a reliance on a particular variety of foreign direct investment (FDI).

China's "East Asian model plus two" formula is specific to its time and place, and may not be readily exportable. Without the unbinding of capital from its moorings in national markets during the 1990s, it is unlikely that such high levels of FDI would have been possible. It is further unlikely that FDI could have been so effectively channelled in the particular manner that it was in China at this crucial time, were it not for a peculiar constellation of Chinese policies and the fact that China is the world's largest country. Also, because of China's size and perceived importance, many foreign investors have chosen to remain heavily involved in its development project, despite possibly better conditions for their own activities in other countries. This further limits the likely chances for any diffusion of China's development framework.

Finally, the instability of the model, even in China, suggests that it may not be one that other countries should seek to emulate. Only time will tell whether China can work its way out of the difficulties it is currently facing in areas such as the environment, public health, asset price inflation, regulation of the banking and financial sectors, unemployment and deficiencies of rural governance. It would certainly be better for the world economy if it can. But until it does, we must remain wary of declaring the China model a success in its own homeland, let alone a blueprint for replication of the "miracle" in distant countries and contexts.

NOTES

1. See, for example, Chalmers A. Johnson, *MITI and the Japanese Miracle: Growth and Industrial Policy, 1925–1975*, Stanford: Stanford University Press, 1982; Alice H. Amsden, *Asia's Next Giant: South Korea and Late Industrialization*, Oxford: Oxford University Press, 1989.

2. Robert Wade, *Governing the Market: Economic Theory and the Role of Government in East Asian Industrialization*, Princeton: Princeton University Press, 1990; Stephen Haggard, *Pathways from the Periphery: The Politics of Growth in the Newly Industrialising Countries*, Ithaca, NY: Cornell University Press, 1990.

3. The World Bank, *The East Asian Miracle: Economic Growth and Public Policy*, Oxford: Oxford University Press, 1993, pp. 13–23.

4. Lowell Dittmer and William Hurst, "Analysis in Limbo: Contemporary Chinese Politics Amid the Maturation of Reform", *Issues and Studies*, vol. 38, no. 4/vol. 39, no. 1, December 2002/March 2003, pp. 11–12.

5. See, for example, Joshua Cooper Ramo, *The Beijing Consensus*, London: The Foreign Policy Centre, 2004.

6. Ibid.

7. For an overview and critical assessment of elements of this policy framework, see Eric Thun, "Industrial Policy, Chinese-style: FDI, Regulation, and Dreams of National Champions in the Auto Sector", *Journal of East Asian Studies*, vol. 4, no. 3, September 2004, pp. 453–89.

8. Dittmer and Hurst, "Analysis in Limbo", p. 36.

9. Mary E. Gallagher, "Reform and Openness: Why China's Economic Reforms Have Delayed Democracy", *World Politics*, vol. 54, no. 3, April 2002, pp. 338–72.

10. Barry Eichengreen and Albert Fishlow, "Contending with Capital Flows: What is Different about the 1990s?", in Miles Kahler (ed.), *Capital Flows and Financial Crises*

(Council on Foreign Relations Book) , Ithaca, NY: Cornell University Press, 1998, pp. 23–68.

11. Mitchell Bernard and John Ravenhill, "Beyond Product Cycles and Flying Geese: Regionalization, Hierarchy, and the Industrialization of Asia", *World Politics*, vol. 47, no. 2, January 1995, pp. 171–209.

12. See, for example, Xue Yong, *Zhongguo Bu Neng Yongyuan wei Shijie Dagong* [China Cannot Toil for the World Forever] , Kunming: Yunnan Renmin Chubanshe, 2006, especially pp. 10–11 and 16–22.

13. William Hurst, *The Chinese Worker After Socialism*, Cambridge: Cambridge University Press, 2009, Introduction.

14. Yongshun Cai, *The State and Laid-off Workers in Reform China: The Silence and Collective Action of the Retrenched*, London: Routledge, 2006; Ching Kwan Lee, *Against the Law: Labour Protests in China's Rustbelt and Sunbelt*, Berkeley, CA: University of California Press, 2007; and Hurst, *The Chinese Worker*, Chapter 5.

15. Hurst, *The Chinese Worker*, Conclusion.

16. See, for example, Victor Shih, "Development the Second Time Around: the Political Logic of Developing Western China" , *Journal of East Asian Studies*, vol. 4, no. 3, September 2004, pp. 427–51; "Zhenxing Dongbei" (rejuvenate the Northeast) *http://news.xinhuanet.com/focus/2004–03/12/content_1359557.htm*.

17. Thomas P. Bernstein, "Farmer Discontent and Regime Responses", in Merle Goldman and Roderick MacFarquhar (eds), *The Paradox of China's Post-Mao Reforms*, Cambridge, MA: Harvard University Press, 1999, pp. 197–219.

18. On fiscal reform, see Donald J. S. Brean (ed.), *Taxation in Modern China*, London: Routledge, 1998; on extra-budgetary funds and "peasant burdens" , see Le-yin Zhang, "Chinese Central-Provincial Fiscal Relationships, Budgetary Decline, and the Impact of the 1994 Fiscal Reform: an Evaluation" , *The China Quarterly*, no. 157, March 1999, pp. 115–41; Thomas P. Bernstein and Xiaobo Lü, *Taxation without Representation in Contemporary Rural China*, Cambridge: Cambridge University Press, 2003.

19. Interviews with central government researcher and Guangdong provincial government researcher, Beijing and Guangzhou, September 2006.

20. Interviews with one county official and three village leaders, Pengze County (Jiangxi Province), April 2007.

21. Hurst, *The Chinese Worker*, Chapter 3.

22. For a general picture of the environmental crises China faces, see Elizabeth C. Economy, *The River Runs Black: The Environmental Challenge to China's Future*, Ithaca, NY: Cornell University Press, 2004.

23. Nicholas R. Lardy, *China's Unfinished Economic Revolution*, Washington, DC: The Brookings Institutions Press, 1998; Victor Shih, *Factions and Finance in China: Elite Conflict and Inflation*, Cambridge: Cambridge University Press, 2007.

CHAPTER 2

Latin America's View of China: Interest, but Scepticism

BARBARA STALLINGS

China's dramatic economic success over the past several decades has attracted worldwide attention. Its high growth rates, however, have caused different effects across regions, countries, sectors and firms. On the one hand, Chinese imports have provided important new markets for exporters throughout the world. Raw materials exporters have benefited disproportionately, but producers of high-tech industrial goods have also taken advantage. On the other hand, China's export juggernaut has outperformed most of its trade partners – especially with respect to light consumer goods – and created large and growing trade deficits. Those deficits, in turn, have been offset by capital outflows of various kinds, which have led to significant international imbalances as well as greater Chinese influence in developed and developing countries alike.

Beyond its economic impact, China is important because some people regard it as a potential model that developing countries might follow to enable them to grow faster and improve the living standard of their populations. Clearly China shares a number of characteristics with the "Asian model", which has been touted for several decades, but there are also significant differences, as will be seen. One of the most important differences is the sheer size of China, which makes its trajectory hard to emulate. Likewise, the authoritarian political system in China is becoming less typical of the rest of Asia. If we are to investigate the attractiveness of the "Chinese model", then, it is necessary to start with a clear understanding of its characteristics, both the upsides and the downsides. Politics clearly play a role here as do economics.

This chapter looks at China's importance for the developing world, with particular emphasis on Latin America, although it also puts Latin America in comparative perspective. The first section begins with a description of the components of the Chinese model as seen from Latin America. These can be summarised as a powerful state with an extensive – though shrinking – role in the economy; a heavy reliance on both trade and foreign investment; low wages, which are seen as giving China an unfair competitive advantage; and an authoritarian political system that operates in a relatively decentralised fashion.

The second section analyses the prerequisites for "Chinese-type success". From the Latin American view, three prerequisites can be highlighted. One is high investment rates and the resources to finance this investment. A second is an educated and motivated population and labour force. A third is the long-term view of the development process and the creation of viable public–private partnerships. None of these prerequisites exists at the moment in the Latin American region as a whole, but some elements can be found in individual countries. A fourth prerequisite, which some have associated with economic success, but which does not seem particularly relevant in the Chinese case, as will be seen, is "good governance".

The third section in this chapter examines the rapidly expanding economic relations between China and Latin America, which in principle might bring them closer together. However, Latin nations have serious concerns about these links. The differing perspectives of the northern and southern parts of the region are emphasised. The differing views of political leaders – ranging from Hugo Chávez to the more moderate leftist leaders and to the centre-right govern-ments – are also discussed.

Finally, the chapter looks at the international context in which Latin American development takes place and asks what a greater Chinese influence – whether economic or ideological – would mean. In general, neither China nor most Latin American elites foresee any likelihood that China will replace the United States as the leading power in the region, despite the concerns of some officials in the former Bush administration. But perhaps the new Chinese interest in the region will serve as a wakeup-call to the US government that it needs to pay more attention to its neighbours.

THE CHINESE MODEL

The vast changes in the Chinese economy in the last twenty-years resulted from reforms that began in 1978 when Deng Xiaoping launched China on a new development strategy that relied heavily on the workings of the market. In the last decade, they have been speeded up by China's accession to the World Trade Organization (WTO) in December 2001.[1] The opening of the economy, both internally and especially externally, led to an average annual growth rate of nearly 10 per cent over the last quarter-century. This growth rate far outpaced that of other economies and moved China up to fourth place in aggregate GDP rankings today. Based on purchasing power parity (PPP) figures, China ranks second after the United States, and some expect it to overtake the USA in PPP terms within the next decade.[2]

The sources of Chinese growth are important in determining the impact on the rest of the world. Demand has depended heavily on investment and net exports, as opposed to government expenditure and private consumption.[3] This pattern is typical of other high-growth East Asian economies, but it is quite different from the type of growth found in other developing regions and in most of the developed world. Furthermore, the investment/export bias has increased substantially during the current decade. In 2001, investment was 34 per cent of GDP, net exports 1 per cent, government consumption 15 per cent and private consumption 50 per cent. By 2005, the numbers had changed to 40, 7, 15 and 38 per cent, respectively.[4] This pattern has exacerbated some of China's problems with its neighbours and other countries due to its seemingly insatiable need for capital and natural resources, as well as its growing trade surpluses.

China's output structure also contributes to worldwide resource needs as industry has grown from around 30 per cent of GDP to nearly 50 per cent between 1980 and 2005, while agriculture has fallen from 40 to 10 per cent. Services have expanded only from 30 to 40 per cent, again much lower than in other econ-omies.[5] The dominance of industry, in lieu of services, exacerbates the resource requirements. China now accounts for 20 to 30 per cent of world consumption of many agricultural commodities (for example, rice, soy, cotton, rubber) and similar amounts of metals (for example, tin, zinc, iron ore and steel). In energy requirements, its main use is coal, but oil is becoming more important. China currently consumes 7 per cent of world oil, but that amount is growing rapidly.[6]

Trade requires special treatment since it is so important in China's relations with other countries. The large size of its economy notwithstanding, China's exports and imports have increased very rapidly. Even after taking GDP growth into account, exports and imports of goods and services as a share of GDP each rose from around 5 per cent in 1978 to around 35 per cent in 2006. In absolute terms (current dollars), the increase in total trade was from $21 billion to $1.8 trillion in the same period. The trade balance shifted back and forth in the early years, but from 1994 it was continually positive. As we will see, however, the positive overall balance was the result of very different trade balances among partners (WTO online database).

While China has an export-led economy, the majority of those exports are produced by multinational corporations.[7] This reflects the enormous amount of foreign direct investment (FDI) that has poured into China in recent years. It is the largest recipient of FDI among developing countries, accounting for over one-quarter of the total between 2000 and 2006, an annual average of $57 billion. In 2002, it surpassed even the United States to become the largest destination for FDI on an annual basis.[8]

A number of the multinationals investing in China are based in the United States, but an even larger number are based in other Asian economies. Japan, South Korea and Taiwan, for example, have shifted important parts of their industrial capacity to China because costs are much lower than at home. This is especially the case for labour-intensive products because Chinese wages – although rising, particularly in coastal provinces – are still only a fraction of those in Northeast Asia. Many of the more complex inputs for the firms relocated in China are imported from the headquarters firms or their suppliers. Some of the goods produced in China by Northeast Asian multinationals are shipped back to their home countries, but most are sold in the United States or in Europe.[9]

This combination of large-scale imports from Northeast (and even Southeast) Asia, without compensating exports, leads to substantial trade deficits for China with these countries. These have been roughly offset by large surpluses with the United States and the European Union. Thus, China itself had relatively balanced trade till the mid-1990s, although we have seen that this turned into a significant overall surplus in the last few years. The shift was due, in part, to the vast increase in textile exports after the end of the Multifiber Agreement, although China also increased its exports in other sectors, including high-technology products. The surpluses have been invested in US treasury securities, partially offsetting US deficits, but the imbalances are seen by many experts as jeopardising the stability of the world economy.[10] Another source of instability is the large bilateral trade deficit that the United States has with China, which produces both economic and political tensions, including demands for protectionist measures to shield US firms that cannot compete.

Finally, it is important to take note of the composition of China's trade. As exports and imports have increased in volume, not surprisingly they have also changed in content. While in the 1980s, primary products and labour- and resource-intensive manufactures together made up nearly 80 per cent of total exports, now their share is less than 40 per cent. The largest category is electronics (around 35 per cent), while other manufactures have also increased significantly. Imports have changed as well. From a fairly balanced import structure in the 1980s, China's main imports now are high-technology equipment, component parts and raw materials.[11]

It should not be assumed from this analysis of China's large and growing economy, and its successful trade strategy, that the country has no problems going forward. Indeed, a number of potential problems loom, some of them stemming from the very reforms that were responsible for its high growth rates. In the economic sphere, China still has a large number of fairly inefficient state-owned enterprises. These firms have traditionally been supported by state-owned banks, leading to massive non-performing loans for the latter. In the last few years, the Chinese government has taken important steps to clean up both financial and non-financial firms, but many problems still remain.[12] One of the reasons for the changes is the Chinese government's decision to join the WTO, which required China to open its economy to foreign competition. The government has since tried to increase the competitiveness of its firms.[13]

In the social area, both open and disguised unemployment are high and are exacerbated by rapid urbanisation. In the last decade, China's urban population has increased by some 200 million people, and the migration continues. Partly as a result of the new urban dwellers, unofficial estimates suggest that open unemployment in the cities has reached 11 to 12 per cent.[14] The other main reason for high unemployment is the shedding of workers by state-owned firms, which have declined to about one-third of the total number of firms – although the share of workers still employed by these firms is much higher. The lower share of public-sector workers has further increased social problems, as services and pensions were previously provided though the workplace.[15]

Unemployment has contributed to increased inequality in the cities, as has the new requirement that citizens be responsible for much of the cost of education, healthcare, housing, and pensions. China's Gini coefficient, the most common measure of income inequality, has gone from among the lowest in the world in the 1970s to levels above most Asian countries – and approaching the levels of Latin America, long known as the most unequal region in the world. A larger problem is inequality between urban and rural areas, or between coastal and interior provinces. After an initial rapid rise of incomes in the countryside with the abolition of the old collective farm system, rural dwellers have now fallen far behind.[16]

Social problems, in turn, are an important cause of growing political unrest. As a result of their low and declining living standards, rural residents and citizens in western provinces have staged a growing number of protests. These are frequently triggered by local government officials expropriating land with little or no compensation. In addition, government expenditures are far lower in rural areas, and until 2006 agricultural producers had to pay a special tax. But urban protests are also increasing, mainly due to poor working conditions or lack of access to affordable services. Demands for greater political freedom have also resumed after a hiatus following the Tiananmen events in 1989.[17]

This brings us, of course, to China's authoritarian political system, under the watchful eye of the Chinese Communist Party, which co-exists with the country's dramatically successful economy. Repression of human rights seems to occur at all levels of government, from the central authorities in Beijing to regional and municipal governments. They infringe on political rights but also on economic rights, as indicated above in reference to expropriation of property. The media is tightly controlled, and religious rights also come under frequent attack. While there has been some improvement in recent years, China continues to be a nation where democracy is an alien concept.[18]

The relationship between economic change and political continuity is a crucial part of analysing the Chinese model. Are we merely dealing with an issue of sequencing, whereby economic liberalisation precedes political liberalisation? This is the pattern that has characterised several other East Asian countries, such as South Korea, Taiwan, Indonesia and the Philippines (and examples as far away as Chile and Mexico, in Latin America itself). Other Asian cases, such as Singapore and Malaysia, have not moved very far in political liberalisation despite a new generation of leaders – although they were never as repressive as China is today.

Alternatively, will the Chinese Communist Party attempt to maintain tight control indefinitely? This seems difficult to imagine, especially with China's fast-growing middle class, but there are few signs of political change until now. Indeed, Chinese authorities themselves portray democracy as an inefficient hindrance to moving ahead in the economic sphere as seen, for example, in recent reports of the advances in infrastructure in China.[19] For many analysts, in trying to compare the future of China and India, it is India's inability to make and implement decisions because of political opposition that distinguishes the two. But for others, India's more open political system is an advantage in obtaining feedback about potential problems before they explode. Of course, these are old debates, but they are crucial in analysing the "Chinese model" and its relevance beyond the country itself, and there are no simple answers.

PREREQUISITES FOR "CHINESE STYLE DEVELOPMENT"

Latin American governments and academics have been interested for years in the "East Asian model" of development. Comparative discussion began to take off in the mid-1980s and expanded rapidly after the publication in 1993 of the World Bank's *East Asian Miracle*.[20] At the regional level, both the Inter-American Development Bank and the UN Economic Commission for Latin America and the Caribbean have been active in promoting research and encounters between the two regions. The centre of attention was traditionally on the four "newly-industrialising countries" or "first-tier NICs" (South Korea, Taiwan, Hong Kong and Singapore) and later on the "second-tier NICs" (Indonesia, Malaysia, the Philippines, and Thailand). Only recently have China and India become a focus of interest.[21] In virtually all of this literature, the focus has been on the economic elements of the Asia model; politics has been notably absent.

If Latin America were to try to emulate either China or other Asian economies in terms of their economic success, three prerequisites stand out. First is the need to raise Latin America's very low investment rate and, of course, to obtain the resources to finance higher investment. Second, it would be necessary to place more emphasis on education and training, and improve their quality. Third, the state would have to step up its activities in support of economic growth. In addition, we will make some comparisons of governance in Latin America, East Asia, and China.

Investment in physical capital is the traditional prerequisite for rapid economic growth. Putting resources into both production facilities and infrastructure not only injects money into the economy in the short run; more importantly, it creates the preconditions for faster growth in the future. Most analysts would argue, then, that those economies that have higher investment coefficients (investment as a share of GDP) will also have higher growth rates. Of course, it is also necessary to take into account the efficiency of investment. It may be that at very high investment rates, investment efficiency declines.

The positive relationship between investment and growth has certainly held for Latin American versus East Asian economies. The former have long had very low investment rates, and they have fallen even lower in recent decades.

Table 1. Investment, Savings and Finance in Latin America and East Asia

Indicator	East Asia	Latin America
Investment rate[*]		
1965	21	21
1990	35	19
2000	32	20
2006	36	20
Savings rate[**]		
1965	24	21
1990	36	22
2000	36	19
2006	40	22
Financial depth[***]		
1990	141	63
1995	185	86
2000	203	104
2003	236	112

Source: World Bank, World Development Indicators online (for investment and savings rates); Stallings and Studart, Finance for Development, p. 119 (for financial depth).
[*] Investment as share of GDP
[**] Savings as share of GDP
[***] Bank credit plus bonds outstanding plus stock market capitalisation as share of GDP

The latter, by contrast, have had very high investment rates, although they also have fallen in some countries since the East Asian financial crisis. As Table 1 indicates, East Asian investment rates have been nearly twice those of Latin America. Among the highest investment rates have been found in China.

Why are Latin American investment rates so low, and what – if anything – can be done about this problem? No simple answer exists, but one aspect clearly concerns savings rates. In growth accounting terms, the relationship is an identity *ex post*, but *ex ante* the question is more interesting. Keynesian answers focus on growth itself as the independent variable, while neo-classical economists worry about why people save. It is important to be clear about who is saving (or not): households, firms, or the government. Part of the difference between Latin America and East Asia has centred on government budget deficits (dissaving), which have been much more common in Latin America than East Asia. But households have also been big savers in Asia. Some would look to cultural variables to explain why Asian households save so much, others to structural factors such as the traditional lack of government programs for social security.

Financial intermediaries are important both as a vehicle for saving and as the main mechanism to transform savings into investment. Here we also see big differences between Latin America and East Asia. The financial sector is about twice as deep in the latter as in the former. The banking system has been especially important as a source of finance in Asian countries. Initially, most of the banks were state-owned (as they were in Latin America), but a wave of privatisation has taken place in the financial sector in both regions.[22] Even in China the banking sector has opened up to allow private – foreign as well as domestic – ownership. Table 1 also shows data on savings and the financial sector in the two regions.

In the recent literature on endogenous growth theory, it has been argued that investment in human capital is more important than physical capital in explaining growth rates.[23] While the essence of human capital tends to focus on formal education, it also involves investments in such areas as health and job training. It is difficult to measure human capital. Schooling is the most common measure, for example, the percentage of particular age groups that are in school or the average years of schooling. Disagreement exists, however, on what level of education is most important and how to deal with educational quality issues.

While Latin American countries generally score as well as Asian countries on quantitative measures of the percentage of primary-age children in school, serious problems of quality are widely recognised. In particular, there is a strong correlation in Latin America between educational quality (however measured) and family income. Children of higher-income families tend to receive better education – often, but not always, at private schools – than their lower-income counterparts. In addition, a smaller share of Latin American students goes on to high school than is the case in Asia. Many stop with a low-quality primary education, which leaves them in a very poor competitive situation in terms of finding well-paying jobs.[24]

Higher education presents a different set of challenges. A larger share of Latin American youth has tended to obtain university education than in Asia – although this is rapidly changing in some Asian countries. But in the Latin American case, the tradition of free university matriculation at public universities has meant a strong bias towards public expenditures on education for middle- and upper-middle-income students, who are the ones who complete high school and whose families can afford the opportunity costs of letting them attend college rather than going to work. The recent increase in expensive private universities also pushes in the same direction of income-based differentiation in the educational profile. Another issue is the subjects studied at the university. Latin American students tend to concentrate on humanities, social

Table 2. Stock of Education among Adult Working Population in Latin America and East Asia

Region/country	Average years	Highest School Level Completed (per cent)		
		Primary or less	Some* secondary	Some tertiary
East Asia	8.3	46.7	39.0	14.3
Cambodia	4.1	86.4	12.6	1.0
Mongolia	9.4	13.6	58.4	28.1
Vietnam	8.8	38.0	56.2	5.8
Indonesia	7.2	60.3	34.4	5.3
Thailand	7.1	66.9	22.7	10.4
Philippines	9.6	52.6	21.7	25.7
China	10.1	19.7	66.4	14.2
Singapore	10.0	36.3	39.9	23.7
Latin America	7.8	57.2	28.5	14.3
Argentina	9.8	51.9	24.0	24.0
Brazil	6.4	69.5	23.2	7.3
Chile	9.4	56.2	33.4	10.4
Colombia	8.9	26.1	36.1	37.8
Guatemala	4.8	79.7	15.8	4.5
Mexico	8.2	46.9	42.6	10.5
Venezuela	8.2	62.9	25.7	11.4
Bolivia	6.9	64.2	27.0	8.8

Source: Emanuela di Gropello (ed.), *Meeting the Challenge of Secondary Education in Latin America and East Asia*, Washington, DC: World Bank, 2006, p. 71.
* Includes vocational education.

sciences, law and (recently) business at the expense of science and engineering, which are more popular in Asia. These differences can be expected to damage Latin American countries" chances to catch up with Asian countries in terms of economic growth. Table 2 presents World Bank data on the stock of education among the working population in the two regions.

While economic fundamentals, such as investment in physical and human capital, are crucial in distinguishing Latin American from Asian countries – including China – in terms of their capacity to generate high growth rates, the better-known distinctions have to do with the role of the state in the economy in the two regions. Japan and most of the first-tier NICs, featured a strong state role and a bias against foreign capital. (This was much less the case for the second-tier NICs, which were both more open and looked to the private sector to a greater extent.) One way in which this distinction has been portrayed is that governments in the former group of countries tended to "pick winners" and to rely on state-owned firms.[25] In so far as that was the case in the earlier post-war years – and not all would agree that it was – it has become less true in the last decade or so. After the Asian financial crisis, and even earlier in some cases, governments began to withdraw in favour of the private sector.

This trend towards a lesser state role can be seen in China as well as the first-tier NICs, but the Chinese experience is more dramatic because China was transitioning from a socialist economy from the early 1980s. Indeed, it was the opening of the Chinese economy, both domestically and internationally, that paved the way for its strong economic performance in the last twenty-five years. Nonetheless, the state has continued to play an important supporting role. This can be seen, for example, in the provision of infrastructure, the support for technology and innovation among Chinese firms, and the multiple rescues of the banking system. The ability to take a long-term, strategic view of the economy has also been singled out as a crucial feature that gives China an advantage in terms of its competitors in the industrial countries as well as other developing regions.

In the Latin American case, there was also a tradition of a large state and a relatively closed economy. This was manifested in Latin America through the development strategy known as import-substitution industrialisation, which was followed from the early post-war period until the debt crisis of the 1980s. At that point, the deficiencies of this strategy became evident, and a dramatic change towards a market-oriented approach took over. In the extreme version of this approach, the strong state was seen as the main stumbling block to economic growth. Thus, various steps were taken to strengthen the private sector as the leading force, including trade liberalisation, privatisation, financial liberalisation, tax reform, and so on.[26] While a few governments would like to see these reforms entirely rolled back, the majority of Latin American governments and civil society prefer a mixed economy in which the state partners with the private sector to increase competitiveness. In this endeavour, the Asian countries – including, but not limited to, China – are seen as having some lessons to offer.

Finally, we close with some attention to the issue of "good governance" as a prerequisite to economic success. This notion has certainly been prevalent in Latin America, sometimes in the form of "corporate governance" and at other times as a broader concept. Using the World Bank concepts and data on governance, it is possible to compare Latin America and East Asia, including China. The Bank has adopted a six-indicator approach to governance and collected an enormous amount of data on these indicators. The six are: voice and accountability, political stability and absence of violence, government effectiveness, regulatory quality, rule of law, and control of corruption.[27]

Table 3 shows the six indicators for the East Asian region as a whole (including China), China, and Latin America for the year 2006. The unweighted average of the six shows East Asia at the top, followed by Latin America, and then China. Rankings differ, however, on some individual indicators. Thus, China is below its East Asian counterparts in all measures of governance except "government effectiveness". Comparing China with Latin America, the former is again higher on "government effectiveness" and also on "rule of law".

Table 3. Governance Indicators for East Asia and Latin America, 2006

Indicator*	East Asia**	China	Latin America
Voice and accountability	49.4	4.8	51.6
Political stability	60.4	33.2	37.7
Government effectiveness	47.1	55.5	43.2
Regulatory quality	47.2	31.7	45.4
Rule of law	54.9	45.2	35.4
Control of corruption	45.6	37.9	42.0
Average (unweighted)	50.8	34.7	42.6

Source: World Bank, Worldwide Governance Indicators online.
* Data indicate per centile rank of country (or regional average) among all countries of the world; 0 corresponds to lowest rank, 100 corresponds to highest rank.
** Includes China.

In so far as these indicators are valid – and they are quite controversial – they would suggest that a fairly poor record on governance has not held China back in a serious way. But this only gets us back to the issue of China's authoritarian political system, and its role in the country's economic success. Clearly the governance indicators are a reflection of the type of political system in China.

CHINA'S ECONOMIC RELATIONS WITH LATIN AMERICA

Beyond discussion of "models", China has suddenly become an important economic actor in Latin America during the last several years. The main element involves trade, the impact of which helped the region to recover from the recession that spilled over from the East Asian financial crisis of 1997. As with other developing regions, Latin America's exports to and imports from China have boomed since the beginning of the present decade. Thus, for example, the region's exports to China were $21.7 billion in 2005, compared with only $4.7 billion in 2000. But these figures represent only 3.7 per cent and 1.3 per cent, respectively, of Latin America's total exports. Table 4 puts Latin America's trade into perspective when compared with Africa and Asia, both of which have stronger trade ties with China. Africa's exports to China are more than 7 per cent of its total, while those of Asia are 22 per cent.

Table 4. Developing Regions" Exports to China, 1996–2006

Region/country	1996		2000		2005	
	$ billions	per cent total exp	$ billions	per cent total exp	$ billions	per cent total exp
Asia*	180.1	18.4	223.1	17.6	511.3	22.3
Korea	14.2	10.9	29.2	16.9	77.4	27.2
Taiwan**	32	24.8	41.5	24.8	96.4	38.9
Singapore	13.6	10.9	16.2	11.8	41.3	20.0
Latin America	4.2	2.6	4.7	1.3	21.7	3.7
Brazil	1.5	3.1	1.6	2.9	6.8	5.8
Chile	0.5	3.0	1.0	5.2	4.4	11.1
Peru	0.5	8.1	0.5	6.7	1.0	11.0
Africa	1.6	1.6	4.8	4.0	17.8	7.4
Angola	0.2	4.4	1.7	23.0	6.0	30.0
Congo	0	0	0.1	5.0	2.1	38.9
Sudan	0.04	7.7	0.7	43.8	3.4	70.8

Source: B. Stallings, "China's Economic Relations with Developing Countries", keynote address at All-China Economics Conference, City University of Hong Kong, 2007.
* Includes HK
** Absolute numbers from Chinese data (reversed); per cent from world data (reversed).

Latin America exports a number of products that are crucial to China's continued industrial success. The top Latin American exports to China are metals (copper, iron ore and scrap metal), foodstuffs (soy, sugar and wheat) and industrial inputs (cotton, wool and leather).[28] Petroleum is noticeably absent from this list, unlike the case of Africa, despite high-profile discussions between

Venezuela's Hugo Chávez and Chinese leaders. There are a variety of obstacles to greater exports of petroleum to China. First is Latin America's declining production; second is the inadequate legal framework for investment in many Latin American exporting countries; third are transportation difficulties. Overall, Latin America provides less than 7 per cent of China's petroleum needs, and most of this comes from Ecuador, not Venezuela.[29] Table 5 shows Latin America's export profile to China, compared to that for other regions. As can be seen, Latin America is more similar to Africa and the Middle East than it is to Asia or the OECD countries.

Table 5. China: Imports by Region and Product, 2006

Region	Agriculture		Fuel/Minerals		Manufactures		Machinery[*]		Total
	$bn	per cent	$bn	per cent	$ bn	per cent	$ bn	per cent	
NEA[**]	1.6	0.9	12.7	7.2	162.4	91.9	85.8	48.5	176.8
Other Asia[***]	15.3	7.7	35.2	17.8	146.7	74.3	112.9	57.2	197.5
Africa	2.0	6.9	24.5	85.1	1.9	6.6	0.4	1.4	28.8
Latin America	9.0	28.6	18.2	57.8	4.3	13.7	2.2	7.0	31.5
Middle East	0.1	0.3	35.2	86.3	5.5	13.5	0.5	1.2	40.8
Industrial Countries[****]	18.5	6.5	17.7	6.3	245.5	86.9	156.0	55.2	282.5
World	51.7	6.5	158.3	20.0	579.5	73.2	357	45.1	791.5

Source: Stallings, "China's Economic Relations with Developing Countries".
[*] Included in manufactures
[**] Korea, Taiwan
[***] Asia minus Japan, Korea, Taiwan
[****] North America, Europe, Japan

While China is only Venezuela's fourteenth-largest market, the situation is quite different for some of its neighbours. For example, China is Peru's second-largest market (mainly through sales of copper and fishmeal), Chile's third-largest (copper), Brazil's third largest (soy and iron ore) and Argentina's fourth-largest (wheat and soy). A similar situation exists with some smaller countries. In all cases except Argentina, the United States remains the number-one export destination, but the gap between the United States and China is closing fast.[30]

Beyond trade, but closely associated, China has also indicated an interest in investing in Latin America. This intention was trumpeted to the world during visits to Latin America by Chinese president Hu Jintao in late 2004 and by vice-president Zeng Qinghong in early 2005. President Hu supposedly promised that China would undertake $100 billion of investment in Latin America over the following ten years. Needless to say, this statement led to high expectations, few of which have been fulfilled. One Chinese expert, however, contends that Latin American newspapers misunderstood Hu's statement, which mentioned the figure of $100 billion only in relation to trade flows. His statement about investment, according to this source, discussed the target of doubling the existing value of investment.[31]

Nonetheless, some investments have materialised, although it remains very difficult to put any aggregate numbers on them due to the serious problems with Chinese statistics.[32] Partial evidence identifies some significant projects, especially copper in Chile ($5 billion in one project and $2 billion in another) and steel in Brazil ($1.4 billion). Negotiations are said to be under way for investments in the energy sector (oil and gas) in Argentina, Brazil, Colombia, and Venezuela; minerals in several countries; and infrastructure for export in Argentina and Brazil. Perhaps the most interesting for the region are some

Table 6. China: Outward Foreign Direct Investment Stock by Region, 2003 and 2006

Region	2003		2006	
	$ bn	Share	$ bn	Share
Asia	26.51	91.40	46.58	83.07
Hong Kong	24.62	84.90	42.27	75.39
ASEAN 10	0.24	0.83	1.76	3.14
Korea	0.15	0.52	0.95	1.69
Africa	0.49	1.69	2.56	4.57
Algeria	0.00	0.00	0.25	0.45
Zambia	0.14	0.48	0.27	0.48
Nigeria	0.03	0.10	0.22	0.39
Sudan	0.00	0.00	0.50	0.89
Latin America*	0.40	1.38	0.74	1.32
Peru	0.13	0.45	0.13	0.23
Mexico	0.10	0.34	0.13	0.23
Brazil	0.05	0.17	0.13	0.23
North America	0.55	1.90	1.59	2.84
Europe	0.49	1.69	2.27	4.05
Other**	0.56	1.94	2.34	4.17
World*	29.0	100.00	56.07	100.00

Source: Stallings, "China's Economic Relations with Developing Countries".
* Excludes tax havens (Cayman Islands, British Virgin Islands).
** Middle East and CIS (except Russia).

high-technology projects between Brazil's Embraer and several Chinese aviation firms.[33] Again, Latin America's share of Chinese FDI stock is small compared to other developing regions, as can be seen in Table 6.

Due to differences in factor endowments (and thus trade structures) in Latin America, Chinese involvement has created both winners and losers in the region. The former tend to be commodity producers and the latter industrial economies. In addition, winners and losers are found across sectors within a given country, where those associated in one way or another with commodities are better off than those in industrial sectors that compete with China. Interestingly, however, both groups of countries have concerns about relations with China. In Mexico and Central America, Chinese competition through low wages is posing a major threat both in export markets and at home. A number of Mexico's assembly plants (maquiladoras) have moved to China to take advantage of lower costs. Cheap exports are flooding the Mexican market itself and threatening the existence of local firms. And Mexico is losing out in the US market, where China has now displaced it as the second-largest supplier.[34]

In South America, by contrast, where exports to China have heightened prosperity, a different kind of concern exists. The fear in South America is that the sub-region is being driven back to the old development model of the nineteenth century, whereby it exports commodities and imports industrial goods. This export profile has proved over the decades to have various disadvantages. Prices of commodities have traditionally been volatile and, some would claim, are likely to fall in the long run in comparison to prices of industrial goods. In terms of labour, production of some commodities relies on unskilled labour, which Latin America has been trying to move away from. In those cases where high-technology processes are used, little labour is employed at all. These concerns are magnified by some of the Chinese "investment" proposals, which have turned out to be long-term loans with the requirement that all of the labour come from China.[35]

Some Latin American countries want simply to strengthen economic relations with China; Chile and Peru would seem to be examples of this approach. Others see the possibility for political or strategic relations as well. Of course, the best-known case of a government's interest in strengthening political ties is Hugo Chávez's Venezuela. Chávez sees China as an important member of his anti-American alliance, but it is unlikely that China will be willing to engage in such ventures (as discussed in the next section). More modest, but more concrete, is Brazil joining with China and other developing countries in the Group of Twenty in the WTO negotiations. The G-20, to which a number of other Latin American countries as well as India and South Africa also belong, is striving to get the best deal possible for developing countries in the WTO's Doha round.

Unlike some other regions discussed in this volume, most Latin American countries do not see China's political model as attractive. That is, despite Hugo Chávez's attempts to muzzle the press and eliminate barriers to indefinite re-election, Latin America in general remains committed to democracy, human rights and the rule of law in a way that China's government makes no pretence to support. Clearly this does not mean that all Latin American democracies are ideal, but the Western hemisphere shares a set of values that binds it together.

As one Latin American intellectual recently put it: values matter. "Latin America shares (and contributes to) the democratic values of the West … Despite clear limitations and inherent internal contradictions, the countries of the region have continued moving forward with democratisation. In this regard, China's internal political model is not especially attractive for Latin America". He goes on to say that China's external diplomatic model is "more seductive", characterised by multi-polarism, multilateralism, non-interference, soft power, pragmatism, collaboration and persuasion – as opposed to their alternatives.[36] Others, however, point out that China's non-interference policy, in particular, has had the effect of supporting some of the least attractive regimes in the world, for example, Sudan, Myanmar, or North Korea.

CHINA, LATIN AMERICA AND THE WORLD

Given China's increased economic presence in Latin America, some have suggested that China also has political ambitions in the region. Despite pronouncements by a few former Bush administration officials, it seems quite unlikely that either China or Latin America will push for an aggressive alliance, where *aggressive* means a set of policies that would restrict US access to the region. Such a move is neither in China's nor in Latin America's interest. On the Chinese side, various factors stand in the way of such an approach. Most important, China has innumerable problems at home, especially in the social and political spheres. These include rapid urbanisation, growing unemployment and inequality, and increasing social protest. The Chinese Communist Party seems determined to maintain power, at least in the medium term, and so must focus on these domestic issues. Environmental problems also weigh heavily on the Chinese government. It might be said that it is precisely because of these domestic problems that China must take risks in Latin America, but this argument does not hold up. In so far as raw materials are the main attraction in Latin America, alternative sources are available elsewhere (especially in Africa), with lower economic and political costs. A low-key approach in Latin America with some countries – especially Brazil and Chile, perhaps also Colombia and Peru – would be advantageous for China. The players who want an aggressive alliance – especially Venezuela, perhaps Bolivia, Ecuador, Nicaragua, even Argentina – are less attractive.

In particular, there is no evidence that China wants to challenge the United States any time soon, which is what an aggressive alliance would imply. As *The Economist* argues,[37] China will be an Asian power for the foreseeable future. It has many problems to resolve in its home region, and Southeast Asian countries also have natural resources to offer if China plays its cards well. Moreover, China needs the United States and its allies (especially Japan) to provide other inputs for its economy. This chapter focuses on China's need for raw materials, but the large majority of China's imports are industrial goods, both inputs and equipment. It needs high-technology products, which generally come as part of the investment process. These goods can come only from the industrial economies at the present time.

China's current economic, social and political situation, as well as what it would gain and lose from an aggressive stance in Latin America, lead to the conclusion that Japan's history in the region could be a fairly good predictor of China's behaviour. Japan started out in a very enthusiastic way in Latin America in the early 1980s, but then this interest fell off. Distance and cultural differences were important obstacles. Issues at home demanded full attention. Integration with Asian neighbours became the main foreign policy priority. And the United States, although it plays a somewhat different role vis-à-vis China than it did with respect to Japan, remains a formidable obstacle to aggressive Chinese measures.[38]

On the Latin American side, the situation is somewhat more ambiguous, since a few governments seem to want to significantly change the status quo. An alliance with China might be useful in promoting their project, although that can be debated. In the meantime, the South American countries that were so enthusiastic about China in the halcyon days of 2004–5 are reconsidering. They have come to realise that Chinese money also comes with strings – if it comes at all. Most of the initial promises (or what were thought to be promises) have not even begun to materialise. Also, a better understanding of how Chinese investment takes place makes it appear less attractive.

Trade relationships, which really have provided copious new resources, are also being questioned. On the one hand is the issue of whether Latin America wants to become primarily a commodity exporter again. On the other hand, even in South America, not to mention Mexico and Central America, there is concern about competition in the industrial sector from a large, low-cost producer. Already barriers are being erected against Chinese exports. Clearly, Latin America will be looking for ways to obtain the advantages from the Chinese relationship without the disadvantages.

Finally, like China, Latin America must consider the implications of confronting the regional hegemon. The United States is still the main market for most of Latin America, especially Mexico and Central America, but South

America as well.[39] Particularly important are the industrial exports that the United States buys. Exports to Europe and Asia – including China – are much more biased towards natural resources. Most, perhaps all, Latin American governments realise that China is neither willing nor able to replace the United States. If this analysis is correct, and no aggressive alliance is likely, what are the implications for the United States? One possibility is that Washington learns nothing and continues to treat Latin America in the heavy-handed way it has typically done – when it focuses on the region at all. A more useful, if less likely, approach is that the Obama administration takes the Chinese presence as a wake-up call and tries to break the syndrome whereby any US attention to Latin America is soon overshadowed by events elsewhere.

CONCLUSION

The purpose of this chapter has been to ask whether the "Chinese model" can offer relevant lessons for Latin America. A tentative answer involved describing the Chinese model in both its economic and political aspects (at least as seen from Latin America); the prerequisites for Chinese-type development to have some chance of success in Latin America; the nature of current relations between China and Latin America; and the context in which the Chinese model emerged in contrast to that of the Latin American approach to development.

Although the introduction to this volume juxtaposes a "neo-liberal" model in Latin America with a state-centred model in China, this is a vision from at least a decade ago. The heyday of anti-statism in Latin America was the late 1980s and early 1990s. Now a much more nuanced approach is being followed in most countries – and an openly populist model in a few (for example, Venezuela, Bolivia, Ecuador and Nicaragua). Latin America is now concerned with public–private partnerships to increase competitiveness and the need to stimulate more investment in physical and human capital. While these were referred to as prerequisites for Chinese-style development, they are also the prerequisites for a centrist (centre-left or centre-right) model of "growth with equity" that most Latin American governments subscribe to.

In the meantime, China has been moving rapidly away from a state-centred model and giving much more space to the private sector. This includes both the domestic private sector and multinational firms. It might not be too far-fetched to think about some kind of convergence in economic policy. In social policy, both face similar problems of inequality and unemployment.

The big difference, however, concerns the political characteristics of the Chinese model. In general, Latin American populations and their political representatives have opted for democratic political systems after a couple of decades of military rule in much of the region. They do not find the political characteristics of the Chinese model to be attractive, and economic reforms and even successes that were carried out under the auspices of authoritarianism are therefore suspect. (A similar doubt has been expressed as to whether the "Chilean model" has lessons for the rest of Latin America, given the authoritarian political system under which Chile's reforms were enacted.)

Some of the international characteristics of the Chinese model are also unattractive for Latin America. On the economic side, China is behaving much as the current industrial powers have traditionally done – despite China's claim to be a developing nation. It wants Latin America to provide it with raw materials and to buy its industrial goods. Latin America thought it had escaped this kind of relationship, so it is not eager to return to it. China's low wages are also seen as providing unfair competition in the production and trade of industrial goods. On the international political front, China's willingness to deal with any country, including some that are known as gross human rights violators, is also a source of scepticism for most Latin American governments and citizens. In this sense, Venezuela is a clear outlier in the Latin American region.

In summary, then, Latin America would certainly like to grow as fast as China, and it has been looking to Asia in general for lessons on how to improve its performance. China, however, has several characteristics that cast doubt on itsef as a source of such lessons: its authoritarian political system, its behaviour in international economic transactions, and the characteristics of its international political relationships. Thus, some of the smaller, more democratic countries of Asia may provide a more compatible development model.

NOTES

1. B. Naughton, *Growing Out of the Plan: Chinese Economic Reform, 1978–1993*, New York: Cambridge University Press, 1995; N. Lardy, *China's Unfinished Economic Revolution*, Washington, DC: The Brookings Institution Press, 1978; and *Integrating China into the Global Economy*, Washington, DC: The Brookings Institution Press, 2002.
2. "The World in 2026: Who Will Be Number One?", *The World in 2006*, London: The Economist, 2005.
3. E. Prasad, "Is the Chinese Growth Miracle Built to Last?", Discussion Paper No. 2995, Bonn: IZA, 2002, Figure 3.
4. IMF, *Direction of Trade Statistics Yearbook, 2006*, Washington, DC: IMF, 2006, pp. 31, 36.
5. B. Naughton, *The Chinese Economy*, Cambridge, MA: MIT Press, 2007, p. 155.
6. S. Streifel, "Impact of China and India on Global Commodity Markets: Focus on Metals, Minerals, and Petroleum", background paper for A. Winters and S. Yusuf, (eds), *Dancing with Giants*, Washington, DC: World Bank, 2007.
7. Naughton, *The Chinese Economy*, Chapter 17.
8. World Bank, *Global Development Finance, 2007*, Washington, DC: World Bank.

9. G. Gaulier, F. Lemoine and D. Ünal-Kesenci, "China's Emergence and the Reorganisation of Trade Flows in Asia", Working Paper 2006–05, Paris: CEPII, 2006.

10. B. Eichengreen and Y. C. Park, "Global Imbalances and Emerging Markets", in J. J. Teunissen and A. Akkerman (eds), *Global Imbalances and the US Debt Problem*, The Hague: Fondad, 2006.

11. A. Winters and S. Yusuf (eds), *Dancing with Giants*, Washington, DC: World Bank, 2007.

12. Naughton, *The Chinese Economy*, Chapter 17; A. García-Herrero, S. Gavilá and D. Santabárbara, "China's Banking Reform: An Assessment of its Evolution and Possible Impact", Occasional Paper 0502, Madrid: Bank of Spain.

13. Lardy, *Integrating China into the Global Economy*; S. Panitchpakdi and M. L. Clifford, *China and the WTO*, New York: John Wiley, 2002.

14. F. Bergsten, et al., *China: The Balance Sheet*, New York: Public Affairs Press, 2006, pp. 31–2. Official figures are much lower, but high enough to alarm the government.

15. Pensions are very important, because China faces a major challenge in its aging population; see analysis in H. Qiao, "Will China Grow Old before Getting Rich?" Global Economics Paper 138, New York: Goldman Sachs, 2006.

16. S. Chauduri and M. Ravallion, "Partially Awakened Dragons: Uneven Growth in China and India", in Winters and Yusuf, *Dancing with Giants*; D. Dollar, "Poverty, Inequality, and Social Disparities during China's Economic Reforms", Policy Research Working Paper 4253, Washington: World Bank, 2007.

17. Bergsten, et al., *China: The Balance Sheet*, Chapter 3.

18. S. Shirk, *China: The Fragile Superpower*, New York: Oxford University Press, 2007; Bergsten, et al., *China: The Balance Sheet*, Chapter 3.

19. *The Economist*, 16 February 2008.

20. One of the earliest discussions comparing East Asia and Latin America is G. Gereffi and D. Wyman (eds) *Manufacturing Miracles: Paths of Industrialization in Latin America and East Asia*, Princeton, NJ: Princeton University Press, 1990. See also The World Bank, *The East Asian Miracle: Economic Growth and Public Policy*, New York: Oxford University Press, 1993, and a volume of commentaries on the East Asian miracle that also compared East Asia and Latin America: N. Birdsall and F. Jasperson (eds), *Pathways to Growth: Comparing East Asia and Latin America*, Washington, DC: Inter-American Development Bank, 1997.

21. See, for example, R. Devlin, A. Estevadeordal and A. Rodríguez (eds), *The Emergence of China: Challenges and Opportunities for Latin America and the Caribbean*, Cambridge, MA: Harvard University Press, 2006, and O. Rosales and M. Kuwayama, "Latin America Meets China and India: Prospects and Challenges for Trade and Investment", *CEPAL Review*, 93, December 2007, pp. 81–104. China's increased importance in Asia has disrupted the so-called flying wild geese model in the region. See K. Lee, "China's Impacts on the Asian Flying Geese and their Adaptation Strategies", Presentation for Conference on the New Asian Giants, Watson Institute for International Studies, Providence, RI: Brown University, 2007.

22. B. Stallings and R. Studart, *Finance for Development: Latin America in Comparative Perspective*, Washington, DC: The Brookings Institution Press, 2006.

23. P. Aghion and P. Howitt, *Endogenous Growth Theory*, Cambridge, MA: MIT Press, 1998.

24. E. di Gropello (ed.), *Meeting the Challenges of Secondary Education in Latin America and East Asia*, Washington, DC: World Bank, 2006.

25. Two of the best-known works making this kind of argument are A. Amsden, *Asia's Next Giant: South Korea and Late Industrialization*, New York: Oxford University Press, 1989, and R. Wade, *Governing the Market: Economic Theory and the Role of Government in East Asian Industrialization*, Princeton, NJ: Princeton University Press, 1990.

26. B. Stallings and W. Peres, *Growth, Employment, and Equity: The Impact of the Economic Reforms in Latin America and the Caribbean*, Washington, DC: The Brookings Institution Press, 2000.

27. Data have been published every two years since 1996. For the latest figures, see D. Kaufmann and A. Kraay, "Governance Matters VI: Governance Indicators for 1996–2006", Policy Research Working Paper 4280, Washington, DC: World Bank, 2007.

28. R. Devlin, "China's Economic Rise", in R. Roett and G. Paz (eds), *China's Expansion into the Western Hemisphere*, Washington, DC: The Brookings Institution Press, 2008, pp. 111–47.

29. L. Palacios, "Latin America as China's Energy Supplier", in Roett and Paz, *China's Expansion into the Western Hemisphere*, pp. 170–89.

30. IMF, *Direction of Trade Statistics Yearbook, 2006*.

31. S. Jiang, "The Chinese Foreign Policy Perspective", in Roett and Paz, *China's Expansion into the Western Hemisphere*, pp. 27–43.

32. One of the main problems with Chinese FDI statistics is that around 75 per cent of the total is listed as going to Hong Kong, which is widely assumed to play a middle man role as a good deal of this investment ultimately goes elsewhere – including back to China itself. This problem is exacerbated by the fact that the other large destination is the Caribbean tax havens. In the tables in this chapter, the latter funds are excluded, since – unlike Hong Kong – virtually none of this money is expended locally.

33. ECLAC, *Latin America and the Caribbean in the World Economy, 2004 and Trends for 2005*, Santiago: ECLAC, 2005.

34. Devlin, Estevadeordal and Rodríguez, *The Emergence of China*; E. Dussel Peters, "Implications of China's Recent Economic Performance for Mexico", Briefing Paper, Dialogue on Globalization, Berlin: Friedrich Ebert Stiftung, 2005.

35. Devlin, Estevadeordal and Rodríguez, *The Emergence of China*; D. Lederman, M. Olarreaga and G. Perry, *Latin American Response to the Growth of China and India*, Washington, DC: World Bank, Office of the Chief Economist for Latin America and the Caribbean, 2006.

36. J.G. Tokatlian, "A View from Latin America", in Roett and Paz, *China's Expansion into the Western Hemisphere*, pp. 59–89.

37. *The Economist*, 31 March 2007.

38. On Japan and Latin America in the 1980s, see B. Stallings and G. Székely (eds), *Japan, the United States, and Latin America: Toward a Trilateral Relationship in the Western Hemisphere*, Baltimore: Johns Hopkins University Press, 1993.

39. IMF, *Direction of Trade Statistics Yearbook, 2006*.

CHAPTER 3

The China Model in Africa: A New Brand of Developmentalism

Catherine Boone with Dhawal Doshi

China has been pushing increased investment and cheap credit into Africa for at least five years. But the astonishing levels of expenditure and the breadth of Chinese involvement reached levels in 2006 that focused minds in the West ... Africa has not seen inward flows of this volume in all the post-independence years.[1]

Introduction

This chapter asks if a China model defines or guides China's economic and diplomatic offensive on the African continent, and whether there is any evidence that Africans themselves see deepening Africa–China ties in this light. We argue that it is indeed possible to speak of a China model in this context. It is possible to discern a China model in two different ways. First, Chinese leaders and many African leaders work deliberately to construct a vision or overarching idea of China's growing involvement in Africa that stands in juxtaposition to the IFI model of economic-cum-political engagement that most countries of sub-Saharan Africa came to know in the mid-1980s. Direct beneficiaries of deepening China–Africa ties have vigorously embraced the opportunity to transcend the IFI model that not only pressured African governments into political, macroeconomic, and sectoral reforms for which most African leaders and technocrats had little enthusiasm or confidence, but also produced little by way of direct stimulus to economic development and growth. Second, it is possible to recognise a China model in the actual patterns of government–business relations and state–society relations that are promoted by Chinese involvement, and with Chinese resources, in Africa.

At the same time, however, African business people in competitive sectors of the economy, African workers, and perhaps those in communities that feel the direct effects of natural resource exploitation (oil, timber, mining), seem to see Chinese involvement as less distinctive – that is, more in keeping with their experiences with other foreign businesses and investors, and perhaps more in keeping with long histories of state–society relations in Africa – and less uniformly beneficial.

This chapter develops these arguments in four steps. In Part I, we offer a sketch of the IFI model of external involvement in African political economies. We will argue that this is a baseline against which African leaders compare their recent experiences with the Chinese. Part II is a brief overview of the volume, composition, and geographic loci of Chinese trade and investment ties with Africa since the late 1990s. Part III argues that Chinese involvement differs from the IFI model in three particular ways, and that, together, these constitute the distinctive China model in Africa: (a) the Chinese government is pumping resources into extractive industries and infrastructural development, often relying on state-owned or state-sponsored companies to do the work; (b) China and Chinese firms, often in public–private partnerships, are investing in a diversified range of export-oriented and domestic market-oriented productive activities, from manufacturing to agriculture to aquaculture; and (c) China supports authoritarian rule more or less overtly by renouncing any intention to "improve" or "democratise" government in Africa, or make it more accountable or transparent. These dimensions of Chinese involvement represent clear contrasts with the IFI model, which is defined by its intense focus on government austerity, the compression of middle-class consumption, export-oriented productive activities, private investment, reliance on market mechanisms to steer investment, and political conditionality.

In Part IV, we present the results of an analysis of African views of Chinese–African ties, with particular attention to the question of whether the idea of a China model is discernable in everyday commentary on this issue. For this, we conducted a content analysis of newspaper articles that appeared in 2006 and 2007 in about ten Nigerian, Kenyan and South African dailies. We inventoried references to different forms of China's economic and diplomatic involvement in Nigeria and South Africa, coded articles for positive or negative views of Chinese involvement, sorted views according to who expressed them (African officials, business people, or person-on-the-street), and recorded the relative frequency with which particular ideas about China appeared in the press (China model, China as a development standard, China as a leader, China as a "no strings attached" partner, the Chinese as competitors, Chinese involvement as exploitative/corrupt, and so on). Although the newspaper search could not give us a complete or robust "sample" of views from these three countries, we present the results as one glimpse of what some African newspapers are publishing about Chinese involvement in their countries. Some particularly interesting press clips are assembled in the Appendix.

I. THE IFI MODEL IN AFRICA

As the 1980s progressed, African countries became more and more dependent upon a creditors cartel headed by the international financial institutions (IFIs), the IMF and the World Bank, for the inflow of loans they needed to sustain trade and to support the operation of governments.[2] For almost all the countries of sub-Saharan Africa, the IFI model of external capital inflows that developed during this period constitutes a standard against which recent experiences with China can be compared.[3]

The specificity of the IFI model is that it links continuing inflows of loans from multilateral sources (and from bilateral sources that make aid inflows conditional on an "IMF seal of approval") to policy reform in an "adjustment regime" designed to improve macroeconomic management, governance and sectoral-specific economic policies in African countries. The IFI model is distinctive in both the policy content it seeks to promote and in its modalities of operation.

The policy content is familiar to all observers of the wave of neo-liberal reform that swept much of the developing world in the 1980s and 1990s. Its main features are those of the Washington Consensus: currency devaluation followed by measures to keep currencies valued at market rates; deflationary measures, including tight credit policies, trade openness, liberalisation of prices and market-access on domestic markets; liberalisation of conditions regulating private investment (domestic and foreign); promoting of export-oriented productive activities (especially in the primary goods sectors wherein Africa was supposed to have a "comparative advantage"); and reduction of fiscal deficits achieved mostly through government austerity. The last of these included cutbacks in public investment and social service delivery, which included trimming health and education delivery until the late 1990s. The overall reform program was characterised by a clear "anti-state bias" and the assumption that markets, once freed from the suffocating hand of government intervention, could restore growth. As van de Walle summarises it, the World Bank/IMF policy agenda called for "the withdrawal of the state from basic developmental activities".[4]

The modalities of operation of the IFI "adjustment regime" are familiar to observers of the structural adjustment programs of the 1980s and 1990s. What is perhaps distinctive about Africa's experience with the IFI model is the heavy-handedness of the IFI role in policy-making, the intensity of their physical presence in African capitals and state agencies, and the intensity of IFI monitoring of the political and policy conditionalities attached to the inflows of loan capital. Van de Walle's analysis is useful in underscoring the extent to which the IFI model of the 1980s and 1990s was, in its general norms and political character, consistent with earlier norms built-into the Western aid regime in Africa: in the IFI model, as in earlier aid relationships, "donors retain the final say over all allocation decisions ... [This is] reflected in preference for project aid and in the presence of conditionality to govern program aid". Van de Walle explains that "the 1980s witnessed the "explosive growth" in the explicitness and detail of the conditions donors attached to their aid". The routines of capital transfer included letters of intent, policy framework chapters, donor-monitoring protocols with deadlines and targets, loans distributed in tranches according to explicit schedules of conditionality, and the "annual ritual of debt rescheduling" ... "Governments were regularly threatened with nondisbursement to encourage them to implement the loan agreements".[5] From 1992 onwards, policy condition-ality has included not only tariff-reduction schedules, privatisation schedules, subsidy-elimination deadlines, debt reimbursement targets, and so on, but also explicit "governance reforms", including requirements for judicial-sector reform, military reform, transparency in government procurement and contracting, civil service reform, reform of monitoring and regulatory agencies, tax and tax admin-istration reform, reform in the modes of delivering essential services, and so on.[6]

By 2000, the IFI model of lending and policy reform had delivered much of the promised macroeconomic stability to Africa, but only limited growth. The general consensus outside of Washington DC is that "structural adjustment", at least as it was actually practised in the 1980s and 1990s, had failed to re-launch economic growth in sub-Saharan Africa. In the late 1990s, the World Bank itself began to experiment with programs and policies that would restore to African governments some of the developmental role that they had forfeited in the 1980s (for example, state investment in infrastructure, investment in primary and even tertiary education, preventative health initiatives).[7] The basic neo-liberal thrust of the IFI model remains well intact, however, as do the disciplining routines and policy "micro-management"[8] that have become the hallmark of the much-resented "conditionalities". Although van de Walle draws a different conclusion from his data, he noted in 2001 that "a majority of decision-makers across Africa [including intellectuals and civil society leaders, not to mention the public do not believe that "adjustment will work" for a variety of reasons ... [F]or the most part, adjustment programs have been imposed from outside on dubious governments ... African governments often remain uncon-vinced by the intellectual logic behind these programs".[9]

By the year 2000, the ground was well-prepared for entry of a new player and new ways of brokering Africa's dependence on external sources of capital, and for new ways of managing its external trading relationships.

II. CHINA'S TRADE AND INVESTMENT TIES TO AFRICA

So marginal was Chinese involvement in Africa c. 2000 that van de Walle does not even mention China as an investor or lender in Africa in his 1999 review of the economic status of the African economies. This changed very rapidly over the course of the next few years. Several sources report total trade flows between China and Africa at about $40 billion in 2005, making China Africa's third-largest trading partner (behind the US and France), to $56 billion for 2006,[10] with increases projected to bring the total to $100 billion in 2010.[11]

a. Africa's Exports to China

Africa's exports to China rose at an annual rate of about 50 per cent between 2000 and 2005[12] fuelled by China's voracious demand for raw materials, especially energy resources. According to Broadman, the dollar value of Africa's sales to China (yearly average, 2002–4), was US $9.2 billion[13] The 2005 total was $16.95 billion.[14] By late 2006, Asia (China, Japan, India, Korea, and others) consumed 27 per cent of all Africa's exports, making the region a destination for African products that is on par with the US and the EU.[15] China itself purchased about 10 per cent of all African exports in 2005. The origins of these commodity outflows are geographically concentrated, with five or six mineral-exporting countries – Angola, Sudan, Libya, Nigeria, Algeria and Gabon – accounting for 85 per cent of Africa's sales to China.[16]

Oil, followed by metals and then agricultural raw materials and timber, are the leading categories of exports to China. Oil and natural gas constituted 62 per cent of the dollar value of all China's purchases from Africa in 2004, with metals and ores constituting another 17 per cent, and agricultural raw materials (apparently including timber, which itself accounted for about 5 per cent of total African exports to China in the 2002–4 period), accounting for 7 per cent.[17] China's Africa purchases satisfied one-quarter of its demand for imported crude oil the following year (2005),[18] making China the second-largest importer of African oil (after the US) in that year.[19] Angola is the single largest supplier of crude oil to China (50 per cent of Chinese imports of African crude in 2005), followed by Sudan (about 20 per cent of China's imports of African crude in 2005).[20] These countries have become heavily dependent on oil sales to China: China buys 50 per cent of Sudan's output, and 25 per cent of Angola's.[21]

b. Africa's Imports from China

Commentary that is concerned with the dynamics of geo-strategic competition between China and the West has paid little attention to China's dramatically successful efforts to access Africa's domestic markets. According to the IMF Direction of Trade Statistics compiled by Joshua Eisenman, China's imports from Africa did not exceed the dollar value of its exports to Africa until 2004. China's exports to Africa climbed sharply after 2000, rising from $5 billion in 2000 to $17.7 billion in 2005. In 2006, China was Africa's second-largest supplier (after France).[23]

China is selling not only machinery and equipment to sustain its spectacular drive to develop African transport, power and telecommunications infrastructure, but also consumer goods, mostly in categories at the cutting edge of China's export drive throughout the world: textile goods (including garments) and consumer electronics.[24] Broadman writes that Chinese consumer goods "have surged into African markets",[25] where they compete against Africa's domestically produced manufactured goods in South Africa and Nigeria, the leading African importers of Chinese products,[26] as well as in Kenya, Botswana, Lesotho, and many other countries.[27] South Africa, with its wide and deep consumer markets, runs a large trade deficit with China: its imports from China exceed its exports to China by a factor of four.[28] Angola and Sudan are also top destinations for Chinese manufactured goods.

Table 1. China's Exports to Selected African Countries (selected countries, in constant USD, 1990–2006)

Country/Region ($ millions)	1990	1995	2000	2005	2006	2007	2008
Angola	39.4	44.6	53.2	401.5	926.4	1283.9	2613.7
Botswana	6.7	7.1	18.2	60.9	75.8	143.5	182.4
Cameroon	22.8	19.4	35.6	164.0	229.4	342.0	414.8
Congo-Brazzaville	26.5	17.0	48.5	156.9	254.4	433.7	607.8
Dem Rep Congo	502.7	137.4	29.0	72.9	89.5	109.4	203.4
Ghana	40.7	124	128.5	690.2	822.1	1251.2	1675.3
Kenya	47.3	181.5	163.1	522.4	689.5	1015.2	1286.7
Namibia	1.6	2	9.7	65.7	143.9	248.9	217.1
Nigeria	310	390.8	717	2392.6	2980.1	3995.7	6647.2
Senegal	43.6	68	77	158.8	207.2	353.3	459.6
Sierra Leone	8.6	7.1	14.8	39.0	47.5	69.1	88.9
South Africa	396.7	1475.9	1612.9	4525.3	6571.3	8211.8	9609.6
Sudan	36.5	44.9	163.5	1302.5	1426.4	1548.4	1864.8

Source: IMF Direction of Trade Statistics 2008.

Table 2. China's Imports from Selected African Countries (selected countries, in constant USD, 1990–2006)

Country/Region ($ millions)	1990	1995	2000	2005	2006	2007	2008
Angola	0.6	136.9	1842.8	6668.8	11081.2	12934.5	24027.6
Botswana	3.2	0.8	0.1	4.0	8.4	26.4	174.6
Cameroon	41.2	39.2	146.8	71.4	213.1	168.2	361.7
Congo-Brazzaville	0.5	4.5	326.6	2284.8	2788.5	2832.8	3832.7
Dem Rep Congo	9.9	2.3	1.1	175.9	368.6	460.5	1365.6
Ghana	2.8	7.8	16.2	97.2	82.1	57.1	107.4
Kenya	3.3	20.2	38.1	55.5	66.9	69.7	96.6
Namibia	0	1.2	4.1	87.1	126.2	159.3	321.0
Nigeria	9.9	63.8	295	552.5	330.4	586.0	566.8
Senegal	2.7	9.4	10.7	20.5	19.9	35.1	24.1
Sierra Leone	0	0	0	2.3	1.1	5.9	7.5
South Africa	372.6	1314.8	1521.3	4063.9	4589.2	7100.6	9274.7
Sudan	62.8	75.7	735.7	2621.7	1949.1	4118.0	6568.5

Source: IMF Direction of Trade Statistics 2008.

c. Chinese FDI in Africa

Broadman[29] reports that the stock of Chinese FDI in Africa (mid-2006) was estimated at $1.18 billion, but this figure is so small that it is hard to guess what Broadman is measuring, since Chinese state enterprises' equity investments in African oil fields alone far exceed this sum. Shinn gives a figure of $6.7 billion for China's direct investment in Africa for 2005 and notes that this sum is "still modest compared to Western investment".[30] It is also small compared to China's worldwide stock of FDI (in 2004) of $45 billion.[31] Leading African destinations for Chinese FDI in 2004 were Sudan, Nigeria, and South Africa.[32]

The UNECA calculated that China and India together accounted for 10 per cent of all greenfield investment in Africa in 2005.[33] This figure should perhaps be considered alongside Chris Alden's observation that most of China's FDI in Africa is equity investment in existing enterprises (joint ventures with African SOEs, purchase of equity in established oil fields, purchases of African SOEs undergoing privatisation (or of shares therein), and so on).[34] French wrote in 2006 that "by one tally, China current has about 900 investment projects on the continent".[35]

It is clear that most Chinese FDI in Africa was been targeted at oil and other mineral extraction, and in infrastructural development that is derivative of China's interest in Africa's oil and metals (railways, roads, ports, and so on). Noteworthy, however, is that since 2000, Chinese FDI has increasingly diversified from extractive industries to other sectors, "including apparel, agro-processing, power generation, road construction, tourism, telecom, and so on".[36] Below we discuss the role of the Chinese government in promoting FDI in Africa in all these sectors.

d. Evaluating the Magnitude of China–Africa Economic Ties

China is also a lender to African governments, and to Chinese firms (including SOEs) that invest in Africa, and well as the source of grants and other concessional flows to Africa. The volumes/sums of these flows are not published for reasons explored by Carol Lancaster,[37] but Howard French does give an idea of the magnitudes involved for some of China's leading African partners: "In 2006, China committed $8.1 billion in lending to Nigeria, Angola, and Mozambique alone", a figure that can be compared with the World Bank's commitment of "$2.3 billion to all of sub-Saharan Africa in the same time span".[38] Total aid inflows to sub-Saharan Africa as of about 2004 are generally estimated at $12–13 billion a year, a figure often compared to outflows of about $15 billion for debt service payments.

Alden[39] and Lancaster[40] have both noted that the multi-stranded nature of China's involvement in particular countries, including its extensive use of "package deal" co-operation projects and in-kind trading relationships, makes it difficult to sort China–Africa flows into the book-keeping categories (loans, grants, export credits, direct investments, debt forgiveness,[41] and so on) employed by Western governments and the international financial institutions. Yet, for the purposes of the present analysis, what is most interesting about China's growing ties with Africa may not be the quantitative reckonings and head-to-head comparisons. Rather, what is most interesting is the particular nature of China's trade and investment ties to Africa, including the credit/lending relationships, the manner in which they are established, and the role of the Chinese government in establishing and managing these relationships.

III. THE CHINA MODEL: FOUR DEPARTURES FROM THE IFI MODEL

China's rulers have undertaken a major, long-term, diplomatic and economic offensive on the African continent, supplying investment capital, capital goods, cash, technology and technical assistance, weapons, and more, in exchange for raw materials, diplomatic support in the UN and WTO, and market access. Lancaster argues that they have deliberately sought "to project their own distinctive image [as a development partner in Africa] ... one that would provide them with a separate and privileged relationship with the governments that they are helping and cultivating".[42] China has courted African leaders with "wave after wave of high-level diplomatic visitors in the continent",[43] wined and dined them "with exquisite courtesy" at China–Africa Cooperation Forum meetings in Beijing in 2000 and 2006 (with a CACF meeting in Addis in 2003), signed deals for huge multi-year mega-projects in a growing number of African states, and provided diplomatic support for African allies such as Zimbabwe's Robert Mugabe, who have come under siege for human rights abuses. Beijing has stepped into strained relationships between the West and the largest African oil and mineral exporters and loudly advertised the fact that China understands Africa's real development needs and aspirations, and that Chinese cash and investment capital comes "without conditionalities".

African resentment of the IFI model – with its punishing conditionalities, micro-management, and cookie-cutter imposition of neo-liberal policy reform – is a force that is itself helping to pave the way for a new model of African partnership with foreign investors and donors. Another factor that is encouraging African governments to look towards the East is the fact that the IFI model has delivered less and less in terms of cash flow and investment capital for African governments.[44] As Chris Alden sees it, "the dramatic fall in foreign assistance and FDI after the end of the Cold War" coincided with "the rise of interference in domestic affairs by both bilateral and multilateral donors ... African leaders sought out new sources of regime [support]".[45] Enter the Chinese, who provide not only capital inflows, but also a development model:

> The symbolic attraction of China, a once-impoverished country victimised by Western imperialism and held back by its own pursuit of disastrous forms of socialism, clearly resonates with African elites looking for a positive development model from the Third World. At the same time, China's rapid rise to power is also appealing for African leaders who are desperately looking for models of success that do not threaten established regime interests ... China holds up a beacon of hope that all the gains of office need not be lost in the process of reform.[46]

Speaking of one of China's most important and least democratic African partners, Amosu writes that the ruling party of Angola has "seized on the idea of a Chinese model of development – involving an autocratic and unaccountable commandist political economy – as an effective alternative to Western-style reform".[47] Other African leaders, intellectuals, opinion-shapers, and civil society leaders, while often nuanced in their assessments, have identified China with a purposeful "developmental state" model that stands in clear contrast to the neoliberal austerity of the IFI model.[48] Walden Bello, in a recent piece in

Foreign Policy in Focus, relays conversations he had at the World Social Forum meeting in Nairobi in January 2007:

> "There is something refreshing to China's approach", said a Nigerian diplomat who asked not to be identified. "They don't attach all those conditionalities that accompany Western loans". Adds Justin Fong, executive director of the Chinese NGO, Moving Mountains: "Whether accurate or not, the image Africans have of the Chinese is that they get things done. They don't waste their time in meetings. They just go ahead and build roads."[49]

We argue here that the contrasts conveyed by these comments are very real: China's relations with its leading African partners differ from the IFI model in three stark ways that together constitute a distinctive China model in Africa.

a. State-to-State Partnerships in Extractive Industries and Infrastructural Development

The Chinese government is pumping resources into extractive industries and infrastructural development, usually relying on Chinese state-owned or state-sponsored companies to do the work, and often in partnership with African SOEs. The leading role of government in these initiatives, and the targeting of infrastructural development, are features of these undertakings that set them apart from standard operating procedure under the IFI model.

African infrastructure – railways, roads, hospitals, power plants, transmission lines, ports, bridges, and so on – suffered years of neglect under the IFI model, which prioritised cutbacks in government spending and dept repayment. Akwe Amosu calls it "a no-go area for Western donors for decades".[50] China's interest in rehabilitating and extending economic infrastructure (usually to make possible the extraction of Africa's raw materials) is perhaps the most dramatic aspect of its current investment offensive. Such investments are sometimes wrapped up in "broad-spectrum package deals" worth many billions of dollars.[51] Examples can be found in Gabon, Angola, DRC, Nigeria and Sudan. Here, Amosu describes the Gabon deal:

> Deep inside the tropical forest of Gabon, 500 miles from the coast, China is going where no other investors dare. A Chinese consortium, led by the China National Machinery and Equipment Import and Export Corporation, has won the contract to develop Gabon's massive Belinga iron ore deposit. In return for purchasing the entire output, Chinese operators will build not only the extractive infrastructure at Belinga but a hydro-electric power dam to power it, a railway to the coast, and a deepwater port north of the capital, Libreville, for exporting the ore. This venture will cost several billion dollars, [and will be undertaken with] the support of [China's] entire state machine.[52]

Amosu also writes of deals with Angola:

> The Chinese agreed to [a broad-spectrum package deal] involving major infra-structural investment for Angola, which is … the continent's lead supplier [of oil] to China. A $2 billion line of credit announced in 2004, … [now raised to] a reported $6 billion, over several years [will] finance a raft of different projects such as hospitals, schools, roads, bridges, housing, office buildings, training programs, and the laying of fiberoptic cable.[53]

Another source cited an Angola government official's response to criticism of the Chinese (for reserving only 30 per cent of the building contracts for Angola companies, with the rest going to Chinese): "'Why would you stop these guys coming?' asks Isaac Maria dos Anjos, a ruling-party MP. 'It absolutely will help the ruling party. We have to build hospitals. We have to build bridges. And we will do a lot of it in just one year," that is, before the next election".[54]

A $5 billion loan deal between China and the Democratic Republic of Congo was announced in September 2007, with capital earmarked for infrastructure and mining. According to the BBC, projects included in the package included roads, some 30 hospitals, 100 health centres, housing developments, two univer-sities, a 3,400 km highway to link Kisangani to Kasumbalesa (on the border with Zambia), a 3,200 km rail to link major mining centres in the south with the Atlantic port of Matadi, and $2 billion in projects "to rehabilitate the crumbling mining infrastructure, and [set up] joint ventures in the mines sector".[55]

In 2006, the Chinese were considering, or had already committed to "some $7 billion of investment in Nigeria across a wide range of sectors".[56] In January 2007, Bello mentioned a $6 billon joint venture between the Chinese Oil and Natural Gas Corporation and the LN Mittal Group to invest in railways, oil refining and power "in exchange for rights to drill oil".[57] The Lagos–Kano rail project may be part of this deal. Other Nigeria investments included $2.3 billion by the China National Offshore Corporation (CNOOC) to buy a 45 per cent working interest in an offshore enterprise called OML 130, also known as the Akpo field,[58] and China National Petroleum Corporation (CNPC) investments in the Port Harcourt oil refinery.[59] In November 2007, the international press reported a possible deal in which CNOOC would buy Royal Dutch Shell's Nigeria assets in the Nigeria Delta (including shares in two offshore oil blocks) for $900 million.[60] China also has projects in Nigeria in power generation, power transmission, hospitals, telecommunications, and beyond.

China's involvement in Sudan follows this pattern. Chinese SOEs established multi-billion dollar joint-venture investments in Sudan's national oil companies, starting in 1995 when China National Petroleum Corporation (CNPC) bought a 40 per cent share in the Greater Nile Petroleum Operating Company. SINOPEC has also invested, and is building a 1,500 km pipeline from the oil fields to Port Sudan on the Red Sea, "where China's Petroleum Engineering Construction Company is constructing a tanker terminal".[61] Chinese firms are "building bridges near the Merowe Dam and two other sites on the River Nile. It is involved in key hydropower projects", including the Marowe Dam project, which involved the forced displacement of a local population of 70,000 people.[62]

The vast majority of companies spearheading or involved in the China-financed projects are state-owned, as the examples cited above suggest. One of the largest road-builders in Africa is China Road and Bridge Construction, which is owned by the Chinese government.[63] In the oil sector, Chinese SOEs are partnering with African SOEs, as in Sudan, Angola, Algeria and Gabon.[64] In mining, Chinese SOEs are purchasing rights to develop sites owned by African governments, and often exploited in earlier periods by African SOEs.[65] French notes that "the African state owned enterprises that sit astride the major extractive industries ... tend to be poorly funded and lacking in the technologies badly needed to upgrade their operations after years of decline and neglect".[66] SOE-plus-SOE joint ventures defy the norms of the IFI model. In extractive industry sectors, in the 1990s, the IFIs promoted the ideals of privatisation, private concessioneering or sub-contracting operations and management to (private) multinational corporations. The vertical integration strategies that are so evident in the energy sector (also typical of Chinese investments in textiles and agroprocessing[67]) also seem distinctively Chinese in today's context – vertical integration as a goal resonates far better with the developmentalist strategies promoted by the World Bank in the 1960s and 1970s than with the IFI's neo-liberalism of the late 1980s and 1990s.

The leading financier of this activity is the China Export-Import Bank, the country's official export credit agency (which is wholly-owned by the Chinese government). Peter Bosshard wrote in 2007 that the Export-Import Bank "has approved at least $6.5 billion in loans for Africa, most of which [80 per cent] is for infrastructure investments. The bank had relations with 36 African countries and had 259 African projects in its portfolio".[68] Bosshard notes that the World Bank estimated the figure of Exim Bank loans to sub-Saharan Africa for infrastructure project alone to exceed $12.5 billion by mid-2006, a figure that Broadman compared to the OECD's total ODA for African infrastructure (as of 2004) of $4 billion.[69]

Lending for prestige projects also constitutes a kind of infrastructural investment, and is also a Chinese departure from the IFI model. Stadiums, government ministry buildings and houses of parliament have all been delivered turnkey-style to African governments, allowing African leaders to display their economic prowess and capacity to deliver, and "revealing China's deep understanding of the imperatives of governance in ... impoverished countr[ies]".[70]

b. State-sponsored Economic Diversification

China and Chinese firms, often in public–private partnerships, are investing in a diversified range of export-oriented and domestic-market-oriented productive activities, from manufacturing to agriculture to aquaculture. Since 2000, the Chinese government has promoted an ever-broader range of productive investment in non-extractive industry in Africa. As in the extractive sector, many or most of these projects are led by Chinese government-owned enterprises, with access to preferential loans and buyer credits provided by the Chinese government, often as part and parcel of larger "general" investment offensives or mega-deals. President Hu Jintao, on an eight-nation African tour in February 2007 (his third such tour in three years) pledged new loans to encourage Chinese companies to "help Africa develop processing and manufacturing industries so as to ease unemployment pressure and enhance the competitiveness of its [processed or manufactured] exports".[71]

Alden describes a push into agriculture and agro-processing that is "related to [China's] food-security concerns. To the end, China's Ministry of Foreign Trade and Economic Cooperation (MOFTEC) has sought to encourage Chinese investment in Africa ... in the production of farm-machinery [and] agricultural processing ... targeted for the world market". He provides examples of Chinese investors setting up "joint-ventures in fish processing in Gabon and Namibia, with some of the richest fisheries in the world, and leas[ing] agricultural land in Zambia, Tanzania, and Zimbabwe.[72] Vertical integration is often a feature of Chinese investment strategies in agro-processing, including joint ventures in textiles between Chinese and African SOEs (as in Zambia, at least before the expiration of the Multifiber Agreement in January 2005).[73]

c. Lending and Investment with "No Strings Attached"

As Alden reports "Beijing has forsworn conditionalities with considerable vigour", thus freeing themselves of onerous complications in their relations with African partner-governments.[74] In doing so, the Chinese are capitalising on African leaders' eagerness to move beyond the IFI model in their dealings with the world. They are also creating a strategic advantage for themselves, for, as French argues, Chinese non-interference gives them "an excuse for doing whatever suits Beijing".[75]

Chinese leaders seem to advertise the "no strings attached" rule at every opportunity. Alden writes that "President Hu Jintao, in a state visit to Gabon in February 2004, declared that Chinese co-operation with Africa was 'free of political conditionality and serving the interests of Africa and China'".[76] Nigeria's *This Day* reported the words of China's ambassador to Nigeria, Mr Xu

Jiangua, who, upon handing over a consignment of anti-malarial drugs to the Nigerian minister of health, "said that China's assistance was devoid of selfish motives, as [it] never attached any political conditionalities or demands to … any aid".[77]

Although the contrast with the IFI model is stark and deliberate, it is not quite true that Chinese aid is conditionality-free: China insists that its African partner-governments frequently reiterate their commitment to the "One China Policy".[78]

China has thus renounced any intention to make government in Africa more accountable, more transparent, or better institutionalised. It supports authoritarian rule overtly in Zimbabwe and Sudan, drawing sharp criticism from many African NGOs, civil society organisations and intellectuals.[79] Many analysts have argued that this aspects of Beijing's African strategy seem short-sighted, in that China, too, will have a medium- and long-term interest in political stability and good governance in Africa, as well as good relations with the workers it employs and the communities in which it works. Bad experiences for the Chinese in Zambia were perhaps a wake-up call in this regard. There are also some signs that Beijing is re-evaluating its blanket approval of and support for Khartoum's Darfur strategy.[80]

IV. Newspaper Content Analysis

For a view of Chinese involvement in Africa that was more "from the field" than secondary analyses could provide, we coded stories on Chinese involvement in Africa that appeared in fifteen Nigerian, South African and Kenyan newspapers. The Factiva search engine allowed us to search by keyword (in headlines and first paragraphs) in order to collect articles published over the last year in Nigeria and South Africa, and over the last two years in Kenya. We inventoried references to different forms of China's economic and diplomatic involvement in Nigeria and South Africa, coded articles for positive or negative views of Chinese involvement, sorted views according to who expressed them (African officials, business people, or person-on-the-street), and recorded the relative frequency with which particular ideas about China appeared in the press (China model, China as a development standard, China as a leader, China as a "no strings attached" partner, the Chinese as competitors, Chinese involvement as exploitative/corrupt, and so on). We paid particular attention to the question of whether the idea of a China model is discernable in everyday commentary on this issue. Here we provide country-by-country overviews. Excerpts from some of the press stories are collected in the Appendix.

Nigeria

Our Factiva search for Nigeria covered articles with "China" or "Chinese" appearing in the headline or lead paragraph of three Nigerian newspapers – *This Day*, *Vanguard* and *News Watch* – for one year, between December 2006 and December 2007. The search yielded 137 results, out of which we deemed 30 to be relevant for our research. The discarded articles dealt with an assortment of topics, most of which were related to sport (usually the Falcons – Nigeria's women's soccer team who played in the FIFA Women's World Cup in China), news and issues within China, and other miscellaneous topics.

Of the 30 articles about China's involvement in Nigeria, 24 had a generally positive tone, while the remaining articles were coded as "negative" or "neutral". Of the total, 25 articles reported on Chinese investment in transport and railway infrastructure, manufacturing and assembly units, oil extraction and pipelines, mining, power plants, tourism, and/or telecommunications. The launching of a Nigerian telecommunication satellite, NIGCOMSAT, in China was a big event, and all four articles specifically related to the development of the telecom sector were related to this event. There were not many news stories about Chinese interest in Nigerian oil (only three of the 30 articles we collected, even though this commodity is the focal point of the China–Nigeria relationship.

Three news stories dealt with Chinese foreign aid in the form of healthcare and technical assistance. One of the articles dealing with foreign aid reported China's donation of US $5.5 million worth of drugs and medical equipment for the eradication of malaria in Nigeria.[81]

Seven of the 30 articles described the Chinese as either presenting Nigeria with a positive development model, greater business opportunities, or no-strings-attached assistance. Two articles carrying a negative tone were ones that focused on corruption in the sale of local companies to Chinese firms. Two articles talked about local politicians regarding Nigeria and China as "natural allies", given the preponderant size and demographic weight of each country in its own regional context.[82]

Although Nigeria received an average of 14 per cent of all Chinese exports to Africa for 2003–6,[83] only one of the articles complained about cheap or poor-quality goods coming from China. This stands in contrast to what we observed in the South African news stories, where such complaints about Chinese goods figured prominently in our sample. At a meeting with US Department of State officials, an unidentified Nigerian politician reportedly said that "Nigeria's pharmaceutical and textile industries are suffering from what appears to be "dumping" of Chinese pharmaceutical and textiles, and from counterfeit goods originating from China", but this comment was balanced by his observation later in the same speech that Nigeria's infrastructure could benefit from Chinese aid.[84]

In almost all the sectors of activity mentioned in our data set, including the high-potential oil, telecom, infrastructure development and tourism sectors, the Chinese were seen as boosting standards and producing benefits for Nigeria.

South Africa

Our Factiva search for South Africa consisted of a keyword search of "China" or "Chinese" in headings and lead paragraphs for a period of one year from January 2007 to January 2008 in ten South African newspapers.[85] The search yielded 318 results, out of which we deemed 78 relevant for our research. Most of the discarded articles were reports about local events in China, views of Chinese politicians, and sports-related events.

Out of the 78 articles considered relevant to our research, 35 had a positive tone about the Chinese involvement in the country, 19 had a neutral tone and 24 were negative. This stood sharp contrast to Nigerian and Kenyan newspapers, where a much smaller proportion of articles had a negative tone. More than 30 of the South African articles expressed viewpoints of editors, scholars from academia and think tanks, while about 20 were straightforward reporting of news. Six articles represented viewpoints of local citizens, and the remaining were divided almost evenly between viewpoints of government officials and private business people.

The South African articles were dominated by news about the commercial sector and South African imports (27 out of 78 stories). Of the 27 articles coded as having to do with Chinese imports or China's presence in South Africa's commercial sector, eight had a negative tone, whereas nine had a positive one. Many of the negative stories were about the low or questionable quality of particular categories of Chinese products (dog food and pharmaceuticals appeared repeatedly), counterfeiting, or import competition that hurt South African industries.

Among these, issues relating to quota restrictions on Chinese imports to South Africa received the most attention. Clothing manufacturers pressured the government to restrict the importation of cheap Chinese garments that were blamed for "massive job losses and factory closures" in South Africa. One article stressed the salutary effects of such restrictions by noting that in the wake of import restrictions on Chinese garments, South African clothing manufacturers had been able to establish multiple long-term contracts with major local chain stores.[86]

Twelve of the 78 articles dealt with Chinese investment in the South African banking sector. The major recent development was the 20 per cent take-over of Standard Bank South Africa by Industrial and Commercial Bank of China (ICBC). Valued at R36.7 billion ($5.6 billion), the deal was described as the biggest foreign investment on the continent.[87] Reacting to the deal, the chief economist of a local consulting firm said, "It suddenly feels as though South Africa is playing a whole new, and very exciting, ball game".[88] Although some scepticism about Beijing's calculated strategic intentions in South Africa was apparent, there seemed to be little doubt that the deal signifies a new level of deepening ties between the two countries. Positive aspects such as easier access to Chinese capital and a huge influx of much-needed foreign exchange reserves stood out, amongst others. Even the pace and simplicity of the whole deal attracted appreciation and in one of the articles, it was compared to the "endless and rather tortuous" take-over deal between the United Kingdom's Barclays and local ABSA.[89]

Some observers warned, however, that South Africa should proceed with caution. Chinese banks, they noted, are different because they are owned by the state, and do not operate on the same market-based business principles as private banks.

Four of the news stories did refer to a "China model", or to China as an example for South Africa to follow. Two themes were seen in this regard. One dealt with China as a leader and partner in the development process, and the other with decisive government action in tackling corruption. Press reports from both South Africa and Nigeria referred favourably to China's recent execution of corrupt government officials for their role in the export of adulterated products. Commentators in both African countries suggested that perhaps their own governments should consider a similarly serious approach to the corruption issue.

South Africa is building sports stadiums as it prepares for the soccer World Cup in 2010. Four of the 78 articles talked about Chinese companies aggressively vying for these construction contracts. The director-general of the World Cup described their approach by saying, "They are coming."[90] Almost all the articles relating to Chinese involvement in infrastructure development in South Africa dealt with the building of stadiums, which differentiated this set of news stories from those collected from Nigeria, where the press also talks about Chinese development of roads, bridges and railways.

South African commentators and reporters seemed to regard China as a peer or partner, whereas the Nigerians more consistently portrayed themselves as beneficiaries of Chinese investment and aid. One South African article referred to China as a standard for measuring South Africa's economic progress, and complemented China's disciplined approach and their ability to attract foreign investment. South Africans, the article argued, could learn from such an approach. Chris Alden, the leading analyst of Africa-China relations at the Johannesburg-based South African Institute of International Affairs (SAIIA), said China had "changed the game of development" after years of domination by Western governments and donors.[91]

Kenya

Our Factiva search for Kenya covered articles appearing in *The Nation* (Nairobi) and *The East African* between January 2006 and January 2008. A keyword search for "China" or "Chinese" in the article headline or first paragraph yielded 107 results, of which we deemed 56 to be relevant to our project. Many of the discarded articles dealt with Kenyan athletes preparing to compete in China, or with crime along China Road in Nairobi.

Of the remaining 56 articles, 17 had a negative tone, while 23 were positive. Only 11 articles were from *The East African*. With the exception of two articles, the viewpoint was either that of an editorialist, an academic, or was the straightforward reporting of facts.

Substantively, 38 of the articles dealt with one or more of the following topics: transport infrastructure, oil extraction, Chinese imports, or miscellaneous diplomatic relations with China. Of these, nine dealt with poor-quality Chinese products (toxic, spoiled, counterfeit), six focused on relations with China presenting opportunities and the need for Kenya to proceed with caution, and six depicted the Chinese as tricky or greedy.

Overall, the Kenyan stories were dominated by reporting on Chinese imports and, more specifically, counterfeit imports. One article estimated an annual loss of Ksh 35 billion, the equivalent of $522 million in government revenue, as a result of the importation of counterfeit and illegal goods, most of which come from Asia.[92] As would be expected, all but one of the nine articles dealing with poor-quality goods had a negative tone. One article discussed Chinese president Hu Jintao's promise to "tame [China's] appetite for counterfeits", and we coded this as having a positive tone (because we are considering the Kenyan perspective).[93]

Articles on Chinese imports were overwhelmingly negative (eight out of nine had a negative tone), and revolved around the issues of counterfeit goods, the trickiness or greediness of China or Chinese traders, and the China–Kenya trade imbalance. Complaints about counterfeit goods mentioned everything from batteries to electronic goods, pharmaceuticals, dolls, toothpaste and pens. A few articles mentioned the growth in trade between 2000 and 2005 (an increase of Ksh 12.79 billion), but viewed China as having the upper hand in this relationship because of its much higher level of industrialisation: Kenya exports raw commodities to the PRC and brings back manufactured goods in exchange.[94] Journalists and observers often note that Africa finds itself, once again, in the role of "raw materials exporter".

In light of these downsides to Kenya's relationship with China, several articles (six) urged Kenyans to proceed with caution. Several commentators supported deepening trade links with China, as long this was done in ways that guard the well-being of Kenyans. While noting the many economic benefits to engaging in trade with China, Kenyans were advised to view Chinese assistance and business ties with a "jaundiced eye"[95] and to "guard [their] rear".[96]

One of China's greatest interests in Kenya is oil. Recent dealings of the Chinese National Oil Corporation (CNOOC) in Kenya were mentioned in eight of the ten Kenyan press articles. A 2006 news story reported that the CNOOC was given contracts to explore six out of eleven highly contested oil blocks, giving the company control over 28 per cent of the total area charted for oil exploration in Kenya.[97] Controversy broke out when the CNOOC turned around and leased these out to third parties – China was depicted as greedy, and Kenya was portrayed as having fallen for the "wiles" of an economic power-house.[98] Chinese financing for the construction of four new pumping stations was mentioned as a positive development.

Many of the positive articles dealt with Chinese construction projects in transportation and other infrastructure. The Chinese led expansion of the Jomo Kenyatta International Airport, which will increase the airport's size and allow for many new non-stop flights to Europe and the East. China is also funding the renovation, expansion, and construction of at least three important roads.[99] Kenyan President Kibaki publicly thanked China for its support, specifically in road construction, referring to China in one report as a "true friend and development partner".[100]

China–Kenya strategic and diplomatic relations are also mentioned in the press. In two articles, Kenya was referred to as a strategic location for China, and as China's "gateway" to the East African region.[101] The headline of an unsigned article that appeared in *The Nation* on 17 November 2006 speaks for itself: "China Offers Military Aid".

The overall tone of the 2006–7 articles was positive. Kenyans are impressed by and value China's important investments in oil exploration and economic infrastructure. Yet the Kenyans do seem to fear that China will gain disproportionately, overwhelm and take advantage of their Kenyan partners, and flood East Africa with cheap manufactured goods. As one writer stated, China's "cheque-book diplomacy" may not produce positive outcomes for Kenya in the long-run.[102]

The view from the news stands across these three countries – Nigeria, South Africa and Kenya – seems focused on the speed and scale of China's emergence as a major player in the economies of these countries. The Chinese government is arguing strenuously that these rapidly developing relationships present win-win opportunities for China and its African partners. On the African side, observers are impressed by China's capacity for action and its economic prowess. Reading the press over time conveys a sense of the wide range of sectors and the diversity of the activities in which the Chinese are now involved. At the same time, however, the questioning and calls for caution that are clearly discernable in the news reports that we collected suggest that observers in Africa believe that African countries need to watch out for their own interests.

CONCLUSION

This chapter has argued that the manner and modalities of China's recent entry into the African political economy differ starkly from those established by the IFIs that have been Africa's prime international interlocateurs and purveyors of investment resources since the early 1990s. One important difference is that China's involvement in Africa is focused on state-to-state partnerships in natural-resource extraction and infrastructural development, unlike IFI support, which prioritised private-sector investment and de-prioritised spending on public infrastructure. Another difference, much commented upon in the literature on China's dramatic new role in Africa, is that Chinese investment comes without the extensive political and economic conditionalities that have structured the Western aid regime in Africa. Finally, Chinese business activities extend to a diversified range of domestic-market-oriented productive and service-sector activities, in contrast to the IFI vision which was more narrowly focused on export-oriented activities.

Viewing the relationship between the IFI model and China model over time, however, does reveal some complementarities and synergies. It is true, for example, that post-1990 trade liberalisation and the marketisation of exchange rate policy opened the door to Chinese private investors, exporters, construction companies, and so on. Complete or partial privatisation of African state-owned enterprises, which was also pushed forward under the structural adjustment programs, created some of the investment opportunities that the Chinese are now taking advantage of. Although China might have invested in resource-extraction in Africa in the earlier period if their incentives and the prices had been right, the extensiveness of the China–Africa ties that we see today is certainly at least partly a result of the reforms that liberalised trade and investment policies in most African countries after 1990.

Two important and interesting questions about the "China model" in Africa have not been addressed adequately, or at all, in this study. The first has to do with what African leaders and policy makers actually see in the China model. It is clear that China stands for rapid economic modernisation propelled and guided by a strong state, and legitimised by a vision that calls for growth now and perhaps democracy later. But does the idea of a China model go beyond that? A thorough study of this issue would ask whether, or to what extent, African policy-makers are studying Chinese policies that have governed the development of export-oriented manufacturing, the operation of domestic agricultural markets, delivery of social services, functioning of civil service or the military, and so on.

Perhaps the biggest question of all is whether the "brand of developmentalism" that the Chinese are selling in Africa will actually promote development. This issue is the pivot of the Africa-centred writing on the China–Africa connection. Most commentators and analysts stress the fact that Chinese investment alone is not a panacea, and that it could, in fact, aggravate the resource-curse syndrome, problems of indebtedness and patterns of misrule that have contributed to the economic frustrations and disappointments that Africans now confront. China is bringing investment capital, ideas, new ways of doing business and new global connections to Africa. Harnessing these to serve Africa's interests is the challenge of the hour for Africa.

Appendix 1
Excerpts from Press Reports on Chinese Activities in Nigeria, South Africa, and Kenya

NIGERIA PRESS CLIPS

Chinese in Infrastructural Development

In an exclusive interview with THISDAY in Abuja, the Executive Secretary of NIPC, Engr.

Mustapha Bello, in addressing a question about the unscrupulous practices of some Chinese companies: According to him, "actually, if you look at the total investment of China in Nigeria, I think it moved from $26 million as at 1999/2000 but today when you include even the facilities the Chinese Government has given Nigeria, it is over $10 billion. If Chinese authorities can commit that to help us develop our railways, which is a major infrastructure, develop dams to be able to produce about $12,000 MW, this is our friendly country. Whatever some of their citizens are doing, we must try to find ways of tolerating them and then stopping them from misbehaving. If I come in to work and I give you over $10 billion, then you have to find ways of making me your friend so that I can give additional billions of dollars."

Kunle Aderinokun, "Foreign Investments in Country Hit $35 Billion", *This Day*, 20 August 2007 (NB-21).

"No strings attached"

Chinese Ambassador to Nigeria, Mr. Xu Jianguo, disclosed this in Abuja, yesterday while presenting a fresh consignment of anti-malaria drugs to the Ministry of Health ... Jianguo described the gesture as a way of promoting friendly relations and boosting economic co-operation between the two countries ... He said China's assistance was devoid of selfish motives, as the Asian country never attached any political condition or demands to any political privileges in providing aids [sic] to friendly developing countries.

Onwuka Nzeshi, "China Donates $5.5m Drugs to Country", *This Day*, 6 November 2007 (NA-13).

China Launches Nigeria's Telecom Satellite

With the successful launch of Nigeria's Communications Satellite, NIGCOMSAT in far away China, Efem Nkanga, appraises the benefits and implications of the historical launch for Nigeria in particular and the African continent as a whole. Nigeria made history last week and reaffirmed its position as the giant of Africa when it launched a satellite project that will revolutionise telecommunications, broadcasting and broadband multimedia services in Nigeria and Africa.

The project called Nigeria Satellite communications, NIGCOMSAT is an icing on the cake to the tremendous gains made in the telecoms sector and a testimony to the benefits of the liberalisation of the telecoms sector spearheaded by President Olusegun Obasanjo six years ago.

The contract for the NIGCOMSAT project which was signed on December 15, 2004 in Abuja between China Great Wall Industry Corporation and the National Space Research and Development Agency was said to have cost the Federal Government over N40 billion. China was awarded the deal after it outbid 21 international rivals to secure the multimillion US dollar deal.

"Gateway to Digitalising Africa?" *This Day*, 16 May 2007 (NC-14).

Golden Dragon Bus Assembly

An automobile firm, Golden Dragon Nigeria Ltd, has … begun moves to bring the assembly plant of one of China's largest automobile companies to Nigeria. According to the company's General Manager, Mr. Dele Ogunsipe, "the wide acceptance of the Golden Dragon buses in Nigeria has encouraged the board of directors of the company to go for the strategic plan of having its assembly plant in the country". He said the buses, which moved into the Nigerian transport market late last year, have been doing well, because they have been fully tropicalised for excellent performance on Nigerian roads.

"Chinese Auto Firm to Build Plant in Nigeria", *This Day*, 19 November 2007 (NA-12)

Railway Construction

Mr Jing Wenchang, Chief Engineer, China Civil Engineering Construction Corporation (CCE-CC), has said work on the Lagos–Kano railway will start by November, this year. Wenchang said this yesterday in Abuja, at a meeting with traditional rulers whose communities would be affected by the project. The 1,315 kilometre double track railway line will pass through Abuja, while a second single track line would run from Minna through Abuja, to Katsina State. Cost for the lines was put at $5.2billion for double lines and $8.3 billion for single lines.

"Lagos–Kano Rail Project Begins November", *This Day*, 27 September 2007 (NA-16).

Nigerian Politician is the Author of China's Development Success (!)

Brimmy Olaghere decamped to Nigeria People's Congress, NPC, under which platform he is contesting the April 21 presidential election. An economist of repute, he was involved in the efforts that saw to the growth of the Chinese economy. China started the implementation of his plan in 1993 and indeed, it worked for them. Prof. Olaghere spoke from Abuja on why he wants to be the president of Nigeria and his plans to turn around the fortunes of the country.

Chioma Gabriel, "There's No Reason for Nigerians to Wallow in Abject Poverty", *Vanguard*, 24 March 2007 (ND-33).

Growth Rate of 10 per cent, Just Like the Chinese

The Nigeria Investment Promotion Commission (NIPC) has said the country is fast becoming the preferred destination for investors, with the total foreign direct investments (FDIs) into the economy now at about $35 billion. Out of this, China's investment alone accounts for $10 billion …

The Executive Secretary of NIPC, Engr. Mustapha Bello, said most of the investments came from telecoms and oil and gas sectors … If we are able to fast-track our growth to a target of 10 per cent, we must be able to drive a minimum of $3 billion a year, then we can keep pace with the 10 per cent growth. If we are able to make much more than that, then we should see a growth of 10 per cent just like the Chinese.

Kunle Aderinokun, "Foreign Investments in Country Hit $35 Billion, *This Day*, 20 August 2007 (NB-21).

Resentment Aroused by Chinese Investment

In the words of a Nigerian government official, while delivering a speech on "Political Dynamics Affecting the Business Climate in Nigeria" during a meeting of the US Department of State Advisory Committee on International Economic Policy:

"The average Nigerian resents the use of Chinese labourers in construction projects and perceives the Chinese as harsh employers. Nigeria's pharmaceutical and textile industries are suffering from what appears to be "dumping" of Chinese pharmaceutical and textiles and from counterfeit goods originating from China".

He described the relationship between China and Nigeria as "strong and cordial" but "complex".

"Nigeria's infrastructure could clearly benefit from Chinese aid, but the Chinese are discovering that their largest and most highly touted, proposed infrastructure projects have not even broken ground because of cultural and market misunderstandings, bureaucratic hurdles and corruption".

Constance Ikokwu, "AAGM: China surpasses US as Country's Import Partner", *This Day*, 3 August 2007 (NB-29).

SOUTH AFRICA PRESS CLIPS

ICBC to buy 20 per cent of Standard Bank

The Industrial and Commercial Bank of China (ICBC), is to buy a 20 per cent stake in our own Standard Bank … It's likely to position it at the centre of the fast-growing trade and investment flows between China and Africa. Standard is already the largest bank in Africa, represented in 18 countries, and it has built an extensive international business that is focused on emerging markets. With China's hunger for resources, its companies want to make inroads into those markets. It is significant that ICBC has picked Standard to do that with. The deal gives Standard the capital it needs to support its rapid international growth but, more importantly, it gives it access to the huge Chinese market and gives it the potential to be a really big emerging market player. And as the latest global economic growth forecasts indicate, emerging markets are where the growth is happening.

Hillary Joffe, "Good lesson in how to clinch a painless deal", *Business Day*, 26 October 2007 (SA2–4).

The Chinese Way: Shoot the Culprits

Those found guilty of misconduct, misappropriation of any nature, or even negligence due to not applying good judgment, should receive the Chinese remedy for their problems. The Chinese have dealt with the corruption problem – they shoot the culprits. I believe this would improve the honesty of the public service.

Joffre Papenfus, "The Chinese Way", *Business Day*, 17 October 2007 (SA2–10).

Bad-quality Products and Unfair Competition

Worse, perhaps, is that our own textile industry has been crippled by cheap Chinese imports made possible only because of China's appallingly poor labour policies. China itself admitted yesterday that its food and drug safety administration was unsatisfactory after the former head of that department was executed for receiving bribes to allow poisoned drugs on to the market.

Kevin O'Grady, "Prickly Lessons", *Business Day*, 11 July 2007 (SA4–6).

South Africa Tracks Chinese Investment in DRC

KINSHASA: The International Monetary Fund warned Congo yesterday to beware of the macroeconomic effects of a planned $5 billion loan from China to modernise the vast African country's decrepit infrastructure and mining industry. President Joseph Kabila's government announced plans last month for the huge loan from China, which would be paid back partly in mining concessions and tolls from roads and railways.

Oscar Stuart, "IMF worries over China's $5bn DRC loan", *Daily News*, 4 October 2007 (SA2–14).

New Development Game

China's push into Africa is prompting growing interest over Beijing's motives in the world's poorest continent, with opinion divided over who stands to benefit most. Speaking at the launch this week of a new China research programme run by the Johannesburg-based South African Institute of International Affairs (SAIIA), its chief academic said China had "changed the game of development" after years of domination by Western governments and donors.

"I think that's probably the most important contribution China has made to date in African development", added Chris Alden, who is also a lecturer on China–Africa relations at the London School of Economics.

Oscar Stuart, "Growing interest in motives, benefits of China's Africa push", *Daily News*, 25 October 2007 (SA2–7).

To Advance, You've Got to have Ties to China

An agreement of intent to invest an initial R1.4 to R1.75 billion in a cement manufacturing plant has been signed by industrial conglomerate, Shandong Xianglong Group – one of many Chinese investments planned in public transport, property and educational exchange, according to MEC for Transport and Public Works Marius Fransman. The cement plant is expected to have a production capacity of 6,000 to 10,000 tons per day and create 500 to 600 production jobs … Fransman said that King Long, possibly China's largest public vehicle manufacturer, had expressed a "strong intention" to set up a manufacturing plant in the Western Cape.

"We have seen a lot of opportunities available to various companies brought along", said Himmer Hou, chairperson of the South Africa Japan China Group (SJC). "Our visit [to Shandong Province] showed us that the world economy is increasingly rotating around the Chinese economy", said Premier Ebrahim Rasool of the China trip last month by a Western Cape delegation … "If you have no relationship with the Chinese economy, you're not going to be able to advance your own economy – especially in a country like South Africa", he said.

Dominque Herman, "R1.75bn cement plant indicates China's desire to invest", *Cape Times*, 6 December 2007 (SA-16).

KENYA PRESS CLIPS

"No strings attached"

The Chinese government has defended its co-operation with African governments. Chinese ambassador to Kenya Zhang Ming ... reiterated that China will offer economic assistance "in a selfless, sincere way and in the purpose of helping African countries in development. We do not attach any political conditions to our assistance nor do we impose our will upon others".

"China Defends Cooperation with Continent", *The Nation*, 12 September 2007 (K1–9).

Import of Counterfeit Goods

The Kenya Bureau of Standards has alerted Kenyans to recall of a toothpaste manufactured by a Chinese company following safety concerns...China is facing a credibility crisis as a manufacturing and exporting country as several of its products in various lines of production have been found to be of low standards and unsafe for consumer use.

"Standards Office Issues Alert on Toothpaste", *The Nation*, 30 August 2007 (K1–10).

Counterfeit Batteries, Electronics and Pharmaceuticals

An OECD report for last June said trade in counterfeits was the equivalent of the national gross domestic product of over 150 countries, based on World Bank data of 2005. Commercial counterfeit costs in 2007 are already over $500 billion, it said. The World Intellectual Property Organisation (WIPO) in a 2006 session in Geneva said the OECD estimates the cost to companies of counterfeiting to be over $630 billion a year. East African governments are losing over Ksh 35 billion ($522 million) as revenue due to importation of fake and illegal goods. According to KAM chairman Steven Smith, counterfeit goods are mainly imported from Asia. Some of the good include batteries, electronic goods, and pharmaceuticals.

Philip Ngunjiri, "Court Release "Fake Biros,'" *East African*, 20 November 2007 (K4–8).

Need to Look Upon China with Caution

Recently, there has been a dizzying parade of high-level visitors between Africa and the People's Republic of China. Some Kenyan officials have suggested that the country should increasingly look East to diversify its economic relationships and reduce dependency on the West. Theoretically, this sounds like a plausible idea. That is until you give it serious thought. China, once upon a time the pivot of the oppressed Third World, has itself become a voracious and cruel imperial overlord. That is why Kenya and Africa must fundamentally recalculate their relationship with the rising Chinese leviathan. China still sings songs about Third World solidarity, but its political and economic actions and interest belie the song. This does not mean that Kenya should not engage China. Rather, it means that Kenya must guard its rear.

Makau Mutua, "Why Country Should Be Wary of China", *The Nation*, 1 July 2007 (K1–24).

Trade Imbalance

Kenyan officials present at the function and who spoke, decried the trade imbalance between Kenya and China, saying it tilted on the side of China more than that of Kenya. Vice President Moody Awori who was present among other Kenya members of Parliament and business leaders, said that while the trade between the two countries continues to grow with the volume of trade in 2000 rising to Sh 7.75 billion and Sh 20.54 billion in 2005, the balance of trade was highly skewed in favour of China, due to the different levels of industrialisation. "Kenya continued to export unprocessed or semi-processed raw materials, while Chinese exports to Kenya comprised mainly of manufacturing goods, machinery and equipment", he said.

"Chinese Government Answers Critics of Its Development Policies", *The Nation*, 26 April 2007 (K1–38).

Natural Allies

The year 2006 is remarkable in one big sense. The Africans and the Asians have renewed their co-operation in ways that are reminiscent of anti-colonialism that was at the expense of the West, mainly Europeans ... The apparent growing closeness of the Africans and the Chinese is beyond personalities. It tends to rekindle the spirit of Afro-Asianism that is based on common experience of exploitation by the West in three stages of classical colonialism, neo-colonialism, and post-modern colonialism.

Macharia Munene, "Africa Edging Closer to Asia Concern for West", *The Nation*, 2 January 2007 (K1–51).

Investment in Manufacturing, Water Services, Telecom, and Other Areas

"For the past five years so, there has been a tremendous acceleration in trade and investment by the two countries [China and India] in Africa. This acceleration has largely been driven by investment and trade in oil. However, this has now extended far beyond natural resources. There are investments in light manufacturing, sophisticated infrastructure, water services, telecommunications and textiles, among others".

Francis Ayieko (Interviewing Dr Harry Broadman), "Rise of India, China Good News for Africa", *East African*, 14 November 2006 (K2–6).

It is Just "Cheque-book Diplomacy"

"Whether our relationship with China is of mutual benefit is an important issue every Kenyan should reflect on. In general, President Hu's visit doesn't serve our national interest. It is just "cheque-book diplomacy" ... Apart from economic prosperity, China has nothing to show to the world. Political repression and religious intolerance are some of the hallmarks of the Chinese government.

Njoroge Wachai, "China Doesn't Serve Our Interests", *The Nation*, 27 April 2006 (K2–42.)

China Snapping Up Oil Contracts

Fuelled by a fast growing economy and increased consumption of fuel, China is snapping up oil contracts and Kenya is its latest hunting ground. The two countries are set to sign an oil exploration agreement that will give the China National Offshore Oil Corporation (CNOOC) a lease to drill for oil and gas in one of the many blocks along Kenya's coastline.

Kennedy Senelwa, "China Joins Search for Oil in Kenya", *The Nation*, 22 April 2006 (K2–46)

Chinese Military Assistance to Kenya

China has offered to help Kenya modernise its armed forces. Chinese Defence Minister Gen. Cao Gangcuan today assured Kenya of his Government's support to the modernisation of the Kenya Armed Forces ... Gen. Gangcuan hailed the continued co-operation between the two countries. President Kibaki thanked China for its continued support especially in roads construction, saying China was a true friend and development partner.

"China Offers Military Aid", *The Nation*, 19 November 2007 (K4–10).

NOTES

1. Akwe Amosu, "China in Africa: It's (Still) the Governance, Stupid", *Foreign Policy in Focus*, 9 March 2007, at www.fpif.org, pp. 1–2.
2. Barbara Stallings (ed.), *Global Change, Regional Response: The New International Context of Development*, Cambridge and New York: Cambridge University Press, 1995.
3. Nicolas van de Walle calls this the "adjustment regime" (of lending) that developed in the 1980s (*African Economies and the Politics of Permanent Crisis, 1979–1999*, Cambridge: Cambridge University Press, 2001, p. 210, inter alia). He reports that, in the 1980s, "some 36 sub-Saharan African countries signed 241 different loans with the Bank and the Fund on behalf of stabilization and adjustment operations". In the 1990s, "almost all African states have engaged in some kind of economic reform program with funding from the West" (p. 7). At the end of 1998, the IMF still had operational loans in 26 African countries, including 22 "enhanced structural adjustment facility loans" (p. 7, note 15).
4. On basic facets of this model, "the new liberal orthodoxy", as it was imposed in Africa, see ibid., pp. 16, 75, 137–9 and 164–6.
5. Ibid., pp. 197, 214, 216 and 215.
6. See Richard Sandbrook, *Closing the Circle: Democratization and Development in Africa*, London and New York: Zed Books, 2000, pp. 13, 16. Although the IFI's embraced the governance reforms, the democratisation reforms (calling for multi-party elections, and so on) were pushed mostly on a bilateral basis, most concertedly by USAID under the Clinton administration. German bilateral aid and EU lending was also linked at various points to democratisation efforts. On this, see van de Walle, *African Economies*, pp. 268–9.
7. van de Walle, *African Economies*, pp. 11–12.
8. Ibid., p 269.
9. Ibid., pp. 57, 145–7, inter alia.
10. For 2006, Peter Bosshard gives the figure of $56 billion, in "China's Role in Financing African Infrastructure", *International Rivers Network*, May 2007, at www.irn.org. For an overview, see Chris Alden, *China in Africa*, London: Zed Press, 2007. See also Daniel Large, "A 'Chinese-Scramble?' The Politics of Contemporary China–Africa Relations", *African Affairs*, vol. 106, no. 422, 2007, pp. 141–3; Firoze Manji and Stephen Marks, *African Perspectives on China in Africa*, Cape Town, Nairobi and Oxford: Fahamu – Networks for Social Justice and Pambazuka.org, 2007; and Alex Vines, "China in Africa: A Mixed Blessing?", *Current History*, May 2007, pp. 213–19.
11. David H. Shinn, "Free Trade, Fair Trade, and Sustainable Trade: The Case of Resource Extraction", Oxford-Uehiro-Carnegie Council Conference, New York City, 7–8 December 2006. Howard W. French also gives the $40 billion figure for trade in 2005, "a four-fold increase since 2001" ("Commentary: China and Africa", *African Affairs*, vol. 106, no. 422, 2007, p. 127).
12. This is compared to an annual growth rate of about 20 per cent in 1990–4 (Harry G. Broadman, *Africa's Silk Road: China and India's New Economic Frontier*, Washington, DC: The World Bank, 2007, p. 11).

13. Ibid., p. 120, Table 2A.4.

14. International Monetary Fund, *Direction of Trade Statistics*, 2006. Prof. Gordon Bennett supplied this data. Available online at http://www.imfstatistics.org/DOT/

15. According to Broadman, the EU's share of SSA exports declined from 50 per cent in 2000 to 27 per cent in 2005 (*Africa's Silk Road*, p. 11 and p. 40, note 3).

16. Ibid., p. 12. Also see ibid. (p. 83, Box 2.1) for share of China's crude oil imports from Africa by country of origin. See also Ian Taylor, "China's Oil Diplomacy in Africa", *International Affairs*, vol. 82, no. 5, 2006, pp. 937–59.

17. Broadman, *Africa's Silk Road*, p. 81, Figure 2.17.

18. Joshua Eisenman, "China's Post-Cold War Strategy in Africa: Examining Beijing's Methods and Objectives", in Joshua Eisenman, Eric Heginbotham and Derek Mitchell (eds), *China and the Developing World*, Armonk, NY and London: M. E. Sharpe, 2007, p. 38.

19. In 2005, China purchased about 770,000 barrels of oil per day from Africa, while the US imported more than three times that amount: 2.4 million barrels per day (Shinn, "Free Trade, Fair Trade", p. 3).

20. Broadman, *Africa's Silk Road*, p. 82, Box 2.1.

21. Eisenman, "China's Post-Cold War Strategy", pp. 38–9.

22. Ibid., p. 220.

23. IMF, *Direction of Trade 2006 Yearbook*. Germany and the US are Africa's third- and fourth-largest suppliers. Professor Gordon Bennett supplied us with this data.

24. This is out of a total of $793 billion in China's exports to the world in 2005 (Eisenman, "China's Post-Cold War Strategy", p. 220, from IMF *Direction of Trade* statistics). Eisenman also reports that "Chinese producers have secured large portions of the African textile and electronics markets and have established *their own sales outlets* throughout the continent" (p. 41, emphasis added).

25. Broadman, *Africa's Silk Road*, p. 12.

26. Ibid., p. 85, Figure 2.18.

27. Eisenman reports that RSA and Lesotho "have seen tens of thousands of workers in the textile sector lose their jobs [to Chinese imports], and there is growing backlash against Chinese products and workers" ("China's Post-Cold War Strategy", p. 42); Amosu, "China in Africa", pp. 4–6.

28. South Africa's share of all outer garments and knitted clothing (SITC 8459) exported by China to Africa in 2002–4 was, on average, 59 per cent (Broadman, *China's Silk Road*, p. 122, Table 2A.6). South Africa's average share of all Chinese colour TVs (SITC 7611) exported to Africa during this period was about the same (55 per cent) (ibid.).

29. Ibid., p. 12.

30. Shinn, "Free Trade, Fair Trade", p. 3.

31. Broadman, *Africa's Silk Road*, pp. 12 and 47. Africa accounted for 5 per cent of all outflows in 2004 (total Chinese outflow in 2004 was $5.5 billion) (ibid.).

32. Ibid., p. 100. Another figure that we can perhaps use for purposes of comparison is the UNECA's reporting of yearly total net inward FDI for SSA. They report yearly inflows of $13.6 billion for 2003, $11.3 billion for 2004, and $17.6 billion for 2005. See United Nations Economic Commission on Africa (UNECA), *Economic Report on Africa 2007: Accelerating Africa's Development Through Diversification*, Addis Ababa: UNECA, 2007, p. 95, Table 3.3.

33. Ibid., p. 26, Box 1.1.
34. Chris Alden, "China in Africa", *Survival*, vol. 47, no. 3, Autumn 2005, p. 149.
35. French, "Commentary: China and Africa", p. 127.
36. Broadman, *Africa's Silk Road*, p. 12.
37. Carol Lancaster, "Center for Global Development Essay: The Chinese Aid System", CGD, June 2007, at www.cgdev.org.
38. French, "Commentary: China and Africa", p. 127. See Deborah Bräutigam, *Chinese Aid and African Development*, New York: Macmillan, 1997, p. 44, for disbursements of Chinese aid to Africa 1960–96. See also Deborah Bräutigam, "Foreign Aid and the Export of Ideas: Chinese Development Aid in the Gambia and Sierra Leone", *Journal of Commonwealth and Comparative Politics*, vol. 32, no. 3, November 1994, pp. 325–49, and Deborah Bräutigam, "Close Encounters: Chinese Business Networks as Industrial Catalysts in Sub-Saharan Africa", *African Affairs*, vol. 102, no. 408, 2003, pp. 447–67.
39. Alden, "China in Africa", pp. 147–64.
40. Lancaster, "Center for Global Development Essay", p. 3.
41. Debt forgiveness is, however, a line-item that the Chinese government does like to announce, for example: "At the China–Africa Cooperative Forum in 2003, China announced debt forgiveness to 31 African countries, amounting to $1.27 B" (Alden, "China in Africa", p. 151).
42. Lancaster, "Center for Global Development Essay", p. 5.
43. French, "Commentary: China and Africa", p. 127.
44. As a per centage of GDP, net official flows ODA to Africa in 2004 ($26 billion, 18 per cent of which was in the form of debt forgiveness, which represented 5 per cent of African GDP) was lower than the figure recorded in 1990 (6 per cent of GDP). ODA in 1992 was $19 billion. (UNECA, *Economic Report on Africa*, pp. 92, 94).
45. Alden, "China in Africa", p. 155.
46. Ibid., p. 156.
47. Amosu, "China in Africa", p. 4.
48. Amosu writes that "For PM Meles Zenawi of Ethiopia, the inflow of investment from China is a concrete demonstration that the Western model of development has failed. He spoke in February 2007 of the need to build 'a strong developmental state," complaining that the 'neo-liberal reforms" advocated by the World Bank and others have failed to 'generate the kind of growth they sought" ... The implication is that African leaders should worry less about meeting demands for transparency, accountability, rule of law, and other such 'neo-liberal" objectives and focus instead on economic growth. With China in the picture, they will get the resources they need." (Ibid., p. 3).
49. Walden Bello, "China Provokes Debate in Africa", *Foreign Policy in Focus*, 9 March 2007, at www.fpif.org/fpiftxt/4065.
50. Amosu, "China in Africa", p. 6. Van de Walle wrote that "under the SAPs, the proportion of expenditures devoted to public infrastructure had declined sharply ... creating a critical obstacle to renewed economic growth" (*African Economies*, pp. 88–9).
51. Bosshard, "China's Role", p. 4.
52. Amosu, "China in Africa", p. 1.

53. Ibid., p. 2.

54. Eisenman explains that the loans to Angola also attracted attention because they "allow[ed] Angola to turn its back on an IMF package that would have demanded greater accountability and the adoption of improved governance measures" (Eisenman, "China's Post-Cold War Strategy", p. 48). He also notes that Beijing's loans to Angola were backed by oil – "if [Angola] cannot repay loans in cash, Beijing will take oil" (ibid., p. 48). In general, the policy of the IFIs was to eliminate such barter deals.

55. BBC, "China opens coffers for minerals", 18 September 2007, posted at BBC.com, hppt://news.bbc.co.uk/2/hi/africa/7000925.stm.

56. Brian Smith, "Western concern at China's growing involvement in Africa", World Socialist Web Site, 10 April 2006, p. 4, at www.wsws.org.

57. Bello, "China Provokes Debate".

58. See Lucy Corkin, "China's Emerging Multinationals in Africa", 21 September 2007, posted at Pambazuka News, Africa and China Forum, at http://www.pambazuka.org/en/category/africa_china/43411.

59. Bello, "China Provokes Debate".

60. "CNOOC may buy Shell's Nigeria Assets", *China Economic Review*, 22 November 2007, posted at www.chinaeconomicreview.com.

61. Bello, "China Provokes Debate".

62. Ibid.

63. BBC, "China opens coffers".

64. Alden, "China in Africa", pp. 148–9.

65. For example, it was China's Nonferrous Metals Corporation (an SOE) that purchased mining rights at Chambishi in 1998. A terrible accident at this mine in 2005 killed 40 Zambian workers and fuelled Zambian resentment of the Chinese. See *The New York Times*, 21 August 2007.

66. French, "Commentary: China and Africa", p. 129.

67. Alden, "China in Africa", pp. 149–50.

68. Bosshard, "China's Role", pp. 1 and 2.

69. Broadman, the source of the $12.5 billion figure, says that "the recent explosion of China's official economic support to Africa has been largely in the form of loans by the Ex-Im Bank" (*Africa's Silk Road*, p. 275). According to Bosshard, the Ex-Im Bank "aims to expand its loans by 15–20 per cent per year. A growth rate of 15 per cent would increase its lending to approximately $40B in 2010 – considerably more than lending by another other export credit agency or the World Bank ("China's Role," p. 4).

70. Alden, "China in Africa", pp. 151. The same could perhaps be said of China's weapons sales to Nigeria, Sudan, Zimbabwe, and the governments of the Great Lakes regions. On weapons sales, see Bello, "China Provokes Debate"; Alden, "China in Africa", pp. 159–61, Eisenman, "China's Post-Cold War Strategy", pp. 48–50.

71. Amosu, "China in Africa", p. 5.

72. Alden, "China in Africa", p. 149.

73. The Zambia–China Mulungushi Textile Joint Venture Ltd. (ZCMT) was thriving in 2003, with out-grower schemes for 5,000 contracted cotton farmers, cotton ginning,

production of yarn, fabric, garments and cotton-seed oil, eighteen retail outlets in Zambia, and exports to the region (*People's Daily*, 27 November 2003). The factories were not operating at all in August 2007, according to *The New York Times*, 21 August 2007.

74. Alden, "China in Africa", p. 155.

75. French, "Commentary: China and Africa", p. 132.

76. Alden, "China in Africa", p. 155. See also Amosu, "China in Africa", p. 4; French, "Commentary: China and Africa", p. 132.

77. *This Day*, 6 November 2007, article A-13.

78. See Alden, "China in Africa", p. 155; Shinn, "Free Trade, Fair Trade", p. 4; Eisenman, "China's Post-Cold War Strategy", p. 36.

79. Bello, "China Provokes Debate".

80. Gareth Evans and Donald Steinberg, "China and Darfur: 'Signs of Evolution'", *Guardian Unlimited*, 11 June 2007, posted by International Crisis Group, www.crisis-group.org/home/index.cfm?id=4891&=1. See Jonathan Holslag, "Friendly Giant? China's Evolving Africa Policy", *Asia Chapter*, vol. 2, no. 5, BICCS Background Chapter, The Brussels Institute of Contemporary China Studies (BICCS), 24 August 2007, pp. 4, 8–9, posted at www.vub.ac.be/biccs.

81. Onwuka Nzeshi, "AAGM: China donates $5.5m Drugs to Country", *This Day*, 6 November 2007 (NA-13).

82. Paul Ibe, "Country targets $10bn Revenue From Tourism in 7 Years", *This Day*, 14 September 2007 (NB-8).

83. Calculated from IMF Direction of Trade Statistics, http:www.imfstatistics.org/DOT/. The denominator is China's exports to all of Africa.

84. Constance Ikokwu, "China Surpasses US and Country's Import Partner", *This Day*, 3 August 2007 (NB-29).

85. *Business Day, Cape Times, Daily News (SA), Johannesburg Stock Exchange, Pretoria News, Rand Merchant Bank Report, Media Institute of South Africa, South Africa Business Intelligence, Independent on Saturday* and *Sunday Independent*.

86. Wendy Jasson da Costa, "Rag trade gains, thanks to quotas", *Pretoria News*, 30 August 2007 (SA3–13).

87. Aneez Salie, "Chinese Bank to buy 20 per cent of Standard Bank for $5.6bn in cash", *Cape Times*, 26 October 2007 (SA2–5).

88. Andrew Walker, "JSE Big on Chinese Fever", *Sunday Independent*, 28 October 2007 (SA2–3).

89. Hillary Joffe, "Good lesson in how to clinch a painless deal", *Business Day*, 26 October 2007.

90. Boyd Webb, "More vying for 2010 contracts", *Pretoria News*, 8 March 2007.

91. Alden, quoted in Oscar Stuart, "Growing Interest in Motives, Benefits, of China's Africa Push", *Daily News*, 25 October 2007 (SA2–7). On the negative side, sceptics warned of some caution, as reflected in the comments of a local citizen who noted that China's involvement in continent was "controversial", in that it failed to put emphasis on human rights and urged South Africans to exercise "moral restraint" while involving them in deals with major stakes (referring to the multi-billion Rand Standard Bank and the ICBC deal). See Ross Harvey, "Chinese Puzzle", *Business Day*, 1 November 2007 (SA1–38).

92. Philip Ngungiri, "Court Release 'Fake Biros'", *The East African*, 20 November 2007 (K4–8).

93. "What China Can Teach Us", *The Nation*, 19 April 2006 (K2–49).

94. "Chinese Government Answers Critics of Its Development Policies", *The Nation*, 26 April 2007 (K1–38).

95. "Yes, Let's Court Libyans", *The Nation*, 7 June 2007 (K1–29).

96. Makau Mutua, "Why Country Should Be Wary of China", *The Nation*, 1 June 2007 (K1–24).

97. "In an unprecedented act of generosity, the government in April gave the state-owned China National Offshore Oil Company Ltd (CNOOC) exclusive rights over a total of 6 out of 11 available blocks, including the hotly contested Blocks 9 and 10A in the Mandera area" ("Country Gifts Six Key Oil Blocks to China", *The East African*, 10 October 2006 (K2–19)). See also Jaindi Kisero, "Region Changing Its Investment Partners", *The Nation*, 16 May 2007. Oil prospecting is taking place along the coast and in northern Kenya.

98. "China Selling Off Oil Rights It Got for Free", *The East African*, 25 February 2007 (K1–46).

99. Jeff Otieno, "Kenya–China Trade to Grow After Accord", *The Nation*, 29 April 2006 (K2–40).

100. "China Offers Military Aid", *The Nation*, 19 November 2007 (K2–10).

101. Gitau Warigi, "Why China Link is Vital for Kenya", *The Nation*, 30 April 2006 (K2–33); Njoroge Wachai, "China Doesn't Serve Our Interests", *The Nation*, 27 April 2006 (K2–42).

102. Wachai, "China Doesn't Serve Our Interests", (K2–42).

PART TWO

The Chinese Model and its Competitors in the Muslim World

CHAPTER 4

Learning the Right Lessons from Beijing: A Model for the Arab World?

EMMA MURPHY

INTRODUCTION

It should not be surprising if Joshua Ramo's "new physics of development and power" hold tremendous appeal for Arab regime elites. Ramo talks of the "electric power" of the Chinese example – its demonstration of an alternative path to development which challenges not only the US-led Washington Consensus for economic liberalism laced with political democratisation, but also offers the potential to translate an economic transformation into global power projection to rival that of America itself. For the authoritarian Arab regimes, with their lack-lustre exercises in structural adjustment, patchy records of economic growth, fragile human development performance and post-colonial resentments at external interventions in regional affairs, what could be more attractive than the so-called Beijing Consensus? As Ramo himself says:

> China is marking a path for other nations around the world who are trying to figure out not simply how to develop their countries, but also how to fit into the international order in a way that allows them to be truly independent, to protect their way of life and political choices in a world with a single massively powerful centre of gravity.[1]

For countries aspiring to comparable development, China's model has become far more than the go-global trade strategy of the 1990s. After all, adherents of the Washington Consensus have been pushing that themselves for decades. The appeal lies instead in the understanding of development as something more than unquestioning engagement with, and submission to, the dictums of global capitalism. The Chinese experience has suggested that success can come without slavishly conforming to the socially painful and ideologically driven economic prescriptions of the global superpower and allied international financial institutions. An alternative recipe for economic development that does not require political concessions to non-regime domestic forces, while simultaneously allowing a country to reposition itself positively in relation to global configurations of power, is bound to be appealing. Add to that the possibility that one can find development solutions within local culture, rather than acquiescing to a global (and essentially alien) process of cultural homogenisation, and it is not surprising that Arab eyes are turning east for inspiration.

However, there are a number of problems with any assertion that the Chinese model either can, or should, be exported to the Arab world (or anywhere else, for that matter). For a start, critics of the Beijing Consensus point to the more problematic aspects of China's recent development, aspects that are hidden from view in Ramo's optimistic assessment, but which may yet see the country spiralling into long-term chaos and disintegration. Second, even if Ramo is right about the reasons for China's rapid growth and rise to economic power, the fundamentals in other parts of the world, and specifically in the Arab world, are very different, and the model cannot be easily superimposed on alternative political, social, cultural and economic formations. Third, the Arab world has its own political economy which suggests that, rather than seeing quick fixes in a Beijing Consensus to rival that of Washington, the solutions for the region lie closer to home. Finally, the reality of the Chinese experience, much as in the Arab world, has been that the erosion of democratic political structures – which does not necessarily mean liberal electoral processes – is ultimately proving to be an obstacle to development, even a regressive dynamic. In the long term, meaningful political reforms which provide transparency and allow populations to hold governing elites accountable are crucial to effective and sustainable economic development.

The Beijing Consensus under Scrutiny

Ramo argued that the Beijing Consensus amounted to three theorems:

1. The centrality of innovation and constant experimentation in development programmes;
2. Rejection of blunt instruments such as per capita GDP growth as the measures of success, in favour of sustainability and improved quality of life;
3. Self-determination and the use of economic leverage against big hegemonic forces which throw their (military) weight around against your interests.

The first of these, innovation and experimentation, has a number of dimensions. The general idea is that, for a country as large as China, with potentially so many problems, the key to sustainable economic development is a burst of momentum in certain key sectors which can then jump-start growth elsewhere. Such momentum does not come from a gradual incorporation and adaptation of technologies developed elsewhere, but rather from innovation of what Ramo calls "bleeding edge" technologies which provide qualitative advantage. This is one step beyond even the leap-frogging qualities of advanced information and communications technologies described by Edward Ayensu;[2] the objective is not to catchup, but to start from the front. With these key sectors pulling others in their wake, the country keeps moving, hopefully solving existing problems faster than new ones occur. For Ramo, the essential quality in innovation is *density*: communications get faster and smoother, networks are woven more tightly and effectively, and increases in output grow relative to increases in input. This approach predicates economic development on the abandonment of conventional ideas of sequential stages, suggesting instead that building high-performance hubs in certain sectors or geographical regions,[3] even at the cost of neglecting others, can have broader developmental dividends, spilling their advantages over into the more backwards sectors even as they surge ahead creating new opportunities and markets.

In the Chinese case, he says, this was first put to work in the agricultural sector, where small-scale liberalisation measures allowed the masses of traditional, conservative peasants to make modest improvements in output.

> Chinese farmers, long considered the most backward and tradition-bound workers in the world, used limited control of their crops and an innovative two-tier price system to optimise output and even, in their spare time, build small businesses. They absorbed new technology such as better rice stocks and improved field drainage. Today Chinese farmers are among the most innovation-hungry in the world. On average, Chinese farmers completely replace their seed stock for newer, engineered seeds *every three years*. Maize farmers entirely replace their seed stock *every 33 months*.[4]

The lesson spread from agriculture into industry. Innovative inputs into production were demanded, rather than settling for cheaper second-best technologies that would reap rewards from the low labour costs but bring little else to the drive for export markets. The realisation also set in that the most crucial input of all was an educated labour force. Unless the skills required to handle such technologies were spread throughout the country, growth would be concentrated in the outward-looking coastal areas and would make few inroads into China's vast interior. Investments in education, both quantitative and qualitative, moved to the heart of government planning: the more highly educated the population, the more China's demographic burden would become its greatest asset. In an ironic reversal of Mao's Cultural Revolution, education – and a willingness to be exposed to new ideas and techniques from the outside world – now became the entry requirement for personal advancement, even into government posts and officialdom.

Such reversals of long-held reliance on seniority, political credentials and defence of the status quo require a willingness to take risks, to experiment, and even to fail. This is a mindset which anticipates crisis and sees forward movement as the only option – under the unique pressures of China's massive population, the greater risk lies in doing nothing.

Beijing's second theorem, according to Ramo, is that growth per se does not equate with development. Indeed, when it is unevenly spread, it carries severe social risks. Stability, equity in distributing the benefits of growth, and effective management, are crucial components for its sustainability. This might sound obvious, but in a country the size of China it means a number of things: first, the relative value of political and civil freedoms is placed lower than that of poverty alleviation and basic well-being. Government should not be dictated by ideology, but rather by the need for sound management, the prevention of chaos and the maintenance of stability through periods of rapid change. The neo-liberal ideological prescriptiveness that views democracy and human rights as prerequisites for capitalist success is rejected for a pragmatic view in favour of balanced development of the whole population's quality of life, articulated in old socialist terminology only because, says Ramo, old China's language has not kept up with the broader pace of change.

The final theorem links China's economic weight with a new determination to exercise global strategic leverage. China's current trade surpluses have given it massive financial clout, not to mention the capacity for financing its own militarisation. Combine these strengths and China can start to manipulate the global environment to create the stability and security it needs to sustain its development project. What seems to be a rising threat for American neo-realists is, for Ramo, an inevitable and defensive strategy which nonetheless seeks to counter US hegemonic ambitions, most of all in China's own back yard. In this, China sees itself as defending the Westphalian state system against the destabilising impact of US militarist adventures and disregard for international law. The notion that democracies do not go to war has, for them, been both disproved by recent American aggressions and even reversed in so far as securing a peaceful environment requires the state to have attributes that preclude democracy, or at least place it very far down the list of priorities.

So far, so good. But this rosy portrayal of China's development path fails to mention some of the crucial failures which threaten its sustainability. For a start,

China's innovation credentials may not be all they are cracked up to be. For sure, the lag-time between innovation elsewhere and its absorption and reproduction in China has collapsed to almost nothing, but, as Thomas Friedman points out in *The World is Flat*, China's own ability to innovate is still circumscribed by insecure capital markets and the precariousness of the rule of law.[5] The willingness and the foundations for scientific innovation are there, but the broader and necessary environment of trust that allows innovation to become embedded in the production cycle is still weak. As illustration, one can point to the World Bank's own Worldwide Governance Indicators, where China still ranked at just 46.3 in the percentile rankings for rule of law in 2006, a small improvement on previous years but still well below other Asian states such as Singapore (95.2), Taiwan (74.8), South Korea (72.9), Malaysia (65.7) and Thailand (55.2). It is worth noting that ten Arab countries also out-perform China in this regard, including Qatar (81.4), Kuwait (74.3), Oman (72.4), the UAE (69.0), Bahrain (66.7), Jordan (62.4), Tunisia (60.5), Saudi Arabia (57.6), Egypt (53.8) and Morocco (53.3).[6]

Bates Gill and Yanzhong Huang go further, arguing that China emulates rather than innovates. Enterprises lack R&D facilities and "Western investors and management styles dominate China's economic achievements".[7] Whilst Chinese products are found en masse around the globe, how many Chinese brands can compete with the McDonald's, Microsofts and MTVs of this world? Improving the technological competitiveness of exports is insufficient: they must achieve the status of global cultural icons before China can claim to have really arrived. Kay Möller reiterates the point: whilst agreeing that the regime under Deng Xiaoping and his successors has made the importing of foreign technology a priority, the argument is made that ultimately foreign investors and governments have been reluctant to assist Chinese entrepreneurs to the point of genuine competitiveness, and that – in the absence of sufficient professional managers – the transfer and development of technology is still overly dependent on public officials and bureaucrats, who resent dependence on learning from abroad and would rather direct resources to promoting basic skills at the expense of creative thinking.[8]

Relatedly, the emphasis on development of human resources is more complicated than Ramo would have us believe. For a start, as Lin Chun points out, in a defence of Chinese socialism, the investment in human resources far predates the era of opening up and subsequent economic success. The decades preceding the reform era witnessed substantial investment in basic needs, public education and health provision, all of which created a ready workforce when export-oriented investors took advantage of the new liberal economic regimes, but which have equally been eroded in recent years.[9] Lin Chun points to the recent decline in universal provision of both public health care and education, with rural areas suffering disproportionately, to the point where what was once a contributing advantage for the Chinese economy now approximates to what Chinese environment expert Elizabeth Economy has termed "a humanitarian disaster".[10] The withdrawal of universal medical provision has not been balanced with private insurance, the costs of which have risen astronomically, whilst public resources have been concentrated in medical facilities in urban areas, government departments or state-owned assets. Meanwhile, whilst the rate of entry into higher education has increased, a report by The International Forum on Globalization[11] argues that basic public education in rural areas has actually declined, stating that "one rural study reveals that 70 per cent of youth finished high school in 1976; but the rate dropped to less than 10 per cent by the late 1990s".[12]

To add insult to injury, the relative quality of the labour force in the hey-day of economic growth did not necessarily translate into highly skilled and well-paid employment. A report highlights the phenomenon of sweatshops, the "result of intense privatisation of industry":

> Today, under the mantra of market competition, Chinese workers now have lower wages in terms of purchasing power, fewer benefits, longer work hours, increasing work-related injuries, and other associated problems. In the Pearl River and Yangtze River delta regions, where most export-oriented industrial plants are located, migrant workers routinely work 12 hours a day, 7 days a week; during the busy season a 13–15-hour day is not uncommon.[13]

Clearly, distribution of the benefits of development is not as equitable as suggested by the second of the theorems. But there is little doubt that there have been astonishing achievements: Ramo refers to 300 million people having been lifted out of poverty.[14] Wen, however, points to the figures of China's own State Statistics Bureau (SSB), which indicate an actual increase in rural poverty and a decrease in the income of rural households in absolute terms. Whilst he acknowledges that fewer people are living in absolute poverty, he points out that the gap between them and those with the highest incomes has grown rapidly. The SSB itself claims that the richest 10 per cent of the population now earn 45 per cent of the income, whilst the poorest 10 per cent earn just 1.4 per cent of the income.[15] Gill and Huang report: "The inequality of income distribution is significantly higher in China than in the United States, with the Gini coefficient – an international measurement of income disparity – reaching 0.53 in 2004."[16]

Whilst Ramo focused on the initial surge in output which accompanied the early privatisation of agriculture, Wen highlights the subsequent lifting of price controls which dampened farmers' ability to continue to utilise new inputs (such as fertilisers, pesticides and hybrid seeds), the declining provision of rural services as the government cut investment, and the massive rural–urban migration that followed. Nor was life much better in the cities. Not only are incomes and relative living standards under threat, but the shift to private and foreign industrial ownership has pulled the carpet of lifetime employment benefits from under the feet of previously state-sector workers. Even worse, international NGOs have increasingly been high-lighting the emergence of slavery, especially among child workers abducted from their homes and forced to labour in unregulated and dangerous environments.[17]

For Wen, it is hardly surprising that the Chinese population has become more politically agitated in recent years. He claims that "the incidence of mass protests, demonstrations and clashes with the government increased from 58,000 in 2003 to 74,000 in 2004, more than 10 times the number of a decade ago".[18] If large swathes of the rural, impoverished population, or indeed the grossly exploited migrants who slave in the coastal city sweatshops for meagre wages that fail to keep up with inflation, are prepared to openly challenge government forces, then the suggestion that political freedoms and civil rights can be at least temporarily forsaken in the greater interest of equitable improvements in quality of life fails to hold water. In other words, if measurements such as GNP per capita are outmoded because they hide a multitude of micro-sins behind macroeconomic statistics, so too are the quality-based measurements of Chinese progress which focus on intent rather than sustained achievement.

Grasping the complexities of Chinese political development is a confusing business. Lin Chun argues that there has, in fact, been a massive reform of politics *within* the Party. A prolonged process of institutional change has led to a reconfiguring of the Party's – and the nation's – objectives towards constitutionalism and legality (not the move from socialism to raw capitalism that some analysts might suggest). The sheer size of the Party has meant that multiple factions, including democratic ones, have been able to contribute to this reformulation, whilst that same national size and diversity has meant that the Party has been the only institution capable of holding national unity in place during the period of transition. Thus, "the CCP must be treated not only as part of the problem but also as carrying with it the needed sources of a solution".[19] Crucial to this analysis is acknowledgement for a start that Chinese identity is not homogeneous. The Chinese Revolution built a political culture that unified the nation through equality, solidarity, and the protective and regulatory state. This was not the same as centralisation – indeed Mao's regime began the process of decentralisation of political authority fairly early on, leading to lively and effective local authorities. This proved a bonus in the early stages of economic opening, when local initiatives could draw energy from empowered local bureaucrats, but was to prove more problematic when those same bureaucrats began to develop rentier or down-right corrupt characteristics. The opportunities presented to them as individuals by incoming foreign investment, and relatively loose central control, made them easy converts to capitalism's vices, even while the government attempted to promote a developmental model which retained its revolutionary emphasis on solidarity, equality and national unity. For Lin Chun, it is this contradiction – whereby individual and local bureaucrats subvert an otherwise solidaristic exercise – that accounts for political protest, rather than angst directed against the system per se. Yet, as the system itself is seen to progressively fail the larger part of its citizenry, and with the Party de facto increasingly subordinating itself to the unrestrained logic of the market, the pressures for more democratic political reform within the Party, if not at the expense of the Party, can only increase.

Lin Chun has her own axe to grind – the abandonment of the normative underpinnings of Chinese socialism – but she does have a point. The devolution of decisions regarding foreign direct investment and the possibilities for private entrepreneurs has been both an asset and, more latterly, a liability for the Chinese project. Initially, it allowed flexibility and rationality in the distribution of investment.[20] However, the growing opportunities for corruption have gone unstemmed by central regulation and anti-corruption campaigns, undermining both popular and investor confidence for the long term. In the World Bank Governance Indicators on Control of Corruption, China's position fell between 1998 and 2006 from a percentile ranking of 52.4 to 37.9, well below Thailand, South Korea, Malaysia, Taiwan, Hong Kong and Singapore, all of whom were in the 50th percentile or above in 2006. It also appears that the Party has become increasingly rigid in its (in)ability to respond to this threat to sustainability, thus drawing criticism towards it for the gap between rhetoric and reality. The most recent illustration of this disparity between local and central policy has come in the wake of the Chegdo earthquake in May 2008. Although the central government was viewed as responding quickly and effectively to the earthquake itself, public anger quickly turned against local officials whose corruption and indifference in terms of their local construction policies and practices were blamed for the fragility of structures and the subsequent loss of lives. Local officials were also accused of intervening to appropriate relief supplies, either for profit or for the wealthier districts.[21] The government anti-corruption body, the Central Commission for Discipline Inspections, responded with promises of "quick, strict and harsh penalties", and the pressure will now be on them, more than ever, to prove that their commitments have teeth. In this regard, it is transparency and accountability that become the immediate imperatives for political reform, not necessarily electoral democracy. The danger, and it is one that has been evident in the manner in which prime minister Wen Jiabao has been fostering his "man of the people" image post-earthquake, is

that the regime will fall back on populism to paper over the cracks. The introduction of a new labour-contract law in January 2008, which makes it harder
for employers to sack under-performing employees, and the promotion of the
children of Revolutionary-era Party elders to senior posts in the legislature, have
been interpreted by some intellectual and media figures as merely short-term
efforts to disguise the real gap between elites and masses.[22]

Perhaps the greatest long-term reservation that analysts have, particularly
regarding the domestic consequences of China's race to development, is the environmental impact of the chemical-based farming and energy-wasteful industry
that has fuelled growth. By 1998, China was home to seven of the world's ten
most-polluted cities, with air pollution claiming 300,000 lives per year. With
coal accounting for two-thirds of the country's energy consumption, sulphur
dioxide emissions are spreading acid rain over 30 per cent of the landscape.
The rapid increase in private car ownership, hailed as evidence of rising living
standards, is taking its environmental toll, too, as are failures to contain sewage
and industrial wastewater drainage into rivers. China is rapidly running out of
"clean" land, water (one-third of Chinese people lack access to clean drinking
water) and air, with life-or-death consequences and little that is convincing
in its attempts to reverse the causes of the problems. In a 2007 report for the
Council on Foreign Relations, Elizabeth Economy dismisses suggestions that
this is no different from the industrialisation experience elsewhere in the world,
arguing that "the scale and scope of pollution far outpaces what occurred in the
United States and Europe" during their own industrial revolutions[23] and is today
actually damaging the economy to the tune of about 9 per cent of its GDP.

A final major cause for concern lies in alternative thinking about China's
external ambitions. Few can argue with Ramo's assertion of a new multilateralism in post-Mao China. Territorial disputes are managed increasingly through
co-operative means, membership has been sought of a whole range of international institutions and organisations, China has participated substantially
in UN peace-keeping operations and has become a net aid donor rather than
recipient.[24] As Gill and Huang demonstrate, Chinese "soft power" is being
wielded in ever more nuanced and considered ways, which do indeed suggest
benign-ness rather than militarism. However, even Gill and Huang admit to the
contradiction between this and a strident Chinese nationalism which reflects
the resentments of past humiliations and gets in the way of its charm offensives
in places such as Japan, South Korea and, of course, Taiwan. It is the fear of
the combination of this nationalism with the growing economic and specifically *military* capabilities of China that instils the threat factor in Western and
regional powers.

If Gill and Huang contest the entirely innocent underpinnings of Chinese
self-assertion, Möller[25] disputes Ramo's theorem of leverage by suggesting that

China actually has little to offer its new multilateral friends other than free trade. It has few real strategic partnerships, and none which give it real hard-power clout or "polar" status. The new-found commitments to international order and organisation amount to little more than a defence of sovereignty and are thus not the basis for real participation in the integrationist project of other East Asian states that would be a better guarantor of long-term competitiveness and sustainability.

A final criticism of China's external policy stems from Beijing's apparent willingness to do business with just about anyone, including international pariahs such as Mugabe's Zimbabwe or the Darfur-purging Sudanese regime. "Coddling dictators can antagonise democratic oppositions and may bode ill for sustaining Beijing's influence in those countries",[26] de-legitimising China as a business partner and global power: it also sends signals to its own population regarding its tolerance of authoritarianism elsewhere and, by extension, the moral bankruptcy of its own governing party. The long-term political costs of such opportunism can only be sustained by China's economic muscle; when the latter is dented, the chickens may come home to roost.

The bottom line here is that, for the Chinese – who themselves claim that the Chinese model works for China, but not necessarily for anyone else – the successes post-1978 (when Deng reversed Mao's ideological rejection of modernisation in favour of a pragmatic market transition)[27] were only possible because the fundamentals for subsequent growth had been put in place during the period from 1949, regardless of its communist and supposedly anti-market credentials. Those very successes, however, have brought a concomitant erosion of economic and political fundamentals that threatens the sustainability of the project as the ideological foundations of Chinese national unity and equitable social organisation have been progressively abandoned. The political protests against inflation and corruption which culminated in the Tiananmen Square incident in 1989 inspired the more conservative generation of Party leaders to initiate an ultimately short-lived retrenchment against the reform process, including an austerity programme which rocked the rural engine for growth. The tide could not be held back, however, and Deng was once again the catalyst when he toured the Special Economic Zones in 1992, and declared them to be the way of the future. The way was then clear to full market transition when the Party endorsed the concept of the "socialist market economy" at the Fourteenth Party Congress in September of that year. It was not until 1994, however, that exchange markets were liberalised, 1995 before the central bank was able to determine monetary policy independently of the government and 1995 that privatisation of state-owned enterprises was introduced onto the agenda. By the end of the 1990s, the central government had essentially succumbed to the market and lost the control which might otherwise have enabled it to restrain the negative side-effects of rapid economic growth. Despite the Party's own internal reforms, the replacement of dictatorship with collective government, and the generation of a new level of factional and contestational politics within it, the regime's growing inability to ensure the material foundations of democracy (improving basic economic and social conditions)[28] is challenging its ability to sustain the social contract of "building socialism with Chinese characteristics".

WHAT CAN BEIJING OFFER THE ARAB WORLD?

We might conclude, then, that China's developmental experience, Ramo's insights notwithstanding, should be considered cautiously by those states which might seek to emulate it, not least because of its evident historical specificity and path-dependency, at least thus far. But there are a number of reasons why Arab regimes are turning their eyes eastwards and stating a desire to emulate China's apparent successes. There is nothing really new in this: throughout the last twenty-five years of Washington Consensus-led structural adjustment, the claim has frequently been made by the governments of countries such as Tunisia and Egypt that this is the path to Singaporean-type export-led success. The attraction lies not only in the rapidly rising standards of living in the East Asian tiger economies, but in the proposition that ruling elites might not have to surrender political power, exercised through the combination of authoritarian political structures and an interventionist state, in order to achieve them. Indeed, was it even possible that, in some instances, authoritarian modes of government might be *necessary* in order to prevent economic reforms from being derailed by popular resistance?

At a polemical level, the Beijing Consensus appears to offers all this and more, including the prospects of international leverage and a way out of the humiliations of past colonial lives, US-led interventions and ongoing Israeli occupation of Arab lands. The suggestion of a culturally authentic path to economic and social development further offers the enticing possibility that Muslim identities and Islamist sympathies among populations can be accommodated without surrendering power or influence to Islamist political competitors. In reality, however, there are significant, even insurmountable obstacles to the simple import of the Chinese model.

Education and Innovation in the Arab World

For a start, the Arab world is largely unprepared for the unrestrained pursuit of innovation. Only five years ago, the Arab Human Development Report, compiled by Arab specialists for the UNDP and the Arab Fund for Economic and Social Development, indentified a string of political and cultural "blocks" that obstruct the building of a knowledge-based society. Young Arabs, it claimed, are actually socialised away from knowledge-generation through authoritarian parenting practices, historically low levels of research and development, intellectual capital flight to the West and elsewhere, the absence of a democratic value system, censorship and the historic political exploitation of religion to denounce original thinking.[29] Most crucially, perhaps, the report highlights the deteriorating quality of formal education, the perpetuation of learning-by-rote and submission to established discourse. This fairly damning critique was echoed in a World Bank report on educational reform in the MENA region, tellingly entitled *The Road Not Travelled*.[30] Although the MENA region, much like China, made tremendous gains during the 1960s and 1970s in terms of increased and more equitable access to formal education, the report concludes that "the relationship between education and economic growth has remained weak, the divide between education and employment has not been bridged, and the quality of education continues to be disappointing".[31]

The problem has not really been one of a lack of investment: over the last forty years around 5 per cent of GDP per annum and 20 per cent of government budgets have been directed towards education. (This is considerably more than the average of 2.3 to 2.4 per cent of GDP per annum invested by China since 1975, and only Malaysia surpasses it from among the other Asian "tigers", at 5.9 per cent per annum). Such expenditure has facilitated near- universal enrolment at the primary level, with only Morocco and Yemen falling substantially short. Rates of enrolment in secondary and tertiary education have also been higher than in China, again with the exception of Morocco and Yemen, although significantly below countries such as the Republic of Korea, the Philippines and Thailand. The telling data refers to the quality of secondary education, where a test of eighth-graders in a large number of MENA, East Asian and Latin American countries found that MENA students scored significantly lower in terms of maths and science achievement than their counterparts in either of the other two regions.[32] Only in Tunisia and Jordan are pedagogical reforms transforming the critical skills of students and encouraging innovative thought processes appropriate to scientific inquiry. In a survey of higher education enrolment carried out between 1994 and 2003, MENA students were overwhelmingly concentrated in the arts, humanities and social sciences (63 per cent) compared to 29.3 per cent in sciences, medicine, technical and engineering subjects. By comparison, China had 32.2 per cent of its higher education students working in the arts, humanities and social sciences and 55.7 per cent working in the science and related fields. The implications for contributions of education to economic growth are significant. Moreover, despite the numbers continuing to secondary and tertiary education, many Arab countries have ongoing problems with high levels of illiteracy in adult populations, particularly among women (as high as

60.4 per cent in Morocco). Increasing private participation in the sector has been to some extent responsible: unlike China where private provision has been introduced principally at higher levels, whilst basic provision is provided by the state and ensures a basic level of equity, in the Arab countries private provision has infiltrated primary-level provision, establishing inequalities from very early on in the educational cycle. In short, despite relatively high levels of investment in human capital, and variations in the detail of provision across the region, the Arab world has failed to consolidate this into a qualitative and equitable output.

Of course, investments in human capital do not themselves generate economic growth. As well as suffering from a relatively poor quality of formal education (at least in the public sector), the report demonstrates that the distribution of labour is poor, with an overly high proportion of university graduates being employed in the public-sector in the absence of a sufficiently large, dynamic and productive private sector.

In sum, there is a crucial need for educational reform, and particularly for the MENA region because it has one of the proportionately largest and fastest-growing youth populations in the world (unlike China, which has an aging population). The challenge of adapting educational systems to provide the new mix of skills and competences required by the global economy at the scale and pace that is necessary gives real urgency to the task. A further task is the translation of such skills and competences into innovation, a task made harder in the Arab world by its poor record of investment in research and development. In 2007, Albert Sasson reported for a UNESCO Forum that:

> The overall spending in R&D [in the Arab world] is about 0.15 per cent of gross domestic product (GDP), compared with an average of 1.4 per cent in the world, and 2.5 per cent in Europe. This spending is provided by the public-sector to a very large extent (97 per cent).
>
> Covering the period 1990–2000, there were about 500 scientists and engineers involved in R&D per million people in the Arab States, compared with more than 4,000 per million people in North America, 2,500 in Europe and about 700 in South and East Asia. The world average was around 1,000 per million.
>
> By the end of the twentieth century, the number of publications – original writings and translations – per million people was around 0.05 in the Arab world, compared with an average of 0.15 worldwide and 0.6 in the industrialised countries ... the number of patents registered in the United States by Arab countries over the twenty-year period 1980–1999/2000 amounted to 171 for Saudi Arabia, 77 for Egypt, 52 for Kuwait, 32 for the United Arab Emirates, 15 for Jordan, 10 for Syria and 6 for Bahrain, compared with 16,328 for South Korea, 7,652 for Israel and 147 for Chile.[33]

Arguably, it is not only education that requires reform in order to generate a culture compatible with innovation. For Ramo, the key characteristic of China's recent development experience has been the sheer pace and scale of change and, since the early 1990s, the willingness of regimes to embrace change despite accompanying risks.[34] Proponents of exceptionalist, culturally-based arguments regarding the resistance of the Arab world to either economic or political reform often cite social conservatism deriving from either Islamic or patrimonial/neo patrimonial cultures, but medieval Islam demonstrated a profound capacity to both adapt to, and generate, change, with consequent and world-changing innovations in the sciences, medicine, manufacturing and the arts. Much as Bernard Lewis might like to brush alternative explanations aside as being merely efforts to pass the blame,[35] it is more likely that the experiences of colonialism, military defeat, failed attempts at post-independence self-sufficiency, and ultimately dependence and political stagnation, have left populations weary of grand promises and fragile or barely legitimate regimes reluctant to stake all on risky ventures. Instead, the preference has been for gradualist, largely risk-averse approaches to reform which do not generate the kind of change-driven momentum experienced by China, and which have proven more socially acceptable and manageable than radical reform programs.

This social conservatism is also evident in approaches to the socio-economic changes fostered by globalisation, in particular the need to move to a knowledge-based economy. As the World Bank report states:

> In today's world, characterised by intense global competition, and rapid technological change, the key to prosperity is a well-educated, technically skilled workforce producing high-value-added, knowledge intensive goods and services; in addition they must be employed in enterprises that have the managerial capacity to find, adapt, and adopt modern, up-to-date technology and sell sophisticated goods and services in local and global markets.[36]

The Arab region was slow to respond to the information technology revolution, but the pace has quickened notably in the past five years (since the AHDR report). By 2007, ICT spend was accounting for around 4 per cent of GDP (compared with 8 per cent in the developed countries)[37] and 17.3 per cent of the region's population were Internet connected.[38] More revealingly, Internet usage had grown by 920.2 per cent (compared with 221.5 per cent in Europe, 117.2 per cent in North America and 540.7 per cent in Latin America) during the period from 2000 to 2007.[39] Internet usage is of course differential across the region, with penetration varying from 42.9 per cent of the population in the UAE to just 1.3 per cent in Yemen, and broadband remains limited, with 7 per cent of households due to be connected in the UAE by 2010, 3 per cent in Saudi Arabia and just 1 per cent in Egypt.

When it comes to telecommunications, the picture is mixed: leisure-based and low-quantity data transfer technologies such as GSM telephones have taken off at an exponential pace. Privatisation in this sector has allowed the emergence of private telecom companies, operating in increasingly tight competition, which are expanding their reach beyond their own region and becoming global players.[40] (Equally, Arab satellite television is becoming a global and multi-lingual product (although without al-Jazeera this would be a less notable phenomenon). However, fixed-line penetration remains relatively low and strategic sectors remain largely the domain of protective regimes and their public sectors. Here, investment and expansion is much slower.

Undoubtedly, Arab governments and private sectors are rising to the ICT challenge, although at varying rates and with different strategies. Jordan and Egypt are focusing educational expenditures on developing a (probably migrant) labour force that can service the technology requirements of the region. Tunisian companies are "Arabising" software and developing new versions for local use. Gulf telecoms markets are engaging with the most recent technological innovations in order to expand their operations globally.

The problem remains, however, that – as Ramo argued – emulation must be surpassed by innovation. If China has made some inroads into this although (according to its critics, not as much as Ramo claims) the Arab world lags well behind. Low expenditures on R&D are compounded by political and cultural resistance to critical and innovative thinking. For example, the Arab state has retained its censorial role, despite the capacity of new technologies to transcend the borders of sovereign nation states. Interestingly, the Arabic Network for Human Rights Information conducted a survey of Internet usage in eleven Arab countries in 2004 and concluded that government policies were largely to blame for the relatively low usage compared to other parts of the world, the only exceptions being Jordan, the UAE and Qatar.[41] Direct modes of censorship have at times been replaced with indirect modes – controlled licensing of Internet service providers, installing filtering mechanisms, co-optation of interested private-sector elites, and recruiting public support in defence of "public morals" or local tradition. They have also been more direct: arbitrary harassment, arresting and imprisonment of Internet users and journalists, the criminalising of public criticism, and the introduction in 2008 of a new Arab Media Charter, which commits the Arab regimes to respecting one another's rights to restrain free media expression.[42]

Arab publics have also shown a resistance to some aspects of the new technologies. Mamoun Fandy has argued that historical experience leads Arabs to place greater trust in oral and unofficial transmissions than formal, public ones. The availability of new information and modes of communicating it does not necessarily translate into trust in such technologies, or a willingness to engage with them.[43] Similarly, there has been evidence of culturally- and religiously-based reservations about the availability of information which the technologies make possible, particularly those which offend certain Muslim sensibilities. This cultural defensiveness, which stems from combinations of colonial history (and legacies), stagnated development, and more recently the need to respond to the implications of the US-led war on terror, is profoundly at odds with the cultural confidence of the Chinese approach to their own development experience, which is that globalisation can be shaped to, and by, embedded Chinese cultural affiliations.

Innovation requires that risk-taking be a social, not merely governmental attribute: in the Arab world, neither are prominent attributes. Those regimes that have pursued even moderately risky strategies (Tunisia's committed approach to quality-enhanced export-driven growth or Dubai's "build-it-and-they'll-come" program) have reaped the rewards of their efforts; but for the most part, and including so-called "radical" regimes such as Syria, governments have proven to be risk-averse and conservative in their policies towards development. Likewise, the Arab private sector (with the possible exception of telecommunications, financial services and property development, largely based in the Gulf) has proven to be lacking in the entrepreneurial flair needed to drive innovative ventures, and this despite the efforts of organisations such as the World Bank to stimulate the adventurous spirit through initiatives such as the Private Enterprise Partnership.[44]

In sum, China and the Arab world demonstrated a shared history of improving access to, and quantity of, education in the pre-economic reform era. Whilst China has built upon this through careful incorporation of private provision at higher levels, a concentration of spending in hubs of educational excellence, increased spending on R&D and a refocusing on scientific development, the Arab world has less successfully opened the whole sector to private provision with fewer favourable results, has failed to generate an emphasis on either science or excellence, and has witnessed an overall diminishment in quality of provision. Some states have fared better than others (Tunisia, for example, has invested heavily in expanding vocational provision, while the Gulf Arab countries have welcomed overseas university provision to the domestic market), but political and cultural constraints remain, which impede them from embracing the educational aspects of globalisation that would enable them to collectively overcome these weaknesses. Moreover, the scale of the problem, given the demographic youth bulge, makes the task of reforming education and creating an innovation-friendly environment all the more daunting. If the Arab world wishes to emulate Chinese success, it must first address issues of educational reform, as well as embracing the cultural and political aspects of innovation and risk-taking. It may equally learn from the Chinese experience that technological emulation is insufficient to sustain development, and that long-term progress requires the qualitative leap to innovative practice that can only happen when the right social and political foundations are in place.

The Primacy of Living Standards and Equality over Democracy

The second theorem of Chinese development, according to Ramo, was the enhancement of living standards and equity, albeit at the cost of democratic reform. There is no shortage of evidence regarding the absence of democracy in the Arab world, or the superficiality and political opportunism that have characterised political reform programs. We may leave aside here discussion as to whether liberal democracy is a culturally appropriate political format for Arab or Muslim countries, or the degree to which the procedural changes that have been wrought in many Arab countries over the last two decades constitute anything more than a façade of liberalisation. Let us accept the weight of the evidence that Arab regimes are, to a greater or lesser extent, essentially auto-cratic or authoritarian. The question, really, is whether this authoritarianism can be justified on the basis that it can in some way facilitate enhanced living standards and social equality? Arab leaders such as Zine el-Abidine Ben Ali of Tunisia, Hosni Mubarak of Egypt or King Abdullah of Jordan might argue that, without tight regime control of the political arena, necessary economic reforms can be de-railed by vested interests such as workers' unions, Islamist oppor-tunists or media provocateurs. Indeed, this logic has underpinned the Tunisian development experience since the political *fermature* of the early 1990s, and to some extent, in that instance, it does hold water. The authoritarian state has been able to take a decisive interventionist and managerial role in the economy, pushing through liberalising reforms and directing resources (both public and private) towards the investment and quality upgrading that were necessary for the country to develop a competitive export-oriented economic base.[45] Unlike most of the Arab world, investment in Tunisia has been of a high quality, demonstrating impressive total factor productivity rates (20 per cent between 1975 and 2000 compared to negative rates in the rest of the region, excluding Egypt).[46] The regime has also operated a programme of carefully targeted welfare assistance to the poorest rural areas and populations, leading to an overall reduction in poverty, a controlled rate of unemployment, rising per capita incomes and a focus on environmental protection to ensure the sustain-ability of the agricultural and tourism sectors. The Tunisian story should be viewed as a success, not least because it has been predicated on the maintenance of political stability through a period and in a region which has experienced serious upheavals over the last two decades, most pertinent of which was the

Algerian civil war taking place next door. The cost of this stability has been the complete exclusion of political Islam from the legal arena, the co-optation and control of legitimate opposition, and a fierce clamp down on media freedom, and civil and human rights. Arguably, however, the formula has reached the end of its shelf-life. The bureaucracy has become entrenched and self-serving, and private-sector elites are closely interwoven with the ruling regime, which has itself maintained gate-keeping and rent-seeking functions that seriously inhibit the deepening of entrepreneurial freedom and undermine trust in both governance structures and the rule of law.[47]

The positive aspects of the Tunisian story are not general to the Arab world. One way to assess the overall standard of living is through measurements of human development, and here we are presented with a mixed story. The Arab Human Development Report of 2002[48] attempted to measure human development in the Arab world against other regions, concluding that:

> The Arab region outperformed sub-Saharan Africa on the overall HDI and on indicators of overall health (life expectancy at birth) and educational attainment (proxied here by adult literacy). It has yet to reach the levels attained by East Asia (with or without China) and Latin America and the Caribbean for these indicators ... The relative position of the Arab region improves with respect to the per capita output indicator (PPP basis), where it outperformed the South-East Asia and Pacific region as well as South Asia and sub-Saharan Africa. The Arab region might thus be said to be richer than it is developed with respect to basic human-development indicators.[49]

Not surprisingly, the best performing Arab countries in terms of the Human Development Index were the oil rich monarchies of the Gulf and Libya, countries which are able to distribute the vast rents accrued from the sale of oil to their citizens in the form of health care, education, welfare provision and other subsidies. At the other end of the scale, population-heavy Egypt and Morocco, war-torn Iraq and Sudan, and impoverished Yemen fared badly on the index. Clearly, the human development components of the standard of living in Arab countries are directly related to the availability of rentier income, and the region is not building its human capital upon more profound social structures (such as the Chinese popular consensus in favour of equality of access to provision). More worryingly, the report highlights a crucial component of Arab human development, or the lack of it. It suggests that probably the single greatest obstacle to the equality of Arab citizens are the social attitudes and norms, reinforced by political structures that exclusively stress women's reproductive role and reinforce the gender-based asymmetry of unpaid care. As a consequence, more than half of Arab women are still illiterate. The region's maternal mortality rate is double that of Latin America and the Caribbean and four times that of East Asia ... The utilisation of Arab women's capabilities through political and economic participation remains the lowest in the world in quantitative terms, as evidenced by the low share of women in parliaments, cabinets and the workforce and in the trend towards feminisation of unemployment.[50]

The report also analysed changing living standards more generally, arguing that, despite fluctuating growth patterns, and an overall apparently respectable regional average growth rate of around 3.3 per cent between 1975 and 1998, the reality was that high population growth rates in the region reduced this in real terms to a stagnant 0.5 per cent per annum, well below the global average of 1.3 per cent and "implying a deterioration in the average standard of living in the Arab world compared to the rest of the world".[51] Ironically (and partly due to fluctuating oil prices), the oil-rich countries fared relatively worst, while Egypt, Morocco, Oman, Syria, Tunisia and the Sudan did marginally better.

When it came to income distribution and poverty reduction, the report concluded that the picture was incomplete due to lack of available and trust-worthy sources. Using World Bank and United Nations figures, the report concluded that the Arab world in general features less absolute poverty than most regions due to historically (post-colonial) egalitarian income distribution practices and periods of economic growth. Nonetheless, "it remains the case that one out of every five people lives on less than $2 per day ... Poor or unavailable health care or opportunities for quality education, a degraded habitat – whether a polluted urban slum or a rural livelihood eked out on exhausted soil – scant or non-existent social safety nets: all form part of the nexus of poverty and are prevalent in Arab countries."[52]

Income distribution represents the positive side of the Arab coin: World Bank and United Nations statistics suggest that, the developing countries of the MENA region now have, on average, one of the most equal income distributions in the world, with an average Gini coefficient of 0.364 for the period 1995–9, and that "the average coefficient has been falling over time",[53] not least due to incomes from migration and remittances which disproportionately benefit those at the bottom of the economic ladder.

This picture compares favourably to China, yet the report argues that there is growing evidence of differentials across the region and of a more recent dimin-ishing of income equality in countries such as Egypt, Iraq and Jordan. Many countries, such as Yemen and Morocco, exhibit a pronounced urban–rural divide (not dissimilar to that in China) and the realities of these income divides are to some extent masked by strong traditions of charitable, family- and religion-based social support on the one hand, and continuing government subsidies on the other. Furthermore, real unemployment rates (which rose during the era of structural adjustment across most parts of the region) have been partially disguised by under-employment, absorption into educational programs (in the Gulf) and the export of labour.

Therefore we may say that, despite a relatively, albeit diminishing, equitable distribution of income in the Arab world, overall living standards have declined in relative terms, with a consequent impact on human development, negating the argument that authoritarianism has been necessary for equity-based rising living standards over recent decades. If anything, the report is adamant that the limits to transparency, accountability, the rule of law, and political freedoms such as that of speech, have worked ultimately to obstruct development.[54]

It is worth pointing out again the diversity among Arab states here. In the World Bank's Governance Indicators, the UAE, Kuwait and Tunisia score relatively much better than the other Arab states for political stability, government effectiveness, regulatory quality, rule of law and control of corruption (although Saudi Arabia and Tunisia both do poorly in the rankings for voice and accountability). They all do badly, however, relative to the developmental giants of East Asia, with the notable exception of China.

Interestingly, Tunisia and the United Arab Emirates – which might be considered regional development success stories (at least thus far) – are also relatively strong regional performers in governance matters, whilst being very definitely not progressive in terms of democratic political systems. That is not to suggest that the sustainability of their development progress is not dependent on greater improvement in these realms (as noted in the case of Tunisia above), but it does support the argument that authoritarianism *with* good governance can move an economy state along the developmental axis and that authoritarianism per se need not be an absolute hindrance to developmental progress. However, for the Arab countries, as for China, there appears to be a limit to this paradigm and, again such as China, the Arab regimes have been trying to internalise political reform within ruling corporate structures rather than opening the party system up to genuine and meaningful competition. Political reforms within ruling parties and regimes in the Arab world have been about two things: broadening coalitions to co-opt private-sector interests and installing technocrats in the place of party functionaries in order to increase the autonomy of elites to act as they choose. Although technocratic change-management teams can work to improve governance, their efforts can only be undermined by the embedded self-interest of governing coalitions and the reduced accountability of regime elites. The end result is decreased rather than increased representativeness, and diminishing legitimacy. The answer for the Arab countries, as indeed it may inevitably be for China, is to look to Singapore and South Korea, both of whom ultimately succumbed to the democratic impulse in order to consolidate their economic success.

Foreign Policy Leverage and Militarisation

China's ability to exercise leverage in the international arena, the third theorem identified by Ramo, is largely a function, not a determinant, of its economic success and the capacity for militarisation that buys. Even a cursory glance at the comparative indicators offered below (Table 1) suggests that the combined economic weight of the Arab states is unable to match the global positioning of China. For a start, despite the nascent development of an Arab free trade area, and the possibilities for complementarities among at least some Arab economies, the barriers to trade between Arab countries remain significant.[55] Given this, and the much smaller total Arab population, they are unable to represent the massive market potential of an increasingly affluent China.

Table 1. Comparative Indicators, China and the Arab Countries (Economic)

Country	Pop. (million)	GDP $US billion	Exports fob $US million	Imports cif
China	1,300	3,241	1,218,000	955,800
Algeria	33	102	54,740	22,335
Bahrain	1	13	11,563	8,941
Egypt	74	107	20,500	33,104
Iraq	28	5*	n/a	n/a
Jordan	5	14	4,041	9,594
Kuwait	1	81	58,638	14,350
Lebanon	4	21	2,282	9,398
Libya	6	45	36,399	13,628
Morocco	31	56	11,500	22,462
Oman	3	36	21,587	10,897
Palestine	4	4	335	2,667
Qatar	1	53	34,051	15,861
Saudi Arabia	24	349	174,635	40,342
Syria	20	30	9,302	10,535
Tunisia	10	30	11,508	14,850
UAE	4	163	142,485	97,850
Yemen	21	13	n/a	n/a
Total Arab	270	1,122	593,566	326,814

Source: *Economist Intelligence Unit, Country Profile: China Main Report*, 12 February 2008. Also country profiles: Algeria, Bahrain, Egypt, Iraq, Jordan, Kuwait, Lebanon, Libya, Morocco, Oman, Palestinian Territories, Qatar, Saudi Arabia, Syria, Tunisia, UAE and Yemen for 2008. Year for which the actual statistics were relevant varied for each country between 2005 and 2007.
*Including grants

Table 2. Arab Trade with the US and EU, 2006

Country		Exports		Imports	
		% of total	rank	% of total	rank
Algeria	US	27.2	2	6.6	3
	EU	52.5	1	54.8	1
Bahrain	US	1.9	3	–	–
	EU	2.1	2	11	1
Egypt	US	8.7	3	7.8	2
	EU	33.9	1	23.2	1
Jordan	US	25.1	1	4.7	4
	EU	–	–	23.6	2
Kuwait	US	11.0	2	10.6	2
	EU	7.8	3	33.2	1
Lebanon	US	–	–	5.9	3
	EU	10.6	3	4.8	1
Libya	US	–	–	–	–
	EU	–	–	47.2	1
Morocco	US	1.9	4	4.5	5
	EU	73.1	1	52.3	1
Oman	US	–	–	5.2	5
	EU	1.2	3	19.2	2
Qatar	US	–	–	9.9	3
	EU	–	–	34.8	1
Saudi Arabia	US	15.1	1	14.5	2
	EU	13.1	2	31.1	1
Syria	US	–	–	–	–
	EU	40.7	1	19.6	1
Tunisia	US	–	–	2.5	5
	EU	80.1	1	69.7	1
UAE	US	–	–	6.3	4
	EU	2.6	4	24.8	1

Source: *World Trade Organisations* profiles, available from http://stat.wto.org/
CountryProfile/WSDBCountryPFHome.aspx?

Nor does the Arab world offer a comparable menu of exports. Those Arab countries with significant trade surpluses only achieve that position by virtue of oil and other hydrocarbon exports. Admittedly these enable them to build up substantial foreign exchange reserves and overseas investment portfolios, but they are essentially rents dependent on a finite and unevenly distributed resource. Moreover, they generate distributive structures rather than employment-based incomes. Of course, in the past, Arab oil exporters have been able to translate this economic wealth and resource control into political leverage, but the growing number of non-OAPEC members, and increasing emphasis on energy-source diversification, suggest that the days of effective oil boycotts are long gone, even if the Arab regimes were able to reconcile their diverse regional strategic and economic interests for long enough to construct one. In the meantime, the dependence of Arab economies on the United States and Europe as sources for their imports and, in some cases, as markets for exports continues, but is not reciprocated in any area other than oil.

China, on the other hand, has become the dominant player in global markets such as textiles, low-value-added manufactures and increasingly higher-technology electrical products. It also offers a lucrative investment market for overseas firms[56] and an increasingly integrated local market for their products. It is worth noting that in 2006 China became the fourth-largest export market for the United States (worth approximately $US55.2 billion) and the second-largest source of imports ($US 287.8 billion). China also overtook the United States as the EU's largest source of imports.[57] The largest slice of the United States' trade deficit lies with its dealing with China, which, despite making commitments in a 1999 WTO agreement to open its own markets more fairly to American exports, is accused of still subsidising its manufactures to a level with which American producers cannot compete. What are perceived as being predatory Chinese export practices have become the subject of calls for renewed American protectionism and boosted by fears of an over-dependence on China's purchases of American Treasury bills, to fend off recession and its energy-thirsty impact on global oil prices. In other words, the American economy (and Europe's, for that matter) is astonishingly reliant on Chinese growth, and yet equally fearful of it.

By contrast, Arab economies only present a threat to the extent that the region's principal export – oil – is a strategic resource in limited supply and, to a lesser extent, when Arab investments overseas are rather bizarrely perceived of as serving a vanguard function for militant Islam (as was the case when the US Congress effectively forced the UAE-based Dubai Portsworld to disinvest from its operations in terminals at six American ports). In short, even if the Arab states could integrate their economies into a single more powerful and co-ordinated engine for trade and investment, they would be unable to exert the kind of influence that China does, as it is out of a combination of dependence and fear among its trading partners. As individual states, the suggestion that Beijing's economy-based foreign policy leverage can be emulated becomes even more ridiculous. The economic solution for the Arab world does not lie in the defence of sovereign interests through regional or international co-operation, but in deeper regional integration, the better synchronisation of local production, markets with global systems of finance and regulation, and the diversification of production, exports and markets. Lacking the economic muscle to re-negotiate the formulations for international trade and investment, they must maximise their ability to extract what they can from existing structures.

Of course, China's economic muscle inspires awe, in part, because it is backed up by a massive militarisation programme. The Middle East and North Africa is one of the most militarised regions of the world, and Arab regimes spend a relatively large proportion of their GDP on their armed forces and security services, so one might expect them to derive some international clout from this. However, as Table 3 demonstrates, here, too, they are thoroughly outclassed by China. Not only does China have a vastly larger military in absolute terms than the combined militaries of the Arab world, funded by an extraordinarily large expenditure, but it also achieves more for less in terms of GDP and per capita spending.

Moreover, while Saudi Arabia's arms purchases might exceed those of China,[58] China has itself become one of the global top-five suppliers of arms, indicating the strength and self-sustainability of the Chinese military–industrial complex. Arab production of weaponry is heavily dependent on technology transfers from outside, on replication and emulation, and is generally of inferior quality and performance to products from industrialised countries. China, by contrast, has

Table 3. Comparative Indicators, China and the Arab World (Military), 2006

Country	Total exp $US million	Def. exp $US per capita	%GDP (000)	No. in armed forces
China	121,872	27	1.3	1,500
Algeria	3,096	94	2.7	187
Bahrain	532	761	3.4	11
Egypt	4,337	55	4.0	397
Iraq	n.a.	n.a.	n.a.	n.a.
Jordan	1,115	189	7.9	10
Kuwait	3,497	1,446	3.4	7
Lebanon	589	152	2.8	20
Libya	593	100	1.1	0
Morocco	2,161	65	3.8	50
Oman	3,276	1,056	9.0	4
Palestine	n.a.	n.a.	n.a.	56
Qatar	2,335	2,638	4.5	0
Saudi Arabia	29,541	1,093	8.5	16
Syria	1,739	92	5.1	108
Tunisia	435	43	1.4	12
UAE	9,482	3,643	6.7	0
Yemen	824	38	4.2	71
Total Arab	63,552	–	–	949

Source: IISS, *The Military Balance 2008*, London: Routledge, 2008. From Table 37: International Comparisons of Defence Expenditure and Military Manpower, 2004–2006.

proved itself a competent innovator and exporter. More crucially, the countries of the Arab world are tied into a complex web of security arrangements with international partners (particularly, but not exclusively, the United States) which constrain their procurement strategies, their operational environments and their regional relations. Their own region is heavily penetrated and fraught with instabilities and local conflicts, and no Arab state has a comparable status as regional hegemon to that which China enjoys. Instead, the Arab world turns its military face inwards, as it tries to balance against the regional aspirations of Iran, the disruptive influence of Israel and the occupation of Palestinian lands, and the ethnic and sectarian rifts spinning out from Iraq. Unlike China, which holds its demographic diversities in check with a unified Chinese nationalism, the Arab world is struggling to reconcile Islamic universalism and aspects of collective Arab identity with individual state sovereignty.

Thus, the Arab world is no more able to direct its militarisation towards global power projection in support of maintaining suitable (peaceful) conditions for economic growth than it is able to utilise economic muscle to fend off the predatory or hegemonic aspirations of an American superpower. Here again, the Arab countries would do better to look elsewhere for inspiration. The region urgently needs meaningful collective security arrangements that engage with, rather than exclude, potential threats to stability and sovereignty. Such arrangements might enable a gradual weaning-away from external guarantors whose interventions are essentially divisive at both regional and domestic levels. More crucially, current Arab regimes would do better to look to enhancing their own legitimacy credentials – and thus internal stability – rather than deflecting domestic unrest by sustaining regional antagonisms, with their accompanying financial and military costs.

LESSONS FROM BEIJING

The assessment given above suggests that the recent Chinese economic experience does not present a straightforward template for development that can be easily imported into the Arab world. As well as containing its own flaws, it has been predicated on a very different set of political, economic and social structures, and is itself still in transition. It does, however, offer a number of interesting insights into what may or may not assist the Arab economies in their developmental struggles. Key requisites for making the qualitative, as well as the quantitative, leap to a globalised economy appear to be educational reform in favour of innovation and critical thinking, the embedding of an appropriately risk-friendly culture in both business and government, recognition of the need to balance equity and living standards on the one hand with growth-oriented policies on the other, and the urgent requirement for good governance, transparency, accountability and the rule of law. Where the Chinese progression appears at risk, this is because the ruling regime has been unable to include the wider population in the benefits of forward momentum, and where political structures have not been sufficiently responsive to contradictions and tensions in economic policy, to adjust it accordingly. Hence, imbalances occur – in income, in rural–urban living standards, in provision of social welfare services, in environmental degradation, or in corruption and graft – which threaten to run the project off the rails. The same political structures have ultimately served to cap the potential for innovation and technology-led growth by resisting the full potential of free thinking, critical research and unrestrained global communication. The Chinese model shows us what Singapore and South Korea taught us ten years ago, and what the populations of the former Soviet Union came to recognise before that: economic development can only progress so far under authoritarian or undemocratic political structures. Without effective means for wider populations to have a voice in calling policy-making elites to account, vested interests hijack economic processes and divert them to particularist ends. When political structures are insufficiently responsive to the demands of populations for a broad level of social equity and a basic provision of welfare support, economic policies serve the interests of capitalist development at the expense of human development. When political structures seek to control communication and knowledge in order to enhance their own capacity to direct populations towards economic ends, then the engine for innovation is constrained. In all this, growth may be enhanced in the short to medium term, but the sustainability of the project comes into question. Thus, the key ingredient for *sustained and sustainable* economic development, which draws upon the energy and potential of the full human resources of a country, is democracy, whether liberal or otherwise.[59] That is not to dispute the usefulness of an interventionist state, or even a non-democratic state during certain earlier phases of development. Gordon White's comment regarding China has indeed proved equally applicable elsewhere, not least in some Arab states such as Tunisia:

> ... in the short to medium term there are strong arguments to suggest that a strong and coherent politico-administrative system is required to manage the process of market transition and tackle the still formidable problems posed by poverty, regional inequality and social disruption ...[60]

But even if one views development as an analytically separate social phenomenon from democracy (that is, that democracy is not considered to be an intimate component of a broad conception of development),[61] one cannot escape the logic of the latter in the advancement of the former when it comes to the project's sustainability. Democracy provides the normative and institutional coherence that facilitates the balance between capitalist and human development.

Given their rhetorical understanding of the Chinese experience as development under authoritarianism, it is perhaps ironic that this is the best lesson that Arab regimes can learn from Beijing.

NOTES

1. Joshua Cooper Ramo, *The Beijing Consensus*, London: The Foreign Policy Centre, 2004, p. 9.
2. Edward Ayensu, "International Management", quoted in Brian Murphy, *The World Wired Up*, London: Comedia, 1983, p. 119.
3. In the early days of opening to foreign trade and investment, the Chinese government decided that Guangdong and Fujian provinces should pursue reform "one step ahead" of other provinces, with special regulatory regimes and flexibilities not available elsewhere. Four Special Economic Zones enabled private enterprises to be concentrated in these provinces, and thus protected from broader political and ideological opposition.
4. Ramo, *The Beijing Consensus*, p. 17.
5. Thomas L. Friedman, *The World is Flat*, London: Penguin Books, 2005, pp. 319–22 and 354–6.
6. World Bank, Governance Matters 2007: Worldwide Governance Indicators, 1996–2006. http://info.worldbank.org/governance/wgi2007/sc_chart.asp.
7. Bates Gill and Yanzhong Huang, "Sources and Limits of Chinese 'Soft Power'", *Survival*, vol. 48, no. 2, Summer 2006, p. 27.
8. Kay Möller, "Review Essay: The Beijing Bluff", in *Survival*, vol. 48, No.2, Summer 2006, p. 142.
9. Lin Chun, "Introduction", in *The Tranformation of Chinese Socialism*, Durham and London: Duke University Press, 2006, pp. 1–17.
10. Susan Lawrence, "The Sickness Trap", in *Far East Economic Review*, 13 June 2002.
11. Dale Wen, *China Copes with Globalization*, San Francisco: International Forum on Globalization, 2006, p. 3.
12. Dongping Han, "Professional bias and its Impact on China's Rural Education: Re-examining the Two models of Rural Education and Their Impact on Rural Development in China", available on http://chinastudygroup.org/article/2/a quoted in Dale Wen, *China Copes*, p. 4.
13. Dale Wen, "China Copes with Globalization: A Mixed Review", International Forum for Globalization, San Fransisco, CA, 2006, p. 3.
14. He also refers to studies suggesting the number is as high as 400 million, including Francois Bourguignon's, "Transition of China's Northeast: The Need for Combining Regional and National Policies", in *The World Bank Seminar: A Development Strategy for Northeast China Shenyang, Liaoning Province*, at worldbank.org, p. 2. Also in Ramo, *The Beijing Consensus*, p.11.
15. "Six Large Gaps Regarding Income: The Top 10% has 45% of the Wealth", *Xinhua Net*, 17 June 2005, available from http://news.xinhuanet.com/fortune/2005–06/17/content_3096235.htm and quoted in Wen, *China Copes*, p. 21.

16. Gill and Huang, "Sources and Limits", p. 27.

17. See for example "China Crisis", *Common Cause*, Summer 2008, pp. 8–9.

18. Wen, *China Copes*, p. 21. Figures taken from Howard French, "Land of 74,000 Protests (but Little is Ever Fixed)", *New York Times*, 24 August 2005.

19. Lin Chun, "Introduction", p. 4.

20. Yingyi Qian, "The Process of China's Market Transition (1978–98): The Evolutionary, Historical and Comparative Perspectives", *Journal of Institutional and Theoretical Economics*, vol. 156, no.1, March 2000, pp. 151–71.

21. BBC News, "China warns over quake corruption" on http://news.bbc.co.uk/2/hi/asia-pacific/7411921.stm . Also Fox News, "China Earthquake Brings Aftershocks of Corruption" on http://www.foxnews.com/stopry/0,2933,359584,00.html.

22. "Why Grandpa Wen has to care", *The Economist*, 14–20 June 2008, p. 72.

23. Economy quoted in Carin Zissis, *China's Environmental Crisis*, Council on Foreign Relations, 2007. Available on http://www.cfr.org/publication/12608/chinas_environmental_crsiis.html.

24. Gill and Huang, "Sources and Limits", p. 21.

25. Möller, "Review Essay", p. 140.

26. Gill and Huang, "Sources and Limits", p. 28.

27. The reform era is widely held to begin at the Third Plenum of the Eleventh Chinese Party Congress, held in December 1978, when a newly rehabilitated Deng announced in response to the ideological diehards' insistence on continuing with Mao's dogmatic policies: "It doesn't matter whether a cat is white or black so long as it catches mice."

28. Manoranjan Mohanty, "Development and Democracy: The Indian and Chinese Experience" in http://igna.nic.in/ks_41030.htm.

29. UNDP/Arab Fund for Economic and Social Development, *Arab Human Development Report, 2003: Building a Knowledge Society*, New York: UNDP, 2003.

30. The World Bank, *The Road Not Travelled: Educational Reform in the Middle East and Africa*, MENA Development Report, IRBD, The World Bank: Washington, DC, 2008.

31. Ibid., p. xvi.

32. Ibid., pp. 17–20. Based on data provided by the International Association for the Evaluation of Educational Achievement) and PISA (Organisation for Economic Co-operation and Development).

33. Albert Sasson, *Research and Development in the Arab States: The Impact of Globalization, Facts and Persectives*, paper presented at UNESCO Forum, Regional Seminar: "The Impact of Globalization on Higher Education and Research in the Arab States", Rabat, 24–5 May 2007, p. 3.

34. Ramo, *The Beijing Consensus*, p. 8.

35. Bernard Lewis, *What Went Wrong?: Western Impact and Middle Eastern Response*, London: Weidenfeld and Nicolson, 2004, pp. 168–79.

36. The World Bank, *The Road Not Travelled*, p. 85.

37. Booz Allen Hamilton, "The Impact of the ICT Sector on Economic Development in the Middle East" from http://www.boozallencom/capabilities/Industries_article.

38. Internet World Statistics, "Usage and Population Statistics" from *http://www.Internetworldstats.com/stats7.html*.

39. It is admitted that these statistics need to be used with caution, as they are based on Internet subscription numbers provided by Internet service providers, rather than on actual individual users.

40. Companies such as UAE-based Etisalaat, Bahrain's Batelco and Kuwaiti-based Zain (a subsidiary of MTC) are expanding their service provision in Africa and South Asia, where the challenges are very different from those in the Arab world, given lower incomes and lower potential revenues).

41. HRINFO, *The Internet in the Arab world and its Users* available on http://www.hrinfo. net/en/reports/net2004/.

42. For a fuller discussion of the issues relating to information and communication technologies in the Arab world, see E. Murphy, "Agency and Space: The Political Impact of Information Technologies in the Gulf Arab States", *Third World Quarterly*, vol. 27, no. 6, 2006, pp. 1059–84.

43. Mamoun Fandy, "Information Technology, Trust and Social Change in the Arab World", *Middle East Journal*, vol. 54, no.3, 2000, pp. 378–94.

44. Tarek Osman, "Risk in the Arab World: Enterprise Versus Politics", *Open Democracy*, Al-Maktoum Institute, available online at http://www.opendemocracy.net/article/ middle_east/risk_in_the_Arab_world.

45. More information on precisely how the Tunisian Government has done this can be found in Emma Murphy, "The Tunisian Mise à Niveau Programme and the Political Economy of Reform", *New Political Economy*, vol. 11, no. 4, December 2006, pp. 519–40.

46. *Arab World Competitiveness Report 2002–3*, quoted in The World Bank, *Project Performance Assessment Report: Republic of Tunisia*, New York: The World Bank, 2004, p. 15

47. The World Bank, *World Bank Country Assistance Strategy Report for 2000–2002*, The World Bank: New York, 2000.

48. UNDP, *The Arab Human Development Report 2002: Creating Opportunities for Future Generations*, UNDP/Arab Fund for Economic and Social Development, 2002.

49. Ibid., p. 26.

50. Ibid., p. 3.

51. Ibid., p. 88.

52. Ibid., p. 5.

53. UNDP, *Arab Human Development Fund Report*, 2002, p. 90.

54. The World Bank, *Governance Matters 2007: Worldwide Governance Indicators, 1996–2006*, available on http://info.worldbank.org/governance/wgi2007/sc_chart.asp.

55. The Greater Arab Free Trade Area was finally implemented fully in January 2005 (the project having been agreed in 1997) and includes seventeen member states of the Arab League, including all members of the Agadir Free Trade Zone that came into existence in 2004. GAFTA is the most far-reaching trade agreement in the area (which displays a proliferation of "spaghetti" regionalism) and it has improved intra-regional trade by a yearly average of 15.1 per cent compared to an average increase in world exports of 7.9 per cent per annum. However, the Gulf countries contribute a disproportionate 70 per cent of intra-regional trade, and the region exhibits a clear dichotomy between surplus- and deficit-trading states.

56. In 2006, it was suggested that foreign invested enterprises (FIEs) produced 31.6 per

cent of gross industrial output value in China and employed 14.1 million people. Economist Intelligence Unit, *Country Profile: China*, 12 February 2008, available on http:www.eiu.com/index.asp?layout=displayIssueAryicle&issue_id=543092639 &opt, accessed on 16 June 2008.

57. Economist Intelligence Unit, *Country Profile: United States of America*, available on http://www.eiu.com/index.asp?layout+displayIssueArticle&Issue_id=1272362712 & opt=full.

58. In 2006, Saudi Arabia was the leading developing nation recipient of arms deliveries, buying $US 4,100 million-worth, compared to second-place China, which purchased $US 2,900-worth. International Institute for Strategic Studies, *The Military Balance 2008*, London: Routledge, 2008. Table 38, p. 449.

59. Gordon White makes a strong case for a more nuanced and geo-historically specific conceptualisation of democratic reform in China in "China: Development and Democratization", in Adrian Leftwich (ed.), *Democracy and Development*, Cambridge: Polity Press, 1996, pp. 209–29.

60. Ibid., 1996, p. 217.

61. See discussion in Adrian Leftwich, "Two Cheers for Democracy", in Leftwich, *Democracy and Development*, p. 281.

CHAPTER 5

Towards an Islamic Model for the Middle East and North Africa?

CLEMENT M. HENRY

Muslim countries, virtually all of which were colonised or brought indirectly under Western non-Muslim domination in the eighteenth and nineteenth centuries, are naturally wary of foreign models of development. The process of globalisation, accelerated by late twentieth-century neo-liberal reforms, bore some resemblance to that earlier period of globalisation, 1870–1914, when virtually all of the territories of Dar al-Islam were consolidated under European flags. Although European gunboats no longer physically threatened debtor states in the 1980s and 1990s, many of these states were obliged to undergo IMF work-outs, followed by structural reforms encouraged by World Bank loans, a process that continues in the current decade.

The Washington Consensus still serves as the intellectual underpinning of second-generation structural reform, although in its most recent ("post-WC") formulation, Dani Rodrik has added an additional ten guidelines to its ten original commandments, albeit with the proviso "do whatever you can, as much as you can, as quickly as you can".[1] To tame the prolific confusion of command-ments, the World Bank commissioned Nobel laureate Michael Spence to lead a distinguished group of world leaders and economists (not the Bank's earlier chief economist and critic, Nobel laureate Joseph Stiglitz) to draft a new consensus. The Spence Report, issued in May 2008, singled out the thirteen countries that had displayed at least thirty years of sustained high (at least 7 per cent) growth rates since the Second World War. They included Oman, Malaysia and Malta, as well as China, Hong Kong and South Korea, and the report concluded that there was no single formula for success and that any sensible approach to development should be diagnostic rather than prescriptive. John Williamson, who had fathered the original ten prescriptions in 1989, took solace in Rodrik's summary of the broad commonalities of these experiences: "they all engage in the global economy, maintain macroeconomic stability, stimulate saving and investment, provide market-oriented incentives, and are reasonably well governed".[2] Williamson also admitted that he had omitted the more recent concerns about good governance. The New Washington Consensus, then, is whittled down to five general points, expandable back to ten if necessary:

1. Openness: import knowledge
2. Openness: exploit global demand
3. Macroeconomic stability: modest inflation
4. Macroeconomic stability: sustainable public finances
5. Future orientation: high investment
6. Future orientation: high savings
7. Market allocation: prices guide resources
8. Leadership and governance: credible commitment to growth
9. Leadership and governance: credible commitment to inclusion
10. Leadership and governance: capable administration[3]

Each country is advised to analyse its competitive strengths and weaknesses in order to devise an appropriate strategy of development. Based on the experiences of those thirteen high-achievers, there is obviously no single model that fits all.

While the Washington Consensus was in flux, however, the Middle East and North Africa (MENA) was exposed to two apparently alternative models: examples of Chinese industriousness in many of their countries and the emergence of Islamic finance, suggesting an "Islamic" variant of capitalism.

The China model could challenge the perception in the MENA, as in many other parts of the developing world, that globalisation is the old imperialism revisited. China, economic victim of the old imperialism, is a principal beneficiary of the freer flow of goods and capital associated with economic globalisation. Does it not, therefore, offer a path of development and integration into the world economy that authoritarian regimes of the Middle East and North Africa – in other words, all but Israel, Turkey, and possibly Lebanon – might emulate? Perhaps the monarchies of the Gulf Cooperation Council and Jordan were less vulnerable than the other states of the region because they had been less heavily colonised than their neighbours and were hence, perhaps, more receptive to Western advisors. But the rest of the region, the core of the Muslim world, had been at least as humiliated as the Chinese and shared experiences of anti-colonial struggle – from Morocco to South Yemen.

And, indeed, a sort of "China model" works by default in the region's two surviving one-party police states, Syria and Tunisia, where any reform is gradual and carefully calibrated to preserve the incumbent authoritarian regime. Both regimes leave some space for token associated parties or, in the case of Tunisia, formal opposition parties; but the political leadership, backed by the dominant party, tightly controls these spaces. In Syria, "Government officials explicitly seek to emulate the Chinese model of reform, where the government promoted economic reform and modernisation in many sectors while retaining complete political control".[4] Yet, as Steve Heydemann observes, "learning goes well beyond fascination with the Chinese model".[5] In Tunisia, officials instead stress the centuries required for democracy to develop in the West and contrast them with Tunisia's lack of progress after Carthaginian and Roman times, when there were germs of democracy, until 1987, when President Ben Ali finally "replanted new seeds".[6] Neither country has any significant Chinese presence, despite the formal similarities of their respective regimes with a Chinese model of authoritarian development. One practical common denominator, however, may be their control over access to the Internet. Information may even be more tightly censored in compact Tunisia than in China, for a few hundred Tunisian cyber police – a promising occupation for young computer engineer graduates[7] – can effectively monitor all personal email communications, block controversial websites and quickly filter out objectionable articles on otherwise open sites.[8] However, Tunisia's official spokespeople, ostensibly committed to Western democracy as a long-term goal, do not highlight such comparisons with China, other than to claim status, as do their Egyptian counterparts from time to time, as new Asian-like dragons of economic development, tagging along after South Korea, Taiwan and Singapore.[9] Most resource-poor MENA countries try, such as China, to attract foreign direct investment, but they also try, with the exception of Syria, to project an image of progress towards liberal democracy.

Nor is the China connection wholeheartedly welcomed in countries such as Algeria, where it is bringing a substantial and growing physical and economic presence. China is indeed gaining footholds in a number of Middle Eastern and North African states, especially the oil states of Sudan and Algeria, but these new presences may turn out to be just as unwelcome as those of the former colonisers. After briefly examining the anecdotal evidence of the Chinese presence in Algeria, this chapter will discuss an alternative model that is projected by the new colonial dialectic that Muslims may associate with globalisation. A post-colonial dialectic of opposition to Western market domination may favour a China model in the short run, associated with Chinese aid and trade, but China, too, has interests that are in conflict with those of Muslim societies (including its own Uyghur population). Trade competition is putting some Muslim export industries at risk, and aid often comes in the form of massive invasions (as in Algeria) of Chinese workers building infrastructures.

Some Muslim countries, such as Morocco or Malaysia, may be developing distinctive national profiles. However, various currents of Islamism are also artic-ulating another, distinctively Islamic response to globalisation. Some Islamic economists think they have an answer: returning to a "moral economy" asso-ciated with Islam.[10] Other, more practical, ones have designed a global archi-tecture paralleling that of conventional banking for Islamic finance. Promoting "Islamic banking", in fact, seems to be the principal economic policy on which most mainstream Muslims and Islamists can agree.[11] In this chapter, after exam-ining the reactions in Algeria to various Chinese presences, I will explore the potential of this "Islamic model" for meeting needs for capital accumulation and credit allocation that Western-style conventional banks may be less capable of satisfying.

CHINESE PRESENCES IN ALGERIA

Algeria underwent the most intensive colonial occupation (1830–1952) of any country in the MENA and experienced the sharpest breaks with its colonial past. Once in the vanguard of Third World revolutionary experiences, elements of its leadership, despite their conservative Islamism, even shared some ideological kinship with the Marxist–Leninist ideology that is China's figleaf for market socialism. Like China's leadership, Algeria's also evolved, so that champions of Algerian state socialism in the 1970s and 1980s now sponsor the privatisation of its state enterprises. Algeria thus offers an interesting testing ground for any China model for the MENA.

The Chinese presence takes three forms in Algeria: 1) oil concessions, 2) labour-intensive construction projects, and 3) retail commerce. Oil, of course, is China's principal strategic concern, and it has carefully targeted African as well as Middle Eastern resources. Its need to expand overseas supplies is evident. Domestic Chinese oil production, averaging an annual increase of less than 1.5 per cent over the decade 1997–2006, has fallen well behind annual Chinese oil consumption, which increased annually by about 6 per cent. In 2007, China imported a record 163 million tons,[12] or about 3.2 million barrels a day, almost half its annual production, and imports were bound to continue surging to keep up with double-digit rates of growth. In 2006, its principal sources of imports were Angola, where China claimed more than half the country's production,[13] Saudi Arabia, Russia, Iran, Oman, Congo-Brazzaville, Equatorial Guinea, and Yemen, in descending order, but new fields in Sudan and Chad were coming online, with Sudan overtaking Congo-Brazzaville in the first quarter of 2007.[14] Algeria, too, supplied China with small amounts of crude petroleum.

The China National Petroleum Corporation (CNPC) signed its first explo-ration contract with Sonatrach, Algeria's national oil company, in late 2003. A map of Algerian concessions shows a large area of three blocks to the east of Ghardaia, in the oil-producing Hassi Messaoud region, under contract with SINOPEC.[15] The Chinese also positioned themselves downstream, contracting to build a $500 million-dollar oil refinery with a capacity of 12,000 barrels a day in Adrar, deep in Algeria's western Sahara; it began operations in 2007, supplying four neighbouring governorates in Algeria's Deep South.[16] China seems to have imported only about 75,000 barrels a day from North Africa, presumably Algeria, but it was positioning itself in Algeria's vast, under-explored potential oil and gas fields. It was also physically positioning itself in the Algerian construction industry and in retail commerce.

With oil revenues sky-rocketing and social pressures mounting, the Algerian government, notably its Agency for Housing Development, engaged in massive construction projects since 2000, and Chinese construction companies, present in Algeria since 1982, took on new prominence, as Chinese labour on work-sites became newsworthy early in the decade. The Chinese embassy in Algiers admitted to 8,000 construction workers in 2005, and the numbers have subse-quently expanded, building most of the East–West Freeway, as well as housing projects, luxury hotels, hospitals, and even mosques. The major hospital in Oran remained unoccupied as of early 2008, four years after being completed,[17] but this is the fault of Algerian management, not the Chinese. The Algerian minister of religious affairs insisted to reluctant religious authorities in Oran that the new mosque, delayed since 1975 when construction began but now being finished by the Chinese, was fit for Muslim worship. After all, some of the local men of religion were living in public housing, he reminded them, that Chinese contractors had constructed, and did they not pray at home?[18] Asked in 2004 about the dangers of Christian Evangelist appeals to Algerian Kabyles, he dismissed them as "a minor deviation from Islam" and added, "actually there are many Chinese in Algeria who have converted to Islam. Why have those of other religions never said that Islam menaces their cults?"[19]

The Chinese presence was mainly in the construction sector, but it was spilling over into the informal sector as well, for "if you want serious, rapid workers for bargain wages, take the Chinese", as a taxi driver advised a reporter.[20] By 2008, journalists estimated that there were some 40,000 Chinese workers in Algeria, a country of high unemployment.[21] Videos online show some Algerian workers to be discontented by the foreign invasion, but other Algerians such as the taxi driver, seemed grateful for the reliable Chinese input, given the perceived lack of motivation of Algerian workers. Without them, the objectives of ambitious construction programs fueled by high oil revenues would have taken longer to meet; in fact, side-by-side housing projects started at the same time by Chinese and Algerian contractors offered tangible evidence in major Algerian cities of Chinese efficiency. The Chinese projects were completed, with people already moved into their new homes, while the Algerian ones were still in process of construction. On the other hand, in the videos, the Chinese were being paid at least twice the salaries of the Algerians for their 12-hour working days. Perhaps an Egyptian blog of 10 January 2008 conveys also some of the ambivalent Algerian elite admiration and fear of the new Chinese migrations: "I always have the feeling when I see those narrow eyes that I am facing an organised army of ants who can do almost anything".[22]

The Egyptian was referring to a slightly different form of activity, the commerce of Chinese retailers who have swarmed en masse into both countries. Commercial penetration, however, seemed less correlated with strategic efforts to develop oil resources than China's construction presence. China sold Egypt almost $3 billion-worth of goods in 2006, compared to $1.9 billion for Algeria and $1.4 billion for Morocco – exports more proportionate to their respective populations and relative wealth than to oil reserves. In Algeria the commercial penetration met with some concerns that workaholic Chinese retailers were grabbing some of the best shopping stalls in downtown markets in Algiers and Oran.[23] They were competing in sectors that *trabendo* retailers also occupied and were possibly useful to authorities who viewed their indigenous competitors as potential Islamist supporters. However, Algeria's self-censored press does not seem to have been publicising the growing Chinese presence after 2004. By 2005, China had invested some $600 million in various construction projects and committed much more in the energy sector. Algeria was also its fifth-most important commercial partner after South Africa, Angola, Sudan and Egypt. By the first quarter of 2007, Chinese exports constituted 9.1 per cent of Algeria's total imports – more than twice those from the United States albeit well under half those from France. Europe, with 53 per cent of Algeria's imports and 55.8 per cent of its exports, remained Algeria's dominant trading partner, led by France, with respectively 20.7 and 7 per cent of its imports and exports, although Chinese market shares were growing rapidly. Their colonies of shopkeepers and workers lived apart from the rest of Algerian society in closed enclaves, concerned for their personal security in an increasingly hostile environment. Even visiting Japanese intellectuals felt threatened by a growing anti-Oriental racism reacting against the Chinese presence.[24]

China may continue to reinforce its multi-dimensional economic relationship with Algeria, but the process is between authoritarian regimes, not their respective societies. There is no "China model" for Algerian politicians to propagate, much as they may desire to retain power and admire the durability of China's single-party system (and even that of their Tunisian neighbours). In the face of the growing foreign presence, they may instead have to cultivate more legitimacy by appealing to an "Islamic" model of development.

The "Islamic" Banking model

"Islamic" banking is a principal manifestation of Islam in matters of economic policy, and it is responding to the Western challenge of globalisation by giving distinctively Muslim institutions a global reach. Applying medieval financial instruments and legal interpretations, this very contemporary movement of "Islamic" finance is extending Islam from matters of personal status into a public policy arena. Although the first "Islamic" bank opened for business only in 1974 in Dubai (in the wake of the first oil boom), the proliferation of these banks across Muslim contexts is also recalling its distinctive past as the global economy prior to the Western Renaissance. Accompanying the new oil boom of the present decade, "Islamic" financiers have dramatically expanded their inventory of financial instruments to compete with conventional financial institutions in expanding global markets. Like political Islamists, they aspire to extend the practical scope of Islam beyond matters of personal status, but they usually try to avoid, or at least pretend to avoid, any taint of political engagement or activity. Yet the effect of an explicitly "Islamic" presence in national banking systems, and on the international financial scene also has political implications.

The emergence of "Islamic" finance coincided with that of political Islam as the principal force of political opposition in a number of Arab countries. These latter movements tended not only to oppose the incumbent authoritarian regimes but also, as the latter were pressed to engage in neo-liberal reforms in the 1980s, to oppose their economic policies. Even here, however, it is important to note some exceptions, notably the Algerian Front Islamique du Salut (FIS), which collaborated implicitly with a reform-minded government in 1989–91 in trying to transform a state-managed economy into one driven by domestic as well as international markets.[25] In fact, the interests of the "Islamic" financiers are congruent with those of putative economic reformers who attempt to open up their economies and position them to benefit from the forces of international capitalism underlying globalisation, rather than to contest them. In seeking "authentic "Islamic" reform", the financiers are reintroducing into the contemporary world financial instruments that were perhaps invented by Muslims, that recall the earlier pre-colonial globalisation of the Muslim *umma*, and that may serve – as the FIS once proposed – as the most distinctive marker of a Muslim economy. The practical operations of "Islamic" finance, however, also require standardisation, a sort of universality to which Islam aspires and yet never quite meets in most spheres of social activity, given the extremely disparate nature of Muslim communities without any exclusive global authority such as a Catholic pope. They require the same sorts of business climates of transparency and accountability that the other conventional economic reformers advocate in line with updated versions of the Washington Consensus.

To cut a long story short, the interest-free banking advocated by "Islamic" financiers experienced greater difficulties than conventional banks did in generating profits from the "investments" (deposits) of Muslim publics. Unlike conventional banks, they are not allowed to engage in term-lending, but instead must resort to the equity-like financing of *mudaraba* and *musharaka*,[26] financial instruments that are too risky, especially in the hazardous business climates of most Muslim majority countries. To keep up with conventional banks, they were obliged to tie up greater proportions of their assets in less lucrative, but "Islamically" permissible, forms of financing than other commercial banks did in making loans and charging interest. Under more investment-friendly business climates characterised by transparent accounting practices, clean and efficient judicial systems and good governance "Islamic" financiers might engage in more profitable but riskier forms of finance because they would be able to monitor their clients more effectively.

Meanwhile, pending more transparent economic environments, incumbent regimes may find "Islamic" financiers useful as allies for economic reform, or for other reasons. By permitting their banks to operate, or at least permiting conventional banks to open "Islamic" windows for their distinctively "Islamic" financial instruments, a regime may attempt to placate popular Islamist sentiment without giving ground to their political opposition. Supposedly secular ex-socialist countries such as Algeria and Egypt tolerate the financiers and also promote official Islam in many ways, whilst repressing any serious Islamist opposition. Even Syria has expressed some interest in "Islamic" banking and has permitted its central bank to join the "Islamic" Financial Standards Board as a full member.

ISLAMIST IMAGES AND COMMERCIAL REALITY

Since the year 2000, "Islamic" banking, swelled by high oil revenues flooding the economies of the GCC states, has consolidated its presence in global markets.[27] "Islamic" financiers have devised an array of controversial new securities and expanded their market shares in many Muslim majority countries. They have also, encouraged by the International Monetary Fund, constructed institutions designed to regulate the burgeoning "Islamic" finance industry and to meet the new guidelines of the 2004 Basel II Accord concerning the capital adequacy requirements of banks. The question to be raised, however, is whether their commercial success is compromising their "Islamic" legitimacy. By successfully competing with conventional banks and harmonising their practices to meet the demands of markets and regulators, the "Islamic" banks may appear to some critics to be losing any distinctively "Islamic" identity, although much of the religious establishment across Muslim contexts supports them.

Their commercial success may also be compromising their legal-religious

Sharia credentials. "Islamic" banks had faced growing problems of excess liquidity and mismatched maturities in their first quarter-century of operations (1975–2000). They could not by definition park funds in conventional interest-bearing financial instruments unless they were ready to commit financial suicide by foregoing the interest payments. They were in need of functional equivalents of T-bills and other tradable securities, overnight inter-bank instruments, and other facilities available as a matter of course to their conventional commercial bank competitors. Finally, in 2000, the Bahrain Monetary Agency introduced the first "Islamic" T-bill, a non-tradable *sukuk al-salam*. The following year Bahrain pioneered a way of bundling Islamically-acceptable leases into the first tradable "Islamic" debt security, a *sukuk al-ijara*. Malaysia followed suit in 2002, this time creating an internationally tradable *sukuk* that met US regulatory requirements for conventional global bonds and was rated by Standard & Poor's and Moody's. The Islamic Development Bank, Qatar, Kuwait, Dubai, and the German state of Saxony-Anhalt subsequently issued a succession of "Islamic" bonds. Dubai formally launched its $750 million *sukuk al-ijara* on 10 October 2004, in partnership with the Hong Kong Shanghai Banking Corporation (HSBC) and other major international and regional banks. Finally, encouraged by Citigroup, which had opened the first "Islamic" window of a major international bank in 1996, a Dow Jones Citigroup Sukuk Index began on 2 April 2006, to track seven outstanding "Islamic" bonds,[28] with expectations of encouraging a secondary market in them. As late as 5 October 2008, "Islamic" financial authorities were claiming that their banks could only be indirectly affected by the global crisis,[29] but fewer new bonds were issued for the first year ever.[30] In the UK, more non-Muslims were running from conventional banks to the Islamic Bank of Britain, which they believed to be better insulated against the credit crisis.[31] And Dubai aspired to be capital of "Islamic" finance and to "develop the same stature as New York".[32]

Investors were acquiring an ever larger menu of choices, sponsored by Citigroup and Hong Kong Shanghai, as well as "Islamic" banks. Teams of London and New York lawyers worked closely with Sharia scholars to devise new packages. Their sheer size, coupled with a degree of standardisation, was reducing cumbersome transaction costs. The driving force consisted of Muslim investors, principally located in Saudi Arabia and neighbouring microstates, who were steadily Islamising their portfolios, diversifying away from the standards accounts of conventional banks to their new "Islamic" windows, admitted in Saudi Arabia in the mid-1990s after being instituted in Egypt a decade earlier. Despite initial concern that "Islamic" finance might fall victim to measures against "Islamic" terrorism in the wake of the 11 September 2001 attacks, the threat of sanctions may have driven some Arab-owned funds from North America and Europe into some of the newer "Islamic" investment vehicles.

An original alliance of ulama, princes and merchants[33] opened up to international banks and lawyers that are reducing the transaction costs of being "Sharia-compliant" to meet the needs of global markets. Some critics argue, however, that "Islamic" finance is compromising its ethics by mimicking international financial practices too closely.[34] Others, in the tradition of the late Ahmad al-Najjar, argue that "Islamic" banks have lost their developmental impetus to service small Muslim businesses, for indeed (like conventional banks in most developing countries) they cater principally to wealthy individuals who place their funds outside the region. One sign of the times is that Faisal Private Bank received a full Swiss banking license in 2006, now that wealthy Gulf individuals were flocking to "Islamic" financial assets.[35]

In this first, neo-liberal moment of economic globalisation "Islamic" finance has indeed evolved remarkable financial instruments. It is possible, for instance, for a Saudi investor to buy into real estate development in South Korea by subscribing to a real estate bond that is certified to be "Islamic". Through a web of special finance vehicles the complex financial package spins off contracts that may meet precise "Islamic" investment criteria, as certified by a Sharia board, even though the overall product is a conventional bond issue.[36] What to some Muslims and outside observers may appear to be legerdemain is to others an illustration of a resurgence of Muslim globalisation. Hong Kong currently competes with Singapore to become one of its financial hubs: "As an international financial centre, Hong Kong is stepping up its efforts to promote its financial services to major "Islamic" countries and regions, and developing an "Islamic" bond market", the chief executive of the Hong Kong Financial Authority explained to a well-attended banking seminar in January 2008.[37]

Virtually all of the 300 entities in 75 countries that call themselves "Islamic" banks[38] today have religious advisory boards, but only recently have efforts been under way to develop international standards of compliance with the Sharia. While institutions with sufficient authority to make universally accepted definitions do not yet govern "Islamic" finance, recent efforts to build a regulatory framework for "Islamic" finance are a significant step forward. The Islamic Financial Services Board (IFSB), established in 2002 in Kuala Lumpur with sponsorship from the International Monetary Fund (IMF), is in effect mandated to define the industry by standardising its products, and the International Islamic Rating Agency, established in Bahrain a year later, was offering ratings of Sharia quality with the help of a panel of nineteen "Islamic" scholars, in addition to credit ratings. In February 2008, for example, it gave an "AA" rating to Bank Muamalat Indonesia.[39] It is to cover both "Islamic" banks and other institutions that produce *sukuk*, and will also provide corporate governance ratings.[40]

These regulatory institutions have materialised just in time – amid an explosion of markets for new securities in response to booming demand from investors. However, they are young, under-staffed and under-funded, more an expression of aspirations for "Islamic" financial order than an established industrial authority. The hope is that the IFSB can set and disseminate international standards for "Islamic" financial institutions. Its full members consist of twenty central banks of Muslim-majority states, including Syria, where there is some interest in "Islamic" finance. The seventeen associate members include the IMF, the World Bank, the Bank of International Settlements, the People's Bank of China and the Central Bank of the Philippines, while a variety of other official authorities and "Islamic" banks are among the seventy-eight observers.[41] As Dr Rifaat Abdel Karim, the secretary general of the IFSB, explained in June 2006, "We do not attempt to reinvent the wheel for 'Islamic" finance as a niche system, rather, we complement the work of the Basel Committee for Banking Supervision by catering for the specificities of "Islamic" banks".[42] Earlier he had successfully lobbied for the creation of the IFSB as general secretary of the Accounting and Auditing Organization for Islamic Financial Institutions (AAOIFI), established in Bahrain in 1991. As of early 2008, AAOIFI has issued seventy standards on accounting, auditing, governance, and ethical and Sharia standards.[43] Meanwhile, the exuberant growth of "Islamic" banks, and Islamisation of existing giants such as Saudi Arabia's National Commerce Bank are generating ever more powerful interests in standardisation. The recent launching, in particular, of an "Islamic" mega-bank, Al-Masref, licensed by the Bahrain Monetary Authority and capitalised at $10 billion – almost four times the capital of the largest existing "Islamic" bank, Al Rajhi of Saudi Arabia – may generate consensus across the Muslim world among its prospective clients.

Were the IFSB to gain the full international authority required to define "Islamic" banking practices, they might still be subject to religious or ethically inspired objections to their "Islamic" identity. Their efforts to join the mainstream of international finance and accommodate the Basel II banking standards are quite explicit. As stated on its website,

> In elaborating the *specificities* [emphasis added] of IIFS, the IFSB Capital Adequacy standard complements Pillar I, Supervisory Review complements Pillar II and Transparency and Market Discipline complements Pillar III of Basel II, respectively. Meanwhile, the Corporate Governance standard is based on the Organisation for Economic Cooperation and Development (OECD) Principles and Basel Paper on Corporate Governance.[44]

Such claims of "specificities" are designed to defend the "Islamic" banks from charges of simply mimicking conventional banks and selling out the essence of Islam to dubious marketing strategies that play on people's piety. There is no infallible authority to define contemporary application of the Sharia. The combined muscle of a rising class of "Islamic" capitalists in Saudi Arabia[45] and elsewhere in Muslim contexts, however, allied to a nucleus of distinguished and representative ulama, may possibly convince more Muslims of the correctness of their interpretations over those of the radical theorists of defensive jihad, other Islamists, or pious sceptics. Substantial financial resources, and the tacit backing of the International Monetary Fund, may empower an expressive myth of a resurgent Islam associated with global finance.

A Second Moment of Islamist Rejection?

To keep the first moment of this dialectic of globalisation in perspective, the financial surface of "Islamic" banking remains a very small part of the global picture. From its beginnings in 1975, when the first privately owned, self-styled "Islamic" bank opened in Dubai, until today "Islamic" banking has gradually acquired the financial surface of a medium-sised international bank. Its total assets are unknown, but estimates range from $250 to $750 billion, with ritual estimates usually echoed in symposia and conferences on the subject since 1995 of an annual growth rate of 15 per cent.[46] Such numbers are quite small in the world of international finance, where the total assets of Citigroup alone amounted to $1.5 trillion in 2005. Without greater standardisation, possibly further compromising "Islamic" finance in the eyes of some critics, secondary markets for the various bond issues will remain problematic.[47] Project finance also features some "Islamic" components in large and complex packages, but we cannot even quantify their dimensions for lack of adequate data.[48]

Penetration of financial markets within Muslim-majority states also remains quite limited and in some cases, such as Egypt, has actually declined since the mid-1980s, when money-changers became "Islamic" investment funds and marketed themselves such as real "Islamic" banks by using religious scholars to validate themselves to a credulous public. When their pyramid schemes burst, the enterprise of legitimate "Islamic" banks suffered, and the Egyptian government, alarmed at any other signs of financial autonomy in the private sector, further curbed their growth by promoting "Islamic" branches in state-owned banks: the latter, in fact, outstripped the former by the late 1990s.

Table 1 shows how much "Islamic" banks have penetrated Muslim markets since the 1970s.[49] Iran is not included for lack of data about privately owned commercial banks, permitted in theory after 2000 to operate alongside the traditional system that had been Islamised and brought under state ownership after 1979. Pakistan's commercial banking was also cosmetically Islamised under General Zia-ul-Haq in the early 1980s, but the table only includes privately owned "Islamic" banks, created recently in the wake of legal contestation about the "Islamic" character of the other banks. It is readily seen that the penetration

Table 1. Evolution of Islamic banks' share of commericial bank deposits by country, 1980–2005 (%)

	Year first established	1986	1996	1997	1998	2000	2001	2004	2005
Algeria	1991		0.4	0.5	0.8	1.0			
Bahrain	1979	6.7	9.8					15.7	
Egypt	1977	9.7	5.1			5.7			
including Banque Misr's Islamic branches' deposits		8.1							
Iraq									
Jordan (JIB)	1978	7.0	8.4	8.2	8.0	6.9	7.1	8.8	
including Islamic International Arab Bank					8.9	9.4		10.7	
Kuwait	1977	18.0	16.2	16.3	15.5			18.1	
Lebanon	1991		0.1	0.0	0.1				
Libya									
Morocco									
Qatar	1982	10.4	17.8	18.1				13.7	14.0
Saudi Arabia	1988		11.3	11.1	11.5	13.9			
Sudan		17.0			27.9				
Syria									
Tunisia	1983	0.2	0.6		0.6	0.8			
Turkey	1985	0.8		3.6	3.6	3.5	1.8		3.4
UAE	1975	3.2	7.9					10.9	
Yemen	1996			4					
Indonesia	1992							1.2	2.0
Malaysia	1983		1.6	1.6					
including Islamic windows of conventional banks (rough estimate)			2	2				10.5	
Pakistan									
Meezan Bank	1997							0.5	0.8

Sources: IMF International Financial Statistics, Harvard Islamic Finance Information Program, various annual reports of banks, author's data set, with additional bold-faced data kindly provided by McKinsey Co., 2005.

of "Islamic" banks has been greatest in Sudan (where the remainder were, in theory, also Islamised after 1983) and in the Gulf Cooperation Council states (except Oman). In Saudi Arabia the penetration was much greater by 2005 than the 13.9 per cent of the market achieved by Al-Rajhi, the kingdom's only self-styled "Islamic" bank in 2000. The National Commerce Bank, with 27.3 per cent of the commercial banking system's deposits at the end of 2005, had become primarily Islamic under new management. In 2006, the bank claimed that 243 of its 263 branches were "dedicated exclusively to Islamic Banking services",[50] but it was not possible to discover the value of the deposits managed by the Islamic branches or whether they were pooled with conventional funds and lent out in conventional ways. SAMBA, another major Saudi bank, also has an "Islamic" banking unit, opened in 1996, which in 2005 accounted for almost one-third of the bank's outstanding loans.[51] The kingdom has, in a sense, contained Islamic financial activity, however, by integrating most of it, as Egypt had done, into these conventional banks. So also in Morocco, where the central bank issued directives in 2007 defining new Islamic financial instruments that existing conventional banks might market in the face of a perceived demand for them. Both kingdoms had rejected Islamic banks on the ground that any new institution claiming an "Islamic" distinction might reflect adversely upon the ruler's legitimacy, but they could still add new kinds of contracts to the repertoires of conventional banks.

In its core areas of strength, "Islamic" finance had faced hard times in the mid-1980s. The Kuwait Finance House, like the conventional banks, had to be rescued by the government in 1984, in the wake of the Souk al-Manakh crisis. In Egypt, so-called "Islamic" fund management companies devised pyramid schemes that collapsed with the devaluation of the Egyptian pound in 1987–8. Although the Faisal Islamic Bank was not associated with these schemes, it lost a quarter of its total assets with the collapse of the rogue Bank of Credit and Commerce International (BCCI) in 1991. It had placed funds with the BCCI, and earlier with the Central Bank of Egypt, for lack of other viable "Islamic" investments. More generally, "Islamic" banks could attract funds as long as they could distribute profits to their "investor"-depositors that were competitive with interest rates offered by conventional banks. Profits stagnated by the late 1980s, and the market shares of these banks peaked at about 10 per cent in their strongholds, Egypt and Jordan, and the microstates of Bahrain and Kuwait. Only in Sudan, where they supported Hassan Turabi's rise to power (1989–99), did they win a greater share of the deposits and total assets of a commercial banking system, all of which had been theoretically Islamised by decree in 1983.

Meanwhile, state sponsored "Islamic" banking in Pakistan and Iran produced only cosmetic changes in the respective commercial banking systems until 2000, when Iran permitted privately owned "Islamic" banks to compete with the public sector. Pakistan, obliged by law to reorganise its "Islamic" system, permitted its first privately owned "Islamic" bank in 2002: the Al-Meezan Bank rapidly gained market share, and other banks opened "Islamic" windows.[52] Likewise in Indonesia, General Suharto supported the founders of the Bank Muamalat Indonesia (BMI) in 1989–92 in order to gain support from Islamists in his bid to stay in power in the early 1990s.[53] BMI and Bank Syariah Mega Indonesia, reinforced by new "Islamic" windows of conventional banks, were aiming for 2 per cent of the market in 2005, and there were plans to establish Jakarta as a leading "Islamic" finance centre, competing with Kuala Lumpur, Malaysia and Bahrain.[54] In Turkey, five "special finance houses", defined by a law passed in 1983 that Turgut Özal's staff had negotiated with Saleh Kamel, were fully integrated into the country's commercial banking system in 1999, survived the financial crisis of 2001, and grew more rapidly than their conventional competitors to gain 5 per cent of the market by 2005.[55]

"Islamic" banks seem to have had little impact on politics in the countries where they operate, except in Sudan in the 1980s. In countries where there is a sharp division between government and Islamist opposition, the "Islamic" banks are obliged to keep a low profile and maintain ties with the government and its official religious establishment, even if the opposition Islamists are of the mainstream rather than radical puritan variety. The business constituencies associated with these banks usually developed some political traction only in countries, such as Kuwait, where the government already tolerated Islamist political forces. At the margins, Turkey's special finance houses may have tipped the balance within the remnants of Erbaken's Welfare/Virtue Party in 1999 towards moderates following Tayyip Erdogan and Abdullah Gul, who had worked as an economist for the Islamic Development Bank from 1983 to 1991. Certainly their victory in the 2002 elections paved the way for a dramatic expansion of these banks. In Saudi Arabia, the rise of "Islamic" finance may benefit some ulama on the supervisory boards of the banks, but it is not clear what relationship, if any, they may have with the "Islamo-liberal" or any other trend among the power elite of Saudi ulama.[56]

What emerges from this brief summary is that "Islamic" banks enjoyed a head start in much of the Arab world, but now seem to be trapped between overbearing authoritarian regimes and Islamist oppositions with which they must at all cost avoid any appearance of association. Only in the GCC and Turkey are there some signs of synergy between the financiers and Islamists. However, even in Saudi Arabia, the two founders of international "Islamic" financial networks, Prince Mohammad al Faisal and Shaikh Saleh Kamel, were not permitted to establish "Islamic" banks for fear that the other institutions permitted by the Defender of the Holy Places would be viewed as un-"Islamic", a clearly unacceptable state of affairs for the kingdom!

Strong Islamist opposition and bitter polarisation between Islamists and incumbent power-holders usually results in stunted growth for "Islamic" finance and leads to excessive dependence upon central banks. Regimes attempt to co-opt the movement, together with any associated by-products of political legitimacy. Islamist political movements may, in turn, harbour a diversity of views about their potential financial ally. In Egypt in the late 1980s until 1992, when Mubarak reversed course and associated the entire political spectrum of Islamists with extremists rather than selectively co-opting them and deepening their divisions, Islamist take-overs of the professional syndicates gave rise to interesting problems. Would the new management try to use "Islamic" or conventional banks? In the case of the engineers, the syndicate already managed a bank – should they then convert it to "Islamic" banking operations, leave it as is, or get out of the banking business altogether? Muslim Brothers within the syndicate's leadership had divided opinions which included all three options. So the verdict is still out on "Islamic" banking. Some pious Muslims and political activists oppose the movement as legalistic trickery or surrender to global capitalism, while others support it as a major standard-bearer for resurgent global Islam.

Conclusion

With further polarisation between regimes and Islamists, exacerbated by a growing US–Muslim divide, the outlook for "Islamic" finance within most Arab countries outside the GCC appears bleak. Presumably the more politically radicalised the Islamists become, the less likely they will be to make common cause with "Islamic" financiers. Any journalistic conflations of "Islamic" finance and terrorism are far off the mark.[57] To this writer's knowledge, the US Treasury's Office of Foreign Assets Control (OFAC), which is well informed about "Islamic" banks, uncovered only one case of an "Islamic" bank being associated with international terrorism – a small agricultural bank in the Sudan. Critics sometimes accuse "Islamic" banks of doing things akin to money laundering when they engage in "Sharia arbitrage", a process whereby a conventional financial instrument (such as the South Korean real estate bond) may be transformed into an Islamically acceptable one by adding one or more degrees of separation between the "Islamic" clients and the underlying financial product.[58] However, they are no more likely than any other bank to engage in real money laundering.

It seems unlikely, then, given the present drift of the Muslim heartland, that the gentle "Islamic" financiers at the heart of Muslim globalisation can somehow tame the passions of those puritan Islamists who tend to reject globalisation because they view it as a new, American form of imperialism. Islamist oppositions become more radical in most Arab countries because of the US occupation of Iraq and the Israeli occupation of Palestine – in which the US is viewed as an accomplice. Regimes become more oppressive in the face of rising opposition to the United States and more generally to economic globalisation, and these oppositions usually adopt an Islamist vocabulary. The "Islamic" financial institutions suffer in the crossfire. "Islamic" finance takes on an ethereal quality associated with the thousands of high-wealth individuals of the oil kingdoms. Middle classes constitute the potential mass clientele of financial institutions, as well as puritan Islam, but their participation is marginalised.

So far it seems to be principally high-net-worth individuals from the GCC states who have diversified their holdings and have some "Islamic" stake in the global economy, among their portfolio of investments. Despite some discussion of an emerging bourgeoisie in Saudi Arabia,[59] "Islamic" finance has yet to coagulate into a relatively autonomous industrial sphere, like that of, say, German bankers at the turn of the twentieth century. "Islamic" capitalism is certainly not yet transforming the spirit of puritan Islamism.

It would not be prudent, however, simply to dismiss "Islamic" finance as wishful thinking. It still serves as an expressive myth and set of discourses uniting growing numbers of bankers and international administrators, as well as high-net-worth individuals. Institutions are taking shape to facilitate those processes of Sharia arbitrage that are essential for the growth of the industry. Sharia law is acquiring new scope and offering new career opportunities for potential opinion-leaders. Pious publics are being instructed into some intricacies of modern financial activity. Most regimes in Muslim-majority states, however authoritarian and however much they repress political Islamists, accept "Islamic" financial institutions co-existing with their state-owned or client private-sector banks. Were the banks to disappear, the big international ones would still be selling "Islamic" instruments to interested Muslim clienteles. It seems safe to conclude, then, that "Islamic" finance, now approaching thirty-five years in its recent reincarnations, will survive as a central symbol of the globalisation of Muslim-majority states linking them to their pre-colonial past. While the financiers cannot stabilise extremist Islam and bring it back to a more pluralistic and tolerant pre-colonial past, they may neverthless offer practical guidelines for military officers or activists seeking safely to forsake politics for business.

To return, finally, to Algeria, where "Islamic" finance has remained marginal, controlling barely 1 per cent of the total banking assets, it is possible that nascent business interests might still try to launder themselves with "Islamic" imagery, now that political Islam has been largely domesticated and the terrorists discredited in the eyes of public opinion. Despite rising tensions elsewhere between moralisers and profit-oriented financiers, "Islamic" finance could offer convenient cover to former military commanders who have retired to the private sector. Financial reform remains a priority in the wake of spectacular private-sector (non-"Islamic") bank failures in recent years that probably cost Algeria more than $3 billion. Despite the legal gymnastics associated with "Islamic" finance, it still offers a model for Muslim governments and private sectors in search of legitimacy and authenticity.

Indeed, credible commitment to development and inclusion, accompanied by competent administration, are the principles of good governance that the Spence Report singled out, along with openness to the world economy, macroeconomic stability, and high savings and investment rates. Much like Marxist–Leninism for the Chinese, "Islamic" capitalism might still serve as a development model for the MENA, if it offers government greater legitimacy and authenticity. With better governance, resource-rich countries such as Algeria and Iraq would only be in need of importing appropriate technology and knowledge for investing those petroleum revenues wisely, while using Islamism to root out corruption. In the final analysis, however, models do not take account of the political networks and infrastructure required to implement them.

NOTES

1. The original Washington Consensus called for:
    1. Fiscal discipline
    2. Reorientation of public expenditures
    3. Tax reform
    4. Interest-rate liberalisation
    5. Unified and competitive exchange rates
    6. Trade liberalisation
    7. Opening for direct foreign investment
    8. Privatisation
    9. Deregulation
    10. Securing of property rights
   To these, Rodrik adds:
    11. Corporate governance
    12. Anti-corruption
    13. Flexible labour markets
    14. Adherence to WTO disciplines
    15. Adherence to international financial codes and standards
    16. "Prudent" capital-account opening
    17. Non-intermediate exchange rate regimes
    18. Independent central bank/inflation-targeting
    19. Social safety nets
    20. Targeted poverty reduction
   See Dani Rodrik, "Rethinking Growth Policies in the Developing World", Luca d'Angliano Lecture in Development Economics, Turin, Italy, 8 October 2004, cited by Alan Richards and John Waterbury, A Political Economy of the Middle East, third edition, Boulder, CO: Westview Press, 2008, p. 229.
2. John Williamson, letter, Economists" Voice – The Berkeley Electronic Press, August

2008, in response to Dani Rodrik, "Spence Christens a New Washington Consensus", *Economists" Voice*, July 2008: www.bepress.com/ev/.

3. Summarising of Figure 2 of *The [Spence] Growth Report: Strategies for Sustained Growth and Inclusive Development*, World Bank, 2008, http://cgd.s3.amazonaws.com/GrowthReportComplete.pdf.

4. Ellen Lust-Okar, "Reform in Syria: Steering between the Chinese model and Regime Change", Carnegie Papers, no. 69, July 2006, www.carnegieendowment.org/.

5. Steven Heydemann, "Upgrading Authoritarianism in the Arab world", Analysis Paper 13, Saban Center, Washington, DC: Brookings Institution, October 2007, p. 2, http://www.arab-reform.net/IMG/pdf/Authoritarianism_in_the_Arab_World.doc.pdf.

6. Sadok Châabane, *Ben Ali, Batir une democratie: de la lutte de croyances a la competition des programmes*, Tunis: Maison du Livre Arabes, 2005.

7. Tunisia has trained a surplus of engineers. See Ridha Ferchiou, "The Role of National Statistics System in Measuring and Fostering National Progress", paper presented to OECD *World Forum on Statistics, Knowledge and Policy*, Istanbul, June 2007.

8. In Tunisia for the celebration of Ben Ali's twentieth anniversary in power, I had the opportunity to read "Tunisie: le système de Ben Ali", *L'Express*, 31 October 2007, which a Tunisian friend who subscribes to *L'Express* had received in the mail. But when, back in the wireless environment of my hotel, I tried to download the article, it was blocked, despite the fact that the rest of *L'Express* was available online. The entire dossier on Tunisia is available outside Tunisia at http://www.lexpress.fr/info/monde/dossier/tunisie/dossier.asp

9. The official website for Ben Ali's re-election in 2004 (www.benali2004.tn) cites support from Mr Zeng Qinghong, vice-president of the People's Republic of China: "President Ben Ali has always adopted a shrewd and thoroughly-studied approach about many questions. I am both impressed and delighted by this attitude". But he is only one of many luminaries that the organisers of the site were desperate to find, even mis-spelling names like that of "March" Brown, then head of the UNDP (Malloch Brown, in fact).

10. Charles Tripp, *Islam and the Moral Economy: The Challenge of Capitalism*, Cambridge: Cambridge University Press, 2006.

11. Clement Henry and Rodney Wilson (eds), *The Politics of Islamic Finance*, Edinburgh: Edinburgh University Press, 2004.

12. AFP staff, "China's crude oil imports hit new record in 2007", *Space Daily*, 11 January 2008. http://www.spacedaily.com/reports/Chinas_crude_oil_imports_hit_new_ record_ in_2007_customs_999.html

13. The US Department of Energy reports that by May 2006 China was importing 750,000 barrels a day from Angola, at a time when Angola was producing a total of roughly 1.4 million barrels a day. See http://www.eia.doe.gov/emeu/cabs/China/Oil.html and British Petroleum, *Statistical Review of World Energy 2007*, at www.bp.com/productlanding.do?categoryId=6929&contentID-7044622. On China's oil strategy in Africa, see Esther Pan, "China, Africa, and Oil", NY Council on Foreign Relations Backgrounder, 26 January 2007: http://www.cfr.org/publication/9557/#4. For a more sanguine view of China's positioning in Africa, see Erica S. Downs, "The Fact

and Fiction of Sino-African Energy Relations", *China Security*, vol. 3 no. 3, Summer 2007, pp. 42 68. http://www.cfr.org/publication/15191/china_security.html

14. IMF, *Direction of Trade Statistics*, September 2007, pp. 96–8.

15. For a map of Algerian contracts with foreign oil companies, see Ministry of Petroleum and Mines: http://www.mem-algeria.org/fr/hydrocarbures/situation-blocs_02_05.pdf

16. CNPC announced the opening of the Soralchin oil refinery on 17 April 2007 and took credit for its "first integrated project combining both upstream and down-stream operations in the African country". http://161.207.1.180/eng/press/newsre-leases/CNPCsrefineryinAlgeriabeginsoperation.htm.

17. In 2003 the Algerian minister of health, after a session of the Council of Ministers devoted to a discussion of the construction delays, was vigorously pressuring the China State Construction Engineering Corporation to complete the hospital. See "Le nouvel hôpital d'Oran compromise", *El Watan*, 19 July 2003.

18. Letter from Robert Parks, Director of the Centre d'Etudes Maghrébines en Algérie, Oran, 24 February 2008. He continued: "The Chinese are getting projects left and right. MobilArt and Plaza Immobilier – the largest Algerian builders in the West – have two high-end projects currently underway. MobilArt's project is six towers along the seaside, traveling from my apartment to the Sheraton. You saw three of the towers already. MobilArt is subcontracting to a Portuguese Engineering firm to build the towers, which, in turn, is subcontracting to the Chinese for labor. Plaza Immobilier also has a big Chinese project near Cité Italien (near the roundabout at the top of the hill near the Sheraton). The Chinese workers live on compounds, work continual eight hour shifts. The beds on the compounds always have someone sleeping in them. We see the Chinese when they come out for holidays, like the Chinese New Year, recently".

19. "L'évangélisation n'est pas un danger", *El Watan*, 8 July 2004.

20. L'Oranais, L'activisme Chinois en Algérie.La postcolonisation en route, 2 November 2006: http://oran.forumactif.com/discussions-generales-f2/l-activisme-chinois-en-algeriela-postcolonisation-en-route-t1115.htm

21. See, for instance, "L'Algérie le nouvel Eldorado Chinois", 23 April 2007 film, http://www.dailymotion.com/video/x1socp_lalgerie-le-nouvel-eldorado-chinois; also this French YouTube video, confirming 40,000 construction workers, including the highway construction: http://www.youtube.com/watch?v=xvNbmknOPUk; and from Algeria's most reliable daily newspaper, *Le Quotidien d'Oran*, "Algérie – Près de 7,000 Chinois sont attendus à Oran", 14 December 2006: http://www.algerie-monde.com/actualite/article1962.html. This was in addition to 3,200 already there, so that there were over 10,000 Chinese workers in the Oran-Tlemcen region alone by 2007.

22. http://www.globalvoicesonline.org/2008/01/10/egypt-chinese-goods/

23. See l'Oranais, "L'activisme Chinois en Algérie. La postcolonisation en route", 2 November 2006: http://oran.forumactif.com/discussions-generales-f2/l-activisme-chinois-en-algeriela-postcolonisation-en-route-t1115.htm.

24. One Chinese professor, reacting to the killing of Chinese workers in Afghanistan, proposed that a insurance fund be set up for China's contracted workers overseas. See "Keeping overseas Chinese workers safe", *People's Daily*, 14 July 2004: http://www.chinadaily.com.cn/english/doc/2004–07/14/content_348368.htm. One Japanese re-

searcher almost burst into tears when I asked her about perceptions of the Chinese in Algiers.

25. The official FIS program published in late 1989 officially called for Islamic banks. One such bank had already been established in Algeria in 1988, before the October riots toppled the single-party regime and led to the Hamrouche government, which attempted simultaneous political and economic reform.

26. In a *mudaraba*, the bank invests in the *mudarib's* business, and they agree to share respective per centages of the profits. In the event of losses, the bank loses its investment. Under the best of circumstances, however, the bank still needs to be confident that the *mudarib* (entrepreneur) is not cooking the books. Similar concerns arise in the case of *musharaka*, or a bank's participation in an investment enterprise.

27. Kristin Smith, "Islamic Banking and the Politics of International Financial Harmonization", in S. Nazim Ali (ed.), *Islamic Finance: Current Legal and Regulatory Issues*, Cambridge, MA: Islamic Finance Project, Harvard Law School, 2005.

28. The seven bonds to be selected were the *sukuk* of the Islamic Development Bank, the *sukuk* of Solidarity Trust Services Ltd, BMA International Sukuk, Qatar Global Sukuk, Malaysia Global Sukuk, Sarawak Global Sukuk and Dubai Global Sukuk. To be listed, a bond must qualify to be Sharia compliant, as determined by the Dow Jones Sharia Board consisting of Muslim scholars from a number of countries, and the Bahrain-based Accounting and Auditing Organization for Islamic Financial Institutions (AAOIFI). See "First Islamic bond index to set global industry standards", 20 March 2006, by Al-Bawaba Reporters (retrieved from Lexis Nexus, 26 April 2006). The Dow Jones Citigroup Sukuk Index is available online at http://www.djindexes.com/mdsidx/?event=Sukuk.

29. Mohammed Al-Hamzani, "Islamic Banks Unaffected by Global Crisis", *Asharq-Alawsat*, 5 October 2008, http://www.asharq-e.com/news.asp?section=6&id=14245

30. "Islamic bond issues slump on US crisis fears", *The Nikkei Weekly* 09/29/2008 Edition.

31. "More non-Muslims turning to safe haven of Islamic finance", *Birmingham Post*, 4 October 2008.

32. "Financial Hubs See an Opening Up at the Top; Wall Street's Long, Dominant Run Is Fading, Global Financiers Say", *Washington Post*, 1 October 2008.

33. See Monzer Kahf, "Islamic Banks: The Rise of a New Power Alliance of Wealth and *Sharia* Scholarship", in Clement M. Henry and Rodney Wilson (eds), *The Politics of Islamic Finance*, Edinburgh: Edinburgh University Press, 2004, pp. 17–36.

34. See the essays, for instance, by Mahmoud A. Al-Gamal and Walid Hegazy, in Ali (ed.), *Islamic Finance*. See also Zuhair Hasan, "Islamic Banking at the Crossroads: Theory vs. Practice", in Munawar Iqbal and Rodney Wilson (eds), *Islamic Perspectives on Wealth Creation*, Edinburgh: Edinburgh University Press, 2007, pp. 11–25, for the traditional critique that Islamic finance uses too much deferred payment financing in place of equity-like risk-sharing.

35. "A Genève, Faisal Finance fonde la première banque privée islamique au monde", ("In Geneva Faisal Finance is founding the first Islamic private bank in the world"), *Le Temps*, 5 October 2006.

36. For an illustration, see Michael J. T. McMillen, "Structuring a Securitised *Sharia*-Compliant Real Estate Acquisition Financing: A South Korean Case Study", in Ali (ed.), *Islamic Finance*.

37. Islamic Financial Services Board, "Seminar on Islamic Finance – Opportunities and Challenges in Hong Kong", 15 January 2008: http://www.ifsb.org/index.php?ch=5&pg=21&ac=81.

38. "A Basic Guide to Islamic Finance", *Grapeshisha*, #013, 19 March 2006: http://www.grapeshisha.com/a-basic-guide-to-Islamic-finance-newsletter.html.

39. http://www.iirating.com/press/20080204_bankmuamalat.pdf

40. Paul McNamara, "The Islamic International Rating Agency", *Islamic Business and Finance*, March 2006, pp. 38–40.

41. The current members are listed on the IFSB website at http://www.ifsb.org/index.php?ch=3&pg=7&ac=10.

42. Keynote address at the "Seminar on Islam and the Global Economy: Malaysian and NZ Perspectives", Wellington, New Zealand, on 13 June 2006, posted on www.ifsb.org.

43. See the AAOIFI website at http://www.aaoifi.com/.

44. http://www.ifsb.org/preess_full.php?id=40&submit=more.

45. See, in particular, Giocomo Luciani, "From Private Sector to National Bourgeoisie: Saudi Arabian Business", in Paul Aarts and Gerd Nonneman (eds), *Saudi Arabia in the Balance*, London: Hurst 2005, pp. 144–81.

46. As observed by Samuel L. Hayes III, chairing the Governors and Institutions Round-table, Seventh Harvard University Forum on Islamic Finance, 22 April 2006. On Lexis Nexus I retrieve $500 billion from "Global Islamic banks must consolidate to be competitive, says industry group", Associated Press (Eileen NG), Kuala Lumpur, 15 November 2005.

47. Michael J. T. McMillen, "*Sukuk* and Islamic Bonds: Toward Viable Secondary Markets", presentation to Seventh Harvard University Forum on Islamic Finance, 23 April 2006.

48. Mohammed El Qorchi, "Islamic Finance Gears Up", *Finance and Development*. December 2005, p. 49, http://www.imf.org/external/pubs/ft/fandd/2005/12/qorchi.htm. The central banks of Bahrain, Malaysia, and Turkey publish aggregate data about Islamic banks, but Qorchi observes that "the lack of adequate data makes it virtually impossible to compare Islamic banks across countries".

49. Taken from Clement M. Henry and Rodney Wilson (eds), *The Politics of Islamic Finance*, Edinburgh: Edinburgh University Press, 2004, p. 7, with additional bold-faced data kindly provided by Javier Jopart, "The Impact of Regulation on the Future of Islamic Finance", presentation to Seventh Harvard University Forum on Islamic Finance, 23 April 2006.

50. National Commercial Bank web page: http://www.alahli.com/personalbanking/aboutus.asp. It claimed 105 billion riyals of customer deposits at the end of 2005, when the Saudi Arabian Monetary Authority indicated a total of 384.5 billion.

51. See SAMBA's financial statements, note 6: http://www.samba.com.sa/about/pdf/FS-2005_FINAL_with_Dir_Report.pdf.

52. International Monetary Fund, Pakistan – Financial Sector Assessment Program – Technical Note – Condition of the Banking System (11 May 2005): http://www.imf.org/external/pubs/ft/scr/2005/cr05157.pdf.

53. Robert Hefner, "Islamising Capitalism: On the Founding of Indonesia's First Islamic Bank", in Arskul Salim and Azyumardi Azva (eds), *Sharia and Politics in Modern Indonesia*, ISEAS Series on Islam, Singapore, 2003, pp. 152–6.

54. Shanthy Nambiar, Bloomberg News, 2 March 2005,www.wwrn.org/parse.php?idd=9518&c=82).

55. Ji-Hyang Jang, "Taming Political Islamists by Islamic Capital: The Passions and the Interests in Turkish Islamic Society", PhD dissertation, University of Texas at Austin, 2005, pp. 158–65. In 2005, the "participation banks" had 4.7 per cent of the outstanding commercial bank credits and 3.4 per cent of the deposits, and their market shares increased to 3.8 and 5.0 per cent, respectively, by the end of September 2006. See Central Bank of the Republic of Turkey, *Quarterly Bulletin* III-2006: http://www.tcmb.gov.tr/yeni/eng/ (present author's estimates from the most recent available data).

56. See Stéphane Lacroix, "Islamo-Liberal Politics in Saudi Arabia", in Paul Aarts and Gerd Nonneman (eds), *Saudi Arabia in the Balance*, London: Hurst 2005, pp. 35–56.

57. Ibrahim Warde, *The Price of Fear: The Truth Behind the Financial War on Terror*, Berkeley, CA: University of California Press, 2007.

58. See Mahmoud El Gamal, *Islamic Finance: Law, Economics, and Practice*, Cambridge University Press, 2006, p.194 note 15: "Arbitrage is the practice of exploiting profitable discrpeencies between markets, usually by buying a financial product in one market and selling it a higher price in another. Regulatory arbitrage is the act of restructuring a financial product that is available in one market to make it tradable in another. Sharia arbitrage is a form of regulatory arbitrage, where the legal restrictions are those perceived to be part of Islamic law." In "Limits and Dangers of Sharia Arbitrage", in Ali, *Islamic Finance*, El-Gamal argues that: "Sharia arbitrage relies on two main tools to achieve its objective: (i) dual characterisation of a financial dealing, one for jurists and one for regulator ... and (ii) addition of one or more degrees of separation between Islamic finance clients and the underlying conventional financial products. The latter is often achieved by inspecting each part of a complex transaction in isolation, rather than studying the entire transaction" (p. 122).

59. Giacomo Luciani, "From Private Sector to National Bourgeoisie: Saudi Arabian Business", in Paul Aarts and Gerd Nonneman (eds), *Saudi Arabia in the Balance*, London: Hurst, 2005, pp. 144–81.

Chapter 6

Democracy, Development and Political Islam: Comparing Iran and Turkey

Mohammed Ayoob

At first glance, Iran and Turkey appear to be an unambiguous study in contrast in both the arenas of politics and economics. In the political sphere, in common parlance, Iran is referred to as a "theocracy" while Turkey is identified as a "secular republic". However, the reality is far more complex than is assumed. Belying the view that Turkey is unequivocally secular in terms of the strict separation of religion and state is that the official Turkish definition of secularism subordinates religion to the state instead of separating the two spheres, thus deviating from the normally accepted meaning of the term, at least in the Anglo-American tradition. Moreover, one finds that the country's public arena is not free from contestation between religiously inclined forces and those espousing a militant and aggressive form of secularism. This contestation, in large measure a reaction to the state's aggressive secularism, has become sharper since the 1970s, as the religiously observant segments of society have regained their political voice suppressed for decades by the Kemalist elite.

Paradoxically, in its attempt to control the public expression of Islam, the Kemalist state has ended up giving Sunni Islam of the Hanafi school of jurisprudence the de facto position of state religion by according it preferential, if subordinate, treatment. The Directorate of Religious Affairs appoints and pays all Sunni imams, the state-funded imam-hatip schools train all Sunni religious functionaries, and the upkeep of Sunni mosques and other religious establishments is the responsibility of the state. Financial subventions provided to Sunni Hanafi institutions are not extended to Alevi or Shia institutions, let alone to institutions that serve non-Muslim minorities. The state's obsession with Sunni Islam demonstrates the fact that, despite all disclaimers, the Republic of Turkey's cultural and political identity is inextricably intertwined with Sunni Islam. It is the mirror in which the state sees its face.

This is borne out by the fact that, at its very inception, the territorial contours of the Turkish republic were defined by the Grand National Assembly as "the territories inhabited by an Ottoman Muslim majority", excepting "territories inhabited by an Arab majority". Furthermore, the exchange-of-population agreement with Greece at the end of the Turkish War of Independence envisaged a transfer to Greece of all Greek Orthodox inhabitants of Turkey outside of Istanbul, and a reciprocal transfer of all Muslims residing in Greece outside of Western Thrace to Turkey. The principle on which this exchange was based was religion, not ethnicity.[1] In fact, the large majority of Muslims transferred to Turkey were Macedonians, Albanians and Greeks, and not Turks. The Republic of Turkey can deny its Muslim roots only at the expense of its national identity.

Iran is thought to fall at the other end of the secular–theocratic continuum, governed as it is supposed to be according to principles of Shia theology. However, once one looks closely at the Iranian political system, its internal contradictions appear to loom very large. Mainstream Shia theologians consider Ayatollah Khomeini's interpretation of Shia doctrine, and his establishment of the institution of the *vali-e-faqih*, as idiosyncratic innovations, if not worse. The very idea that the Shia ulama could directly rule over a polity, and that one of them could be designated as a surrogate for the twelfth imam in the latter's absence, and arrogate much of the absent but awaited imam's powers to himself, sounds blasphemous to many Shia, theologians and lay people alike. Moreover, this has been seen as obliterating the distinction between Sunni and Shia Islam by creating a Shia caliph on the Sunni model.[2] In other words, the entire theological justification for Iran's political structure appears to be on very shaky grounds.

The role of the Shia clergy in governing Iran has, therefore, constantly faced intellectual and political challenges both from lay opponents and from within the ranks of the ulama themselves. A leading opponent of clerical involvement in governance is Grand Ayatollah Montazeri, Khomeini's chosen successor for the position of *vali-i-faqih*, who was relieved of his position during the last year of Khomeini's life because of his differences with the latter. Ayatollah Montazeri has gone to the extent of calling the present system in Iran "a monarchical setup", an obvious reference to the vast powers exercised by the Supreme Jurist.[3] Furthermore, the fact that a human-made constitution was considered necessary to define the institution of the *vali* (the Supreme Jurist), whose powers are supposed to be divinely sanctioned if not divinely derived, sums up the conundrum faced by a political system that is, on the one hand, purportedly divinely ordained and, on the other, very much a human invention (some would say one human's invention).

In the same dichotomous vein as the "theocratic–secular" contrast between

Iran and Turkey, the Iranian political system is described as "autocratic" while its Turkish counterpart is referred to as "democratic". However, these descriptions hide as much as they convey. Iran demonstrates a significant amount of popular input in how it is governed, with representative institutions co-existing with unelected and appointed clerical ones. Despite the Council of Guardians' attempts to control electoral outcomes, Iranian elections have produced surprising outcomes in the 1997, 2001 and 2005 presidential contests, with the reformist Khatami winning the first two and the darkhorse neo-conservative Ahmadinejad winning the third. Parliamentary elections have also produced reformist majorities in the past that have been unwelcome from the perspective of the hardline clergy. In addition, there are multiple cross-cutting cleavages in the Iranian body politic that make political bargaining and coalition-building essential thus precluding undiluted authoritarianism and promoting "continuous regime change".[4]

The parallel structures of authority, one representative the other clerical, were the deliberate creation of the post-revolutionary elite in part because of the mixture of democratic and clerical elements within the anti-Shah movement. The composition of the popular movement in 1978–9 was similar to that of the movement that led to the constitutionalist revolution of 1905–6. The constitution of 1908, which was a product of the constitutionalist revolution, established a set of representative institutions, as well as a clerical body with supervisory powers. The parallel structures created in 1979 were also the result of interal contradictions within Khomeini's political preferences that were simultaneously democratic and authoritarian in nature.[5] Khomeini saw these institutions balancing each other under his benign guidance and prevented as far as possible direct intervention by the Council of Guardians into the day-to-day politics and administration of the country. However, his successor, Ayatollah Khamenei, has politicised clerical structures to a much larger degree, thus throwing into sharp relief the contradictions inherent in the constitution. As a result of these contradictions, and the actions of the Iranian ruling elite, the political system has been left in what has been termed a state of "suspended equilibrium".[6]

Turkey's political system may be democratic in form, but its representative institutions are constantly hampered in the exercise of their functions by the existence of un-elected power centres collectively known as the "deep state". The role of the military, which has staged several coups in the past decades, and even last year issued veiled threats to deter parliament from electing Abdullah Gul to the presidency, detracts significantly from Turkey's democratic credentials. Similar noises were made more recently, by the military and its allies, regarding the constitutional amendment permitting women students to wear headscarves in universities, thus raising further questions about Turkey's democratic claims.

Of late, the Turkish military has exercised much of its political influence through the National Security Council (NSC), which includes top military brass and important cabinet ministers, and is chaired by the President of the Republic. Established by Article 118 of the 1982 constitution, which was adopted after the military coup of 1980, the NSC affords the military high command the opportunity to influence, pressure, and often dictate to the government in matters of national security. Since "security" has been traditionally defined in Turkey as embracing internal as well as external issues that the secular elite finds "threatening", the military has traditionally exercised virtual veto-power on issues relating to political Islam and Kurdish ethno-nationalism that the Kemalists perceive as threats to national security.[7] Although the role of the military brass within the NSC has been reduced in recent years, in response to pressure exercised by the EU, the institution continues to be a major avenue through which military commanders can influence civilian decision-making on "security"-related issues, including the state's response to Islamist political activity.

In both the Iranian and Turkish case, the picture is far too complicated to merit simplistic descriptions of autocracy-versus-democracy and theocratic-versus-secular. In fact, the similarities in the constitutional and political structures of the two states are especially striking in the area of executive functions. Both the Turkish and Iranian constitutions are democratic in form and make provision for representative institutions and the separation of functions among the legislative, executive and judicial institutions. Periodic elections to the legislature and the executive are also mandated by their constitutions. However, both allot supervisory functions to non-elected institutions – the Supreme Jurist and the Council of Guardians in the case of Iran, the military high command and the National Security Council in the case of Turkey. In both cases these institutions are flaunted as repositories and guardians of the fundamental values on which the two political systems are based. They are, therefore, seen to be above and outside the normal political process, and indeed above the countries' written constitutions.

In actual fact, they are not outside the political process of the two countries. They are integral parts of that process, and constantly interfere in it, but without the accountability to the people that representative institutions are required to demonstrate in a democracy. Just as the president of Iran is persistently constrained in his role as the chief executive by the superior authority vested in the Supreme Leader, the Turkish prime minister has to constantly make sure that his or her policies and decisions do not cross the limits of what is considered appropriate by the military top brass. In this sense, both Turkey and Iran possess twin executives rather than a single locus of executive authority.

One could, in fact, argue that the locus of executive authority is clearer in Iran, where the Supreme Leader holds a constitutionally designated position that puts him above the president. In the case of Turkey, the military's political role, whether direct or through the National Security Council, is far more opaque, thus creating great uncertainty in times of heated political contestation, such as over the headscarves issue. The clear line of control over the armed forces in Iran, which is vested in the Supreme Leader, by and large rules out military coups in the country. This is not true in the case of Turkey, though, where several coups have been staged in the past and the threat of future coups cannot be discounted.

What makes the comparison between Iran and Turkey most interesting, however, is the fact that the political groups who are currently in government in both countries, trace their roots to Islamist movements, explicitly in the case of Iran and implicitly in the case of Turkey, and draw at least part of their legitimacy from their Islamist antecedents. The Iranian regime is the direct descendant of the Islamic Revolution, while the Justice and Development Party (AKP) is the latest incarnation of Islamist political parties in Turkey. Although the AKP has attempted to present itself as a "conservative democratic" party, and to distance itself from its leaders' Islamist past, it continues to have a solid base of support among religiously observant segments of the population, especially in the provincial cities and towns of Anatolia. Many people consider the use of terms such as "conservative" and "traditional" in its rhetoric as signifying "Islamic", without it having to utter the taboo word for fear of the party being declared "illegal" by the Constitutional Court or the military staging a coup to safeguard "Kemalism" and "secularism".

It is also instructive to note in this context the contrasting uses of Islam by the principal agents of political Islam in Iran and Turkey. In Iran, political Islam is used to justify restraints on unfettered democratic functioning through institutions such as that of the *vali-i-faqih* and the Council of Guardians. Political Islam in Iran has, therefore, taken on an undemocratic image, despite the presence of representative institutions in the country. This image has been reinforced since the parliamentary elections of 2004 and the presidential elections of 2005, when the Council of Guardians rejected the nomination papers of large numbers of reformist candidates whose commitment to strengthening democratic institutions (as against appointed ones) was clearly on display.

In contrast, in Turkey political Islam has of late become the primary vehicle for the expression of the population's democratic aspirations. This was driven home forcefully by the performance of the AKP in the last two parliamentary elections in 2002 and 2007, in which it garnered 35 and 47 per cent of the popular vote respectively, and emerged as the ruling party in parliament, able to form governments without the support of any other party or grouping. The election of former foreign minister Abdullah Gul to the presidency in 2007 has further reinforced this image. This is the result of the fact that, in Turkey, secularism has become identified with authoritarianism primarily because the

Kemalist elite – both aggressively secular and instinctively authoritarian – has been in control of the state and of the constitutional process for most of the time the republic has been in existence. The civilian Kemalists have openly allied themselves with the military to prevent challenges from popular forces that they deemed as weakening the secular basis of the Turkish political system or the Kemalist definition of a unitary Turkish national identity. It is largely as a reaction to this authoritarian secularism of the Kemalist state that freedom of religious expression (principally of Islamic practices free from the fetters of the state) has come to be identified with democracy in the minds of substantial segments of the Turkish population, a majority of whom have always been religiously observant.[8] This has given Islamically-inclined political formations a major boost in terms of electoral support.

Current Iranian and Turkish developmental strategies, like their political systems, also appear at first sight to be a study in contrasts. The Iranian state, if you go by its rhetoric, seems to be ever more involved in managing the country's economy and in promoting a near-autarkic approach in terms of the country's relationship with the global economy. Consequently, in the economic sphere, Islam is used by segments of the Iranian ruling elite to promote the state's control of the economy because they are the principal beneficiaries of a statist or semi-statist economy, controlling as they do, much of the state's institutions and its resources. Leading members of Iran's ruling elite have been beneficiaries of the state-controlled or state-manipulated sectors of the economy, especially the bonyads (foundations). Also, rising prices of oil, which accounts for more than 80 per cent of the country's export earnings and is controlled by the state, have provided the regime with surplus resources that can be used to increase its patronage of those loyal to the regime and to buy-off or neutralise opposition.

On the other hand, the Turkish state, since the coming-to-power of the AKP in 2002, has been engaged in progressively reducing its role in the arena of economic management, is promoting economic liberalisation, and is committed to integrating the country into the global economy. This process started in the early 1980s, with the coming-to-office of Turgut Ozal, first as prime minister and then as president. It accelerated in the second half of the 1990s under pressure from the IMF and the World Bank, when the Turkish economy faltered and needed to be bailed out, and as a result of the emergence of the provincial bourgeoisie in cities such as Kayseri and Konya independent of state patronage and engaged in export-oriented industries.

In contrast with Iran, in Turkey the Islamically-inclined social forces, principally the religiously observant provincial Anatolian bourgeoisie, are interested in dismantling the state's control of the economy and integrating the Turkish economy into the global market. The Anatolian bourgeoisie, as distinct from large manufacturing enterprises located in Istanbul, Izmir and Ankara,

are export-oriented and not dependent on state largesse, unlike the established "national" bourgeoisie that traditionally have had a very close and often
dependent relationship with the Kemalist state. As Ayse Bugra points out, "The
role of the state in the Turkish economy has not only been much more significant than in Western developed economies, but it also has been more crucial
than in many other late industrialising countries as far as its impact on private-
sector development is concerned". State-business relations are, therefore, as
Bugra notes, "The most salient features of the societal context of private-sector
development in Turkey".[9] The entrenched bourgeoisie concentrated in Istanbul,
Izmir and Ankara were a product of this state–business nexus, whereas the new
provincial bourgeoisie have emerged independently of state patronage. While
the latter are interested in integrating into the global economy, the former have
a protectionist mindset that is a product of the import-substitution industrialisation model adopted by the Turkish Republic from its inception until the
1980s.[10] According to one analyst, "In Turkey, the success of the AKP's Muslim
Democratic platform is less a triumph of religious piety over Kemalist secularism
than of an independent bourgeoisie over a centralising state".[11]

It is interesting to note that the religiously observant provincial bourgeoisie
have created their own association known as MUSIAD, separate from the association of the established big business houses known as TUSIAD. Not only do
the former's economic interests differ from those of the latter, but its economic
culture, based on the Islamic concept of "trust", is also remarkably different from
that of TUSIAD. In the words of one author, "without state support, economic
Islam is functioning effectively, its role being an articulating principle between
the free market and local communities by providing medium and small-sized
enterprises with a powerful network based on trust relations".[12]

The Anatolian bourgeoisie also admire the East Asian model of development, which they believe has not sacrificed "tradition" in order to develop,
and has maintained its cultural moorings unlike the Westernisation-equals-
modernisation model adopted by the Kemalist elite represented in TUSIAD.[13]
However, MUSIAD's admiration for the East Asian model does not go so far as
to embrace the latter's authoritarian state form (that is, a relatively free economy
mixed with a regimented polity à la China). Members of MUSIAD distinctly
prefer democracy to authoritarianism, an attribute of the Kemalist elite whom
they oppose.[14] Indeed, it is the Kemalists who probably find inspiration from the
Chinese model of governance, especially its combination of authoritarianism
and ideological regimentation.

Both the Iranian regime since the revolution of 1979 and the Turkish government since the coming to power of the Justice and Development Party (AKP)
in 2002 have attempted to distance themselves from the developmental models
pursued by their predecessors – the Shah's regime, in the case of Iran, and the

Kemalist elites who had been in power in Turkey almost continuously since the creation of the republic. While there is a considerable degree of substance to these claims, one also sees elements of continuity in both cases that should not be ignored.

In the case of Iran, the Shah's regime was considerably statist in character. It had, in fact, created a state-dependent "modern" bourgeoisie that became the principal beneficiary of the state's largesse, to the considerable unease of the traditional Iranian merchant class, the *bazaaris*. The latter had close connections to the Shia clergy and financially supported the anti-Shah movement during the crucial years 1978–9.[15] However, in somewhat of a paradox, the bazaar's close relationship with the clerical establishment, rather than ensuring its independence from the state, eroded its autonomy after the Revolution. This was due to the fact that various elements from the bazaar became intimately connected with the political aspirations of multiple factions trying to control the Iranian state. In fact, it has been argued by some that the bazaar retained a greater degree of autonomy from the state during the time of the Shah than it did in the post-Revolutionary period because the Shah's regime was largely indifferent towards the traditional merchant class.[16]

It should also be noted that the statist rhetoric of Iran's current rulers hides a substantial degree of free-market activity outside of the oil sector, although the operation of the free market is distorted by the intervention of religio-political elites who use their political clout to garner disproportionate benefits, especially through the operation of the *bonyads*. "Although bonyads are technically separate from the state, their management is chosen from the clerical order close to the supreme leader. Because they are intertwined with the regime, the bonyads have effectively displaced any independent industrial class through political pressures and economic favouritism ... By some estimates, the total share of bonyads amounts to at least 20 per cent of GDP".[17]

In the case of Turkey, while economic liberalisation has proceeded apace under AKP, previous governments in the 1990s had already considerably aided the process of liberalisation, primarily under IMF and World Bank pressure. In fact, as stated earlier, the beginnings of liberalisation of the Turkish economy can be traced to Turgut Ozal's government in the early 1980s, which opened the economy to global competition and also encouraged Turkish businesses to enter the global market in considerable numbers. Ozal prefigured the current Islamist elite both in terms of his publicly displayed religiosity and his links to the emerging provincial bourgeoisie who came of age in the 1990s and who were, like Ozal himself, religiously observant and economically liberal.[18] It needs to be pointed out, however, that substantial portions of the Turkish economy continue to be under state control, despite the AKP government's efforts at divestment.

The international environment, whether mainly supportive as in the case of Turkey, or largely obstructive as in the case of Iran, is another factor that helps explain the developmental strategies and the political trajectories of the two countries. The democratisation of the Turkish polity has been helped considerably by ongoing negotiations with the EU for Turkey's entry into that organisation. In order for Turkey to enter the EU, it has to meet the Copenhagen criteria that encompass the supremacy of civilian institutions over the military, as well as respect for human rights, including minority rights. It is interesting to note that the AKP, supposedly the heir to Islamist attitudes of suspicion and mistrust vis-à-vis the West, has become the prime promoter of Turkey's accession to the European Union. At the same time, the Kemalist military and civilian elites – the Turkish modernisers, according to conventional wisdom – have become lukewarm towards the European project they had initially espoused.[19] This has been the case largely because of their apprehension that EU pressure will force the military to stay out of the political arena and might also provide greater rights and freedoms to both Islamists and the Kurdish minority, outcomes that the Kemalists consider to be anathema.[20]

The hostile political environment, at least as it pertains to the policies of the United States and its European allies, has worked to the disadvantage of democratic forces in Iran by strengthening hyper-nationalist sentiments and by making it easy for the hardliners, both traditional conservatives and neo-conservatives, to brand reformists and democrats as agents of the West, thus detracting from their credibility and legitimacy. The former Bush administration's policy was very short-sighted in this regard, and played into the hands of the neo-conservatives in Iran – represented by figures such as President Ahmadinejad – who demonstrate a visceral antagonism towards the United States, just as their American counterparts do towards Iran.[21] Ahmadinejad's election to the presidency in 2005 has had the concomitant effect of bringing into positions of power and authority non-clerical hardline elements that are very different in their approach to both domestic and international politics than are the traditional, mostly clerical, conservatives. This, as one analyst points out, "indicates that Iran is, in fact, undergoing a gradual process of regime change, not moving towards democracy but rather modifying Iran's brand of authoritarianism. It constitutes the beginning of a marked shift from the existing clerical theocracy towards a more conventional authoritarian regime…The consolidation of conservative power in the Iranian state is proceeding along conventional authoritarian patterns with an increasing shift of power to the state security services".[22]

Turkey has also operated in a favourable global economic environment that has welcomed the Turkish engagement with the global economy. This has strengthened the hand of economic liberalisers in Turkey, who also happen to be democrats and Islamically-inclined, as opposed to the statist elites, many of whom are dyed-in-the-wool Kemalists and aggressive secularists. On the other hand, the imposition of economic sanctions on Iran, and the threats to pile on more if Tehran does not do the Western powers' bidding on the nuclear issue, has strengthened the hand of the neo-conservatives in the country, who also happen to be economic statists not particularly interested in engaging with the global economy, and certainly not if the costs are too high politically. This has worked to the disadvantage of economic liberalisers, many of whom also happen to be political reformists. International variables have, therefore, had an important impact on the political trajectories and economic development strategies of Iran and Turkey, and need to be taken into consideration while comparing the two countries.

Finally, the rentier nature of the Iranian state, with its heavy dependence on oil revenues, helps explain major differences with Turkey economically and politically. Oil revenues strengthen the hand of those in control of the state in both spheres by reducing their dependence on resources that have to be raised by taxation, thus making a social compact between the rulers and the ruled less important, if not redundant. Increasing oil revenues also help those in control of the state by providing them with the surplus that can be used to reward loyalist constituencies and subsidise the population at large. Oil revenues, which account for more than 80 per cent of Iran's export earnings, therefore make the state largely immune to societal pressure, and at the same time allow state elites to build patronage networks in order to shore up the regime over which they preside. This is particularly the case currently, when oil prices have hit record highs and produced unprecedented surpluses for state elites, such as those in Iran, to utilise for their own purposes.[23] Furthermore, as Fred Halliday points out, "While oil has bought [social] peace it has also ... inhibited engagement with the world economy: Iran's main non-oil exports remain in traditional sectors – carpets and pistachio nuts – while foreign direct investment outside the oil sector is minimal".[24]

Turkey, on the other hand, is a "normal" state that has to depend largely on resources raised from its population through direct and indirect taxation in order to be able to provide security and services in return. Those in control of the levers of power in Turkey, therefore, have to be far more sensitive to popular concerns than do their counterparts in Iran. This also substantially explains the trajectory of political Islam in the country, as it is clearly linked to the increasing clout within the Turkish economy of the observant, provincial bourgeoisie of Anatolia, who have been traditionally linked to Islamist political parties since the 1970s and are the principal financial supporters of the AKP that currently governs. In Turkey, the extraction of economic resources and their distribution is central to governmental policy. The sorry plight of the parties that dominated the political landscape in the 1990s attests to the importance of economics in Turkish politics. They were wiped off the political map in 2002 because of their miserable performance in terms of economic management. This lesson has been driven home so well to the current political players, that even the post-Islamist party – the AKP – feels it necessary to couch its differences with other parties in economic terms and cater assiduously to the needs of its social and economic constituencies. In the words of Hakan Yavuz, the AKP is no longer "a party of identity but rather a party that strives to provide better services".[25] In Iran, on the other hand, political contestation is couched largely in religio-cultural terms with debate about economic issues playing, at best, a secondary role. This is the case because "when the government is financially autonomous from its citizens, conditions are ripe for challenging the state on noneconomic grounds. In rentier states only moral and ideological commitment obliges the government to increase the national wealth, to provide services, and to consult the population. In other words, the relation between the ruled and the rulers is defined in moral and ideological, not economic terms".[26] This factor explains the large difference between Iran and Turkey regarding the terms of political debate going on currently in the two countries.

Iran and Turkey provide very interesting comparisons – both in terms of similarities and contrasts – in the political and economic arenas. In the political arena, we see democratic and authoritarian impulses, as well as secular and religious elements, operating within them, although in different mixes and in different degrees. Similarly, in the economic arena, statist and liberal impulses are evident in both cases, although again in different combinations and in different degrees. The operation of the variable referred to as political Islam, in both contexts, makes the comparisons and contrasts between Iran and Turkey even more interesting, especially for scholars and analysts engaged in unravelling the relationship between Islam on the one hand, and democracy and development on the other. The two cases clearly demonstrate that Islam does not prescribe a single political or economic model. Where Islam does seem to have some influence in shaping political systems or economic trajectories of predominantly Muslim states, this influence is mediated through a number of contextual variables that render generalisation about this relationship all but impossible.

Political Islam is a very malleable ideology in both the economic and political arenas. It can be used to justify a state-controlled economy as well as a free-market economy. Similarly, it can be used to rationalise authoritarian control over the political system as well as representative democracy. It all depends on who is using it for what ends, and whether the proponents of political Islam in particular milieux have a proper understanding of the contextual variables operating in their societies, and the way such variables shape the political economy of discrete countries. As the Iranian and Turkish cases clearly demonstrate, context matters hugely in the interaction between democracy, development and political Islam.[27]

NOTES

1. Mohammed Ayoob, "Turkey's Multiple Paradoxes", *Orbis*, vol. 48, no. 3, 2004, pp. 451–63.
2. Hamid Enayat, "Khumayni's Concept of the 'Guardianship of the Jurisconsult'", in James P. Piscatori, *Islam in the Political Process*, New York: Cambridge University Press, 1983, pp. 160–80. Also, see H. E. Chehabi, "Religion and Politics in Iran", *Daedalus* vol. 120, no. 3, 1991, pp. 69–91.
3. For more on Montazeri's views, see Christopher de Bellaigue, "Who Rules Iran?" *New York Review of Books*, vol. 49 no. 11, 2002, pp. 17–19.
4. Ali M. Ansari, "Continuous Regime Change from Within", *Washington Quarterly*, vol. 26, no. 4, 2003, pp. 53–67.
5. Daniel Brumberg, *Reinventing Khomeini: The Struggle for Reform in Iran*, Chicago: University of Chicago Press, 2001.
6. Mahran Kamrava and Houchang Hassan-Yari, "Suspended Equilibrium in Iran's Political System", *The Muslim World*, vol. 94, no. 4, 2004, pp. 495–524.
7. For the National Security Council and the military's role in the politics of Turkey, see Metin Heper and Aylin Guney, "The Military and the Consolidation of Democracy: The Recent Turkish Experience", *Armed Forces and Society*, vol. 26, no. 4, 2000, pp. 635–57. Also, see Umit Cizre Sakallioglu, "The Anatomy of the Turkish Military's Political Autonomy", *Comparative Politics*, vol. 29, no. 2, 1997, pp. 151–66.
8. Omer Taspinar, *An Uneven Fit? The "Turkish model" and the Arab world*, Washington, DC: The Brookings Institution, 2003.
9. Ayse Bugra, "Class, Culture, and State: An Analysis of Interest Representation by Two Turkish Business Associations", *International Journal of Middle East Studies*, vol. 30, no. 4, 1998, p. 523.
10. Hasan Kosebalaban, "The Impact of Globalization on Islamic Political Identity", *World Affairs*, vol. 168, no. 1, 2005, pp. 27–37.
11. Vali Nasr, "The Rise of "Muslim Democracy"", *Journal of Democracy*, vol. 16, no. 2, 2005, p. 18.
12. E. Fuat Keyman, "Modernity, Secularism, and Islam: The Case of Turkey", *Theory, Culture and Society*, vol. 24, no. 2, 2007, p. 221.
13. Ayse Bugra, "Labor, Capital, and Religion: Harmony and Conflict Among the Constituency of Political Islam in Turkey", *Middle Eastern Studies*, vol. 38, no. 2, April 2002, p. 194.
14. E. Fuat Keyman and Berrin Koyuncu, "Globalization, Alternative Modernities and the Political Economy of Turkey", *Review of International Political Economy*, vol. 12, no. 1, February 2005, 105–28
15. Misagh Parsa, *Social Origins of the Iranian Revolution*, New Brunswick: Rutgers University Press, 1989.
16. Arang Keshavarzian, *Bazaar and State in Iran: The Politics of the Tehran Marketplace*, New York: Cambridge University Press, 2007.

17. Elliot Hen-Tov, "Understanding Iran's New Authoritarianism", *Washington Quarterly*, vol. 30, no. 1, 2006–7, p. 174.

18. John Waterbury, "Export-Led Growth and the Center-Right Coalition in Turkey", *Comparative Politics*, vol. 24, no. 2, 1992, pp. 127–45.

19. Hasan Kosebalaban, "The Permanent "Other"? Turkey and the Question of European Identity", *Mediterranean Quarterly*, vol. 18, no. 4, 2007, pp. 87–111.

20. Omer Taspinar, *Kurdish Nationalism and Political Islam in Turkey: Kemalist Identity in Transition*, New York: Routledge, 2005.

21. For the difference between traditional conservatives, many of whom come from the ranks of Shia clergy, and neo-conservatives, most of whom are not religiously trained and many of whom have been associated with the Revolutionary Guards and other para-military outfits, see Anoushiravan Ehteshami and Mahjoob Zweiri, *Iran and the Rise of Its Neoconservatives: The Politics of Tehran's Silent Revolution*, London: I. B. Tauris, 2007.

22. Hen-Tov, "Understanding Iran's New Authoritarianism", pp. 163, 165.

23. According to the Economist Intelligence Unit, Iran's GDP doubled between 2003 and 2007 from US$129.3 billion to US$256.5 billion thanks to sky-rocketing oil prices. As a result its current account surplus increased twenty-fold during the same period. http://www.economist.com/countries/Iran/profile.cfm?folder=Profile&2DEconomic%20Structure.

24. Fred Halliday, "Foreword", in Ali Mohammedi (ed.), *Iran Encountering Globalization: Problems and Prospects*, New York: RoutledgeCurzon, 2003, p. xiii.

25. M. Hakan Yavuz, "The Role of the New Bourgeoisie in the Transformation of the Turkish Islamic Movement". in M. Hakan Yavuz (ed.), *The Emergence of a New Turkey: Democracy and the AK Parti*, Salt Lake City, UT: University of Utah Press, p. 2.

26. Hootan Shambayati, "The Rentier State, Interest Groups, and the Paradox of Autonomy: State and Business in Turkey and Iran", *Comparative Politics*, vol. 26, no. 3, 1994, p. 329.

27. For a detailed analysis of the importance of context in shaping the discrete manifestations of political Islam, see Mohammed Ayoob, *The Many Faces of Political Islam*, Ann Arbor, MI: University of Michigan Press, 2008.

PART THREE

The Role of Governance in Development Models

CHAPTER 7

Can the East Asian Developmental State be Replicated? The Case of Malaysia

JEFF TAN

INTRODUCTION

This chapter seeks to explain Malaysia's industrialisation in terms of the East Asian developmental state model. This "model" generally refers to a developmental state characterised by the capacity to manage the process of late industrialisation, specifically: 1) the transfer of resources to more productive groups and sectors; and 2) learning and "catching up". In particular, the disciplinary capacity of the state to ensure that learning rents are not wasted is seen as central to successful late industrialisation.[1] However, this capacity was rooted in historically specific social relations that reduced the need of the state to accommodate political opposition, whether this was a powerful landed class or organised middle class. At the same time, there were geo-political contingencies that provided the impetus to industrialise, supported by substantial amounts of US aid.

The question, then, is whether the East Asian developmental state can be transferred to developing countries, given its historical specificity. While it may be relatively easy to replicate the sorts of capacities related to making the correct economic decisions by improving the quality (and autonomy) of the bureaucracy, the political capacity of the state to implement decisions and enforce discipline is far more difficult to replicate because this will be contingent on political factors specific to a country. The notion of state capacity therefore needs to be understood in terms of historically specific social contexts, and in particular the balance of political forces that shape state motivations and constrain policy design and implementation. Here, the usefulness of the East Asian developmental state model for other countries will depend on the compatibility of institutions and policies with existing power structures.

Malaysia provides a useful case study of how the state's political capacity is shaped by wider social forces, and how this subsequently affects the quality of policy and institutions, and ultimately economic performance. The government's attempt to replicate the East Asian development path, in particular Japan's and South Korea's, aimed to address weaknesses in industrial structure through direct state intervention and a heavy industries policy. However, despite strong manufacturing-led export growth from the 1970s to late 1990s, these policies and industrial performance were qualitatively poorer than those of the East Asian newly industrialised countries (NICs), posing long-term problems in technology upgrading.

Weaknesses can be traced back to policy design and implementation, in particular the management of learning rents. Here, the state's disciplinary capacity was constrained by changes in the balance of political forces. In particular, the emergence of, and subsequent differentiation within, the Malay middle class affected resource allocation and subsequently the ability of the state to manage the learning process necessary for industrial upgrading. Growing competition for rents led to increasing political contestation and subsequent factionalisation of the ruling Malay political party. This compromised the political leadership's ability to discipline Malay capitalists because their support was increasingly crucial in intra-party leadership contests. As a result, the state could not ensure that rents were conditional upon learning. This, in turn, undermined the emergence of efficient domestic industrialists and industrial deepening, with Malay capitalists moving into non-tradable or protected sectors such as construction and real estate.

This chapter will: 1) identify the challenges specific to late industrialisation, looking at the role of the developmental state; 2) examine the sources of state capacity, drawing from the East Asian experience and locating this in historical perspective; and 3) explain Malaysia's policy choices and industrial performance from 1970 to 1997 in terms of developmental state theories.

LATE INDUSTRIALISATION AND THE DEVELOPMENTAL STATE

The role of the developmental state can only be understood in terms of the development process, and late industrialisation in particular. The development process has historically entailed the transfer of productive resources from one group to another, and is closely related to the transition to capitalism. These resource transfers are inherently political and have taken place largely through non-market processes often involving compulsion or force, with the state playing a central role. We can trace this back to the English enclosures of common land from the sixteenth to the eighteenth century that created a class of capitalist farmers, through to the dispensing of licences, loans, and mining and land concessions that have been associated with the emergence of an entrepreneurial class in Europe and the US.[2]

The development process today is very similar to the early stage of capitalist development, with the state needing to allocate resources to productive groups through the creation of property rights in the face of often intense competition. Moreover, economic development has also historically been characterised by structural change associated with industrialisation and reflected in the growth of industry's share of GDP. This means that development not only hinges on the transfer of resources to an emerging capitalist class, but to a class of capitalists engaged in manufacturing. As this process will be inherently political and keenly contested, the state will need to ensure that: (1) resources are transferred to productive groups able and willing to invest in industry; and (2) it can accommodate or override potential opposition to these transfers by groups that are left out. The ability of the state to manage the development process will, in turn, depend on the balance of political forces, in particular the strength of the state in relation to an emerging capitalist class and other social groups contesting for resources.

As latecomers, developing countries face the additional challenge of late industrialisation. Developing countries are characterised by low levels of technology, and hence efficiency, particularly in relation to incumbent firms in advanced countries, along with institutional constraints and market failures related to information and co-ordination externalities.[3] As a result, there are few incentives for domestic entrepreneurs to invest in manufacturing, and indeed there is every reason not to, given the very high risks, their initial lack of competitiveness, and the existence of less risky investment alternatives which offer better returns in the short term. This means that late industrialisation is inherently risky and the state will need to provide incentives for capitalists in developing countries to move into manufacturing, and adopt new technologies in order to become competitive. Historically, the process of late industrialisation has necessitated some form of state intervention, usually through the creation of "functional substitutes" in the context of market failures[4] and the provision of subsidies in the form of infant-industry protection to promote learning and "catching up".[5]

Successful late industrialisation will therefore depend on the state's capacity to: (1) transfer resources to productive groups (that is, emerging capitalists) and specific industries; (2) manage potential opposition to this process; and (3) promote learning through learning rents that are conditional upon meeting performance targets. The discussion of development thus necessitates a prior examination of the role of the state and the issue of state capacity.

STATE CAPACITY AND THE EAST ASIAN EXPERIENCE

The idea of state capacity is closely related to that of state autonomy. State capacity has been defined in terms of the ability to implement economic policies effectively, and to exercise a large measure of control over the behaviours of domestic and foreign capital[6]. The state must be able to manage conflict (for example, between different capitals), allocate resources to the most productive sectors and enforce discipline. It must be able to construct economic rules that advance the long-term interests of capital and the technological character of the nation as a whole and, as such, promote growth.[7] The capacity to do this will depend on the bureaucracy's autonomy or degree of insulation from political interference. Bureaucratic capacity, coherence and autonomy from societal forces are said to provide the ability to devise long-term economic policies without interference from private interests.

However, this autonomy is, in turn, only relative because the state "cannot go as far as acting against the long-run interest of the dominant class as a whole".[8] This is because the basis of the developmental state's legitimacy is its ability to promote and sustain development through a "combination of high rates of growth and structural change in the productive system".[9] It is the implementation of strategies by a comparatively autonomous technocratic elite, and the institutionalising of close relationships between business leaders and state officials in the formation of a dynamic export-oriented regime of capital accumulation, that is seen to characterise the developmental state.[10]

Here, the idea of state autonomy is explained in terms of its "embedded autonomy" – the combination of an autonomous bureaucracy (that is, "Weberian bureaucratic insulation") and thick external ties to the economy's organised agents.[11] That is to say, the state needs to be insulated enough to be able to independently formulate and implement policy, but also connected to productive groups in society. As capital accumulation demands close connections to private capital, such connections have to be with industrial capital, enabling state elites to incorporate these powerful groups in the state's economic project.[12] The discussion of state capacity thus provides the framework to explain the East Asian development experience in terms of the three conditions identified for successful late industrialisation.

Here, the contrast between East Asia (in particular, South Korea and Taiwan) and Latin America (notably Argentina, Brazil and Mexico) is useful in highlighting the main features of the East Asian developmental state. The East Asian developmental state was able to transfer resources from agriculture to industry because it could implement the necessary agrarian reforms to raise agricultural productivity to create a surplus.[13] It was able to do this because it could override political opposition in the countryside, unlike in Latin America, where the state faced considerable resistance from large landowners. At the same time, South Korea and Taiwan were able to ensure that learning took place in order to shift from import-substituting industrialisation (ISI) to export-oriented industrialisation (EOI). In contrast, Latin American countries were characterised by infant industries that failed to mature because the state was unable to make protection conditional upon learning.

The differences between the two regions have thus been attributed to the effectiveness of state intervention which was, in turn, due to the different degrees of state capacities. Unlike Latin America, effective industrial policies in East Asia were characterised by flexibility, selectivity and coherence.[14] South Korea, for example, was highly selective in targeting particular industries or firms for promotion, but was also willing and able to change policies, withdrawing subsidies from unviable sectors or inefficient firms, and refusing to bail out firms that got into difficulties.[15] Latin American industrialisation, in contrast, was characterised by the ongoing support of inefficient industries, indiscriminate protection of consumer goods, policy inconsistency and the bail-out of firms for political reasons.[16]

Here, the "relative autonomy" (insulation) of the East Asian state from dominant and subordinate classes, along with an efficient and cohesive bureaucratic machinery, facilitated the formulation and implementation of coherent economic strategies.[17] State autonomy was backed by "effective state structures with a strong commitment to economic growth which formed the basis for the South Korean and Taiwanese 'miracles'".[18] Here, economic decision-making was highly centralised through the Economic Planning Board in South Korea and Economic Planning Council in Taiwan. The state directed capital flows through control of the financial sector and FDI regulations, allowing it to target key economic sectors and develop local technological capabilities through joint ventures and licensing. This state capacity can, in turn, be traced to specific social structures in both regions.

The main difference here was that Latin American countries generally featured more established social classes, namely landowners, an industrial bourgeoisie, a business and middle class, and an organised labour movement, each exercising varying degrees of political influence that undermined policy and bureaucratic autonomy. This resulted in fragmented and incoherent decision-making and policy, a much more politicised bureaucracy subject to capture by particular interest groups, and the reduction of state goals to private interests.[19]. Thus, landlords in Latin America were able to prevent reforms in the countryside and the transfer of agricultural surplus to industry; sections of the industrial bourgeoisie, along with workers, were able to resist the dismantling of early protection; and the state was also susceptible to pressures from business and the middle class.[20]

In contrast, both South Korea and Taiwan inherited relatively egalitarian social structures and unified bureaucracies. In particular, the absence of a landlord class meant that there was no opposition from powerful interests to industrial policy, as was the case in Brazil, Argentina and Mexico.[21] At the same time, the industrial bourgeoisie in South Korea and Taiwan were relatively new and less able to influence the state, compared to Latin America,[22] while labour was more repressed and thus easier to accommodate in East Asia, in part because of the gender division of labour.[23] These social conditions are seen to have provided the East Asian state with the autonomy and capacity to implement policy that promoted economic growth.

Social structures are, in turn, rooted in historical specific contexts. Thus, in the case of South Korea and Taiwan, this included a Japanese colonial legacy and geo-political considerations related to the Cold War. Japanese colonialism "severely weakened the traditional governing class and landed aristocracy, robbing them of much of their political power, appropriating large portions of their material base and causing them, particularly in Korea, to be tarred with the collaborationist brush".[24] This paved the way for subsequent land reforms to promote political stability in South Korea and destroy the base of the emergent middle class in Taiwan.[25] Both countries inherited effective colonial bureaucracies and Japanese industries that were nationalised and, in the case of South Korea, subsequently sold off to selected families. Finally, the external military threat facing both countries provided the imperative for economic growth and, more importantly, drew in substantial amounts of US aid. This financed investments and provided a degree of independence from local classes and interests, "in certain respects strengthening the state apparatus vis-à-vis the local bourgeoisie, especially in Taiwan in the early 1950s".[26]

State Motivation

The discussion of state capacity in the context of the East Asian developmental state raises the question about state motivation. Why does the state do what it does? In other words, why should a state be developmental? The state's motivation is usually left unexplained in the developmental state literature and the state is generally assumed to be benevolent. Policies in favour of capital are explained in terms of a mutually dependent relationship between government and big business,[27] where success depends on the fortunes of the other partner.[28] This "strategic interdependence" ensured that both business cartels and state economic bodies in South Korea were "committed to high growth, realising that they would have to swim or sink together".[29]

In reality, the state is neither inherently predatory nor benevolent. Rather, state motivation needs to be understood in specific social contexts, taking into account the state's relationship with both productive and unproductive groups, and locating these in the wider context of the economic imperatives imposed by the dynamic (logic) of capital accumulation. Rather than benevolent or predatory, it would be more useful to assume that the dominant political objective of any regime is to remain in power, and that policies and strategies are formulated around this.[30] The issue is whether this manifests itself in terms of developmental (growth-enhancing) or predatory (growth-reducing) policies. These will, in turn, depend on the nature of social formations and power structures in a country.

State actions and policies will therefore reflect the interests of the more powerful groups in society, as well as political (and bureaucratic) elites. This provides us with a more nuanced explanation of the failure of Latin American countries to shift from ISI to EOI due to the weakness, and hence inability, of segments of the industrial bourgeoisie (vis-à-vis ISI industrialists and landed interests) to influence the broader macroeconomic policies necessary to reduce the risks associated with moving into export manufacturing.[31] South Korea and Taiwan made the transition from ISI to EOI because the state was not constrained by an established industrial bourgeoisie. In South Korea's case, the state could allocate and reallocate resources without significant political constraints to efficient entrepreneurs, and these were also the entrepreneurs who could offer the highest pay-offs to the state.[32] In principle, the state could enforce both predatory and developmental actions, but chose the latter because it offered bigger pay-offs in the long run. In other words, the size of the bribe was a function of entrepreneurial efficiency that, in turn, facilitated economic growth.

Conversely, if political conditions do not favour the pursuit of long-term policies, the state may instead seek short-term gains, and this may be manifested in predatory behaviour and growth-reducing outcomes. The state thus becomes predatory because it lacks the political capacity to govern and hence to maximise gains through long-term developmental strategies that also allow it to stay in power longer. This could help explain the transformation of the Kuomintang from predatory or failed state in mainland China to developmental state in Taiwan. In contrast to South Korea's creation of large conglomerates or *chaebol*, the Kuomintang promoted small- and medium-sized industries (SMIs) and retained control of strategic industries because it did not have popular support as an outside political party.

REPLICATING THE EAST ASIAN DEVELOPMENTAL STATE

As we have seen, the political circumstances that facilitated the emergence of the East Asian developmental state were historically specific. This raises the question of whether the model can be replicated elsewhere. Indeed, arguments against state intervention have cautioned developing countries against attempting similar industrial policies because the conditions for the East Asian developmental state were too context-specific.[33] However, the usefulness of the East Asian model lies not in the specificities, institutional details, bureaucratic capacity, policies and the like, but rather in our analysis of state capacity rooted in social relations and shaped by the dynamic of capital accumulation. By identifying the main features of the development process and conditions in specific countries, we can better understand why many developing countries may lack the state capacity to implement developmental policies.

Here, one of the main differences between East Asia and developing countries is the nature of class formations that, in turn, shape the type of state–society relationship. In South Korea and Taiwan, the state's relationship was with productive segments of society, namely industrial capital, in part because of the earlier Japanese colonial emphasis on manufacturing. More crucially, effective state intervention was possible because of the absence of powerful groups in society which allowed the state to enforce decisions by penalising poor performers and rewarding good performers. In contrast, most developing countries typically have powerful factions, often led by unproductive social groups, who can, for a price, protect inefficient enterprises. These countries also have a far more limited pool of qualified candidates to select from and impose discipline on through the threat of replacement. These conditions can effectively constrain the state's ability to transform those initially selected into efficient capitalists through the effective management of rents. State capacity thus does not only depend on the state's reach (its connections with capitalist groups or other productive relationships), but also on its ability to overcome political constraints (that is, resistance to discipline). Hence, while the South Korean state could maximise rents extracted from capitalists, and at the same time ensure compliance with productivity maximisation, many developing country states are faced with the problem of incompetent (non-capitalist) candidates who are also harder to discipline.

As the state's connection with society in developing countries may not be through production-oriented alliances but instead with unproductive "non-capitalist" classes created and brought together by the colonial legacy and struggle for independence, these groups have had to be accommodated. These groups have been variously described as "a well-educated but economically unproductive professional class",[34] the "educated salaried middle classes",[35] and the intermediate class left behind in the development process, whose political role is of considerable importance in that it involves organising resistance and developing ways to "modify certain market outcomes 'politically'".[36] State capacity, therefore, not only depends on the state's relationship with segments of capital, but also on political constraints posed by other groups in society outside the "developmental alliance".

Furthermore, the state–society relationship in developing countries is not necessarily formalised or "institutionalised" (as has been argued by some in the South Korean case),[37] but personalised, usually between patrons and clients. Patron–client relationships are repeated relationships of exchange between specific patrons and their clients. The nature of this relationship (in terms of how it is likely to influence economic decisions) depends on the objectives and ideologies of the patrons and clients; the number of potential clients and their degree of organisation; the homogeneity of clients; and the institutions through which patrons and clients interact, including the degree of fragmentation of institutions.[38] More critically, the relative power of patrons and clients can determine how resources are allocated. As mentioned, it was possible for the state to extract the maximum economic pay-off in South Korea, while ensuring that resource allocation was efficient, because clients of the state in both the business sector and in politics were weak. Inefficient clients could not defend themselves and the state had no interest in defending them. This could also explain why the South Korean state chose to damage business interests (as in the case of the Kukje *chaebol*) when state demands for bribes or political subservience were not met.[39]

However, where the patron is politically weak, inefficient clients may easily survive because clients in this context may be offering political support (or the absence of political opposition) rather than an economic pay-off. This political corruption may be necessary to ensure stability, but it can also be growth-reducing. This depends in part on the degree of centralisation, with centralised corruption being potentially less harmful,[40] as reflected in the different impact of corruption on economic growth in South Korea and South Asia.[41] Patron–client networks in India and Pakistan reveal the substantial political power of clients from intermediate "non-capitalist" classes, whose necessary accommodation made it more difficult for the state to reallocate rents more efficiently. This partly explains the persistence of inefficient rents in the Indian subcontinent.[42] Thus, state capacity does not necessarily increase with a deeper and broader social base,[43] as this may lead to greater fragmentation in patron–client relationships.

Rather, state capacity depends to a considerable extent on the balance of power in society determined by a country's social relations, including the factional composition of various interest groups, the nature of their relationship with the state, and the strength of the state in relation to these groups. The assessment of state capacity must, therefore, take into account the country's political context, looking specifically at how patron–client relationships affect the allocation of economic resources and the capacity of the state to allocate resources productively and enforce discipline. This will, in turn, allow us to explain institutional and political constraints. In particular, the enforcement requirements need to be compatible with existing power structures in order for institutions to perform efficiently, and to be effectively enforced by the state.[44] The incompatibility of the enforcement requirements of particular institutions with pre-existing social power structures can explain why similar state policies and institutions can lead to very different outcomes.

The Malaysian "Developmental" State

Malaysia provides a very useful case study, given the government's attempts to emulate the East Asian developmental state model, and its impressive economic performance in terms of industrialisation and growth. From our discussion so far, we have identified strong institutional and political capacities as important factors that enabled the East Asian developmental state to pursue and implement targeted and effective industrial policy. These capacities were, in turn, rooted in historical and social conditions that allowed for the alignment of interests between the state and an industrial capitalist class, and provided the state with relative autonomy from various factional or class interests in society. As a result, policy-making was centralised and coherent, learning rents were conditional upon performance targets and, most crucially, the state had the political capacity to enforce discipline to ensure that learning took place.

In the case of Malaysia, despite active intervention and similarities in the types of institutions and policies, the state's capacity to transfer resources to productive groups and promote learning necessary for late industrialisation was shaped and constrained by a very different set of social conditions characterised by the emergence of, and subsequent differentiation within, a Malay middle class. The need to politically accommodate factions within this class ultimately affected industrial and technology acquisition policies, the state's disciplinary capacity and, consequently, the quality of Malaysia's industrial performance. We will look at two broad phases of industrial policies in Malaysia: (1) import-substituting industrialisation (ISI) under the New Economic Policy (1970–early 1980s); and (2) export-oriented industrialisation (EOI) during the privatisation programme (1985–97).

New Economic Policy (NEP)

The NEP was introduced in 1970 in response to pressure for greater government intervention from the emerging Malay middle class in general, and Malay businessmen specifically.[45] The thrust of the NEP was largely shaped by these demands and involved the redistribution of wealth to this class through substantial increases in education, (public) employment and business opportunities, and the ownership of corporate equity with the aim of creating a Bumiputera [Malay] Commercial and Industrial Community (BCIC). By 1985, the government had created around 700 state-owned enterprises (SOEs) that were engaged in a variety of economic activity and provided entrepreneurial training for Malays, while the state acquisition of well-managed, profitable companies increased de facto Malay corporate ownership and provided further management opportunities. These measures were facilitated by the 1975 Industrial Coordination Act (ICA), which required companies to set aside 30 per cent of shares issued for Malay equity, with (below-market) share prices set by the Capital Issues Committee (CIC) for Malay individuals and SOEs. Efforts to promote a Malay industrial capitalist class were thus closely linked with industrial policy, and need to be considered together.

Unlike South Korea and Taiwan under the Japanese, the British colonial authorities discouraged local industries in Malaysia, confining these to processing raw materials for export and some domestic consumption.[46] As such, early industrial policies (late 1950s–mid 1960s) sought to expand the domestic manufacturing base through ISI by identifying new products and processes to promote "learning by doing".[47] The NEP coincided with a shift in industrial policy from ISI to EOI, prompted by the inherent limitations of ISI in a small, open capitalist economy.[48] EOI was spearheaded by the Federal Industrial Development Authority (FIDA) and supported by the 1968 Investment Incentives Act (IIA) to encourage diversification and manufactured exports through various tax incentives and the 1971 FTZ Act to promote free trade zones.[49] The Malaysian Industrial Development Authority (MIDA) worked with state government corporations to attract foreign investment, with the main emphasis on labour-intensive manufacturing in export-processing or free trade zones.[50]

The government sought to promote technology acquisition (mainly through technology transfer and licensing agreements) under the Ministry of International Trade and Industry (MITI) and the Ministry of Science, Technology and Environment (MOSTE).[51] Technology acquisition was overseen by MITI through its Technology Transfer Unit (TTU), MIDA and the Industrial Master Plan (IMP) Sectoral Task Force. The TTU approved technology transfer agreements to safeguard the "national interest", prevent unfair restrictions on Malaysian firms, and ensure fees were reasonable and technology transfer was meaningful.[52] MIDA evaluated industrial projects and the IMP Sectoral Task Force reviewed priority products and industries according to IMP priorities.[53]

MOSTE facilitated technology transfer by: providing linkages between technology acquisition and industrial development (through the Standards and Industrial Research Institute of Malaysia-Technology Transfer Centre); assisting entrepreneurs with information on technology selection and acquisition (Malaysian Science and Technology Information Centre); formulating science and technology policies and R&D priorities (National Council for Scientific Research and Development); identifying priority sectors, formulating technology transfer plans and policies, and ensuring the growth of the industrial sector (Coordinating Council for Industrial Technology Transfer); and promoting the development of technology parks and selected industries, products and technologies (the Science Advisor to the Prime Minister).[54] Public-sector agencies were supported by policies to promote technology acquisition, including the Intensification of Research Priority Areas program (1986) and the Action Plan for Industrial Technology Development (1990) along with tax incentives and research grants for small- and medium-size industries (SMIs).[55]

Malaysia's manufacturing growth was impressive. As a result of EOI, the GDP share of manufacturing grew from 13.1 per cent in 1970 to 20 per cent by 1985, while the manufacturing share of exports grew from 11.9 per cent to 33 per cent in the same period.[56] Furthermore, Malaysia's manufactured exports were based on high-skill and technologically complex products (as opposed to garments, for example), with EOI dominated by electronics and electrical goods, which increased from 8.5 per cent of manufactured exports in 1970 to 47.7 per cent by 1980.[57] Between 1971 and 1990, manufactured exports grew at a rate of 24 per cent per annum, enabling Malaysia to become the world's largest exporter of semiconductors and among the largest exporters of disk drives, telecommunications apparatus, audio equipment, room air-conditioners, calculators, colour televisions, and various household and electrical appliances.[58]

However, the rapid growth of manufacturing and manufactured exports relied heavily on foreign direct investment (FDI), with EOI dominated by the subsidiaries, affiliates or licensees of multinational companies. This was, in part, shaped by NEP considerations to bypass Malaysian Chinese capital, but arguably also because of limited existing domestic production capabilities and the preference of Chinese capital for commercial over industrial investments.[59] The reliance on foreign investment had several consequences for Malaysia's industrial structure, in terms of depth and domestic technological capabilities. First, the foreign domination of almost all internationally competitive non-resource based industrial capability restricted domestic firms mainly to assembly and subcontracting as original equipment manufacturer (OEM).[60] Local firms generally demonstrated minimum technological dynamism and most of the domestic industrial sector remained technologically passive, with few intra- and inter-industry linkages, and little diversification into the export market.[61]

Second, the export base remained narrow. The 1986 Industrial Master Plan (IMP)[62] highlighted the heavy dependence on components-production for export, in particular semiconductors, with consumer and industrial electronics only contributing between 15 and 20 per cent of total output (compared to between 55 and 70 per cent in South Korea and Taiwan). Third, manufactured exports had a high import content, indicating a fairly shallow industrialisation process.[63] The share of intermediate goods in total imports, for example, rose from 35 per cent in 1970 to 47 per cent in 1985, with the share of imported inputs in the gross export value of manufactured exports as high as 75 per cent.[64]

Fourth, low local content, especially in electronics, meant that there were limited linkages and technology transfer between the foreign-dominated manufacturing export sector and domestic firms outside the free trade zones.[65] Despite the increasing number of technology transfer agreements (mainly in electronics and electrical, chemical and fabricated metal industries), and the relative size and sophistication of Malaysia's manufacturing sector and export profile, the local technological base remained shallow, with excessive dependence on technology, marketing, management and components supply.[66] This also meant that there was an outflow of royalty payments, fees and other charges for technology use, with little net foreign exchange savings.[67]

Poor progress in technology acquisition has generally been blamed on institutional (bureaucratic) failures and industry's lack of capacity to learn.[68] Here, MITI lacked the "assessment capability" (the experience and expertise) to evaluate technology content and thus ensure the real transfer of technology.[69] The National Council for Scientific Research and Development and MOSTE had little political and financial clout to influence the broader range of trade and industry policies affecting technological development, and institutional arrangements to promote technology acquisition also suffered serious co-ordination failures.[70]

Failure was also due to the complex nature of the technology and lack of (Malay) skills. The capacity to learn is said to depend on industry's "collective learning" ability (facilitated by the country's human capital and competitive pressures from exporting) and "knowledge accumulation" (for example, on-the-job learning and "learning by doing" and "using", in order to learn how to produce before learning how to export).[71] Malaysia's low skill endowments reflected weaknesses in the education system that restricted innovation[72]. Little attention was given to viability and managerial competence, with state agencies not interested in building up an indigenous technological capacity, preferring easy access to foreign partners and technology.[73] As a result, Malaysian firms had limited capabilities to choose and assimilate imported technologies, especially in the context of imperfect information.[74] The failure to learn can also be traced back to an efficiency trade-off under the NEP arising from the political (and ethnic) imperative to develop (Malay) entrepreneurs through the quick transfer of assets to state agencies.[75]

The government sought to create Malay capitalists through ownership and management, supported by preferential treatment. However, there were no

performance targets or conditionalities, and insulation from market competition, along with easy access to finance, undermined business discipline and
"learning by doing".[76] There was little pressure for infant industries to grow
up, with concerns raised in two Malaysia Plans regarding the efficiency losses
due to protection, and again in 1983 by the Malaysian Industrial Policy Study,
which recommended the halving of average levels of protection.[77] Despite this,
inefficient import-substituting industries continued to receive high (and even
increasing) levels of protection without proper evaluation, monitoring or performance conditions, and irrespective of productive capabilities, allowing unsuc-
cessful firms to waste rents.[78] As a result, the NEP did not increase business
acumen or produce a class of dynamic Malay entrepreneurs.[79] Over-expansion of
the public-sector under the NEP also created a small but powerful "bureaucratic-
capitalist elite" able to largely resist government attempts to impose budgetary
discipline, making policy adjustments increasingly difficult.[80]

This led to public- and private-sector inefficiency, and a lack of a productive
base, reflected in the divestment for quick profits and a preference for investments
in protected or non-tradable sectors which contributed least towards independent
industrialisation, namely services, property development and construction.[81] The
accelerated expansion of construction and services at a time when Malaysian
manufacturing was still dominated by low value-added OEM activities undermined technological deepening.[82] The preference for investment outside of
manufacturing was reinforced by the industrial finance and banking systems.
Unlike South Korea, Malaysia's industrial finance system was weak in design and
execution, in part because of the dominance of foreign firms in large-scale manufacturing and Chinese firms in SMIs.[83] Furthermore, banks in Malaysia were based
on the Anglo-American model, acting as passive intermediaries and lending
tended to be conservative and based on collateral rather than project viability,
with a preference for general commerce at the expense of manufacturing.[84]
Loans to manufacturing rose from the 1970s, but only modestly compared to the
increasing share of loans for property, stocks and shares, again reflecting lending
preferences.[85] The lack of incentives for Malaysian banks to favour long-term
lending reflected weaknesses in financial policy and is seen to have limited the
development of (non-resource-based) domestic manufacturing.[86]

Privatisation

Privatisation was introduced in 1983, in part to address NEP inefficiencies, and
coincided with a second round of ISI from the mid-1980s. It is here that Malaysia
attempted to replicate many of the East Asian NIC institutions, replacing the
NEP with the New Development Policy (NDP) in order to provide "a more
coherent and systematic analysis of the needs and capabilities of manufacturing

activities" and move "much closer to the kind of industrial intervention practised by the East Asian NIEs".[87] Policy-making was centralised in the Economic
Planning Unit (EPU) in the Prime Minister's Department (mirroring South
Korea's Economic Planning Board and Taiwan's Economic Planning Council)
and the government attempted to recreate Japan's institutionalised state–business
relationships. The "Look East" policy in 1981 sought to raise productivity and
competitiveness by instilling Japanese attitudes and work habits in order to
raise productivity rates and competitiveness.[88] This was followed by "Malaysia
Incorporated" in 1983 which aimed to foster private–public co-operation and
consultation for industrial upgrading.[89] The institutionalising of direct, high-
level, public–private networks aimed to free policy-making and the industrialisation project from the distributional constraints and inefficiencies of the NEP
by centralising decision-making and rent allocation more narrowly among a
smaller group of entrepreneurs through the management of key government-
linked projects.[90]

The government followed South Korea's Heavy and Chemical Industry drive
of the 1970s, targeting the same industries (iron, steel, cement and automobile
production); and the state-owned Heavy Industries Corporation of Malaysia
(HICOM) sought to address the issue of absorbing complex organisational
and production processes necessary for technological upgrading and industry
linkages.[91] State-led industrialisation was seen as necessary because Malaysia,
unlike South Korea, did not have large industrial conglomerates or many
(non-resource-based) major manufacturers with strong records of international
competitiveness who could undertake industrial upgrading.[92] The creation of
HICOM – encompassing steel, cement and automobile production – and its
subsequent privatisation was an attempt to develop large Malaysian conglomerates along the lines of South Korea's *chaebol* and Japan's *zaibatsu*.

The government sought to shift into higher technology sectors through the
Malaysian Industry–Government Group for High Technology (MIGHT) (a
government–business technology forum formed in 1993 to track emerging technologies and encourage ventures exploiting new technological innovations),
the Intensification of Research Priority Areas program (to provide a conceptual
view of technology development), Technology Action Plan, Malaysian Technology Development Corporation (MTDC), Advanced Manufacturing Technology Centre, Malaysian Institute for Microelectronics Systems (MIMOS) and
Technology Park Malaysia.[93] It also launched a second round of FDI-led EOI in
the second half of the 1980s through the 1986 Promotion of Investment Act
that provided generous incentives, and relaxed some NEP ethnic requirements,
but also added technological and domestic content conditions.[94] This led to a
new round of FDI, mainly from NICs and Japan, facilitated by a strengthening
Japanese yen.

Despite these interventions, Malaysia's industrialisation remained largely "technology-less", without real technological strength or capacity in product development or capital goods production, and with no internationally recognisable brands.[95] Malaysia's industrialisation continued to be characterised by:[96]

1. A very high degree of concentration – the top five products accounted for 58.9 per cent of total exports in 1990, with electronics accounting for 67.5 per cent of manufactured exports in 1995 and 68.2 per cent of total export value in 1998.
2. Foreign domination – foreign firms accounted for more than 70 per cent of the total value of manufactured exports in the early 1990s and 91 per cent of electronics by 1993.
3. Low levels of local content (and high import content) with weak linkages;
4. Relatively low technological capabilities restricted to assembly and finishing operations, with few high-value-added and technologically demanding tasks (as even subsidiaries of multinational companies undertook no design functions, sourcing other product technology from parent companies or major buyers).
5. The absence of independent marketing capabilities necessary to upgrade into higher value added products and markets.

The inability to address industrial deepening and technology acquisition meant that Malaysia's industrialisation remained vulnerable to changes in FDI flows to countries with lower wage costs, higher skill endowments and engineering capabilities, and larger domestic markets, such as India and China.[97] Failing to improve competitiveness and moving into higher technological sectors, Malaysian firms continued to rely on state subsidies and protection, and shifted into non-tradable sectors. Malays in particular remained restricted to property, construction and finance, and dependent on government contracts, continued state support and intervention. This was reflected in the sectoral distribution of privatisation that reflected the ongoing preference of Malay businessmen for these sectors.[98] More tellingly, privatisation was characterised by the state restructuring, bail-outs and takeovers of companies owned by the small group of Malay businessmen who received the bulk of privatisation, with significant dilutions of Malay interests in privatised enterprises overall.[99] A prominent example was HICOM (which included the national car project, Proton), which was re-nationalised following insufficient technological progress, with its private owner subsequently moving into largely protected, non-tradable sectors.[100]

These problems can be largely attributed to institutional failure. As heavy industries were set up to serve domestic rather than export markets, there was no systematic attempt to guide or monitor the technology-development process, with the sector characterised by soft budgets and a lack of performance targets and conditionalities.[101] Selective state intervention was of a much poorer quality and considerably less effective than in Taiwan and South Korea in the 1960s and 1970s, with industrial policy characterised by very high protection rates and little evidence of rent deployment favouring industrialisation or productive use.[102] Instead, rents provided the wrong incentives, even encouraging previously efficient companies into protected sectors.[103] Not surprisingly, lower protection levels following liberalisation from the mid-1980s pushed private interests into other rentier activities such as property and share purchases, with construction and real estate growing significantly faster than GDP.[104]

SOCIAL STRUCTURE AND STATE CAPACITY

Underlying these institutional failures were changes in social relations that affected the state's capacity to address the three conditions necessary for late industrialisation, namely the transfer of resources to productive groups, management of conflict arising from potential challenges by losers, and promotion of learning. Under the NEP, the government was able to centralise redistribution without state capture due to a unified party elite under a strong leadership which had the support of a large middle class and rural populace (as a result of bureaucratic expansion and rural development).[105] This centralised patronage allowed UMNO, the ruling Malay party, to control resources, providing benefits to its supporters and strengthening party loyalty.[106] The government was also able to strengthen and insulate the state's planning and economic agencies, with bureaucrats controlling resources through the management of state assets, and initially with minimal private business influence on economic policies.[107]

However, over-expansion of the public-sector also created a small but powerful "bureaucratic–capitalist elite" able to largely resist government attempts to impose budgetary discipline, making policy adjustments increasingly difficult.[108] More crucially, despite its continued dependence on the state, the Malay business class grew in organisation and influence,[109] with the growing number of Malay businessmen fostered by the NEP becoming an increasingly important element in the Malay political elite by the 1980s. This was reflected in the changing composition of UMNO leaders from politicians and "administocrats" to a combination of politicians and businessmen,[110] with significantly more Malay politicians active as businessmen (on their own and on UMNO's behalf) and Malay businessmen active in politics after the NEP.[111] State efforts to control the "commanding heights of the economy" (for example, plantations and tin mines) also produced a powerful group of former state managers increasingly active in business.[112]

The late 1970s saw the emergence and transformation of the Malay bourgeoisie from primarily directors – not owners – of large corporations (before
the mid-1970s) to Malay millionaires,[113] with professional and trustee Malay
executive directors becoming prominent by the late 1980s.[114] This paralleled
changes in the occupational background and outlook of UMNO leaders and
grass-roots members, with school teachers and other local leaders replaced by
businessmen and university-educated professionals produced by the NEP.[115]
"Middle-class elements" were able to completely take over UMNO by the early
1980s,[116] and by the time privatisation was introduced, there was already a large
Malay middle class, including a younger, more professionally trained managerial
cadre whose support was important and who had to be accommodated.[117]

The changing composition of the Malay middle class re-shaped the internal
politics within UMNO local branches. Increasing economic patronage changed
the nature of the patron–client relationships, transforming local UMNO representatives into political patrons. Elected members of parliament who were
previously political patrons (providing political support in return for economic
benefits) greatly increased their control of the district development machinery,
allowing them to distribute development benefits and purchase continued
support.[118] While Malay businessmen were heavily dependent on their access to
government patronage, they became an important force in the internal politics
of UMNO through the party's extensive patronage network,[119] increasing
factional struggles for nomination and outbreaks of violence at UMNO branch
and division meetings after 1984.[120] Although factions were already present in
all levels of UMNO,[121] the rise of "money politics" was closely related to (if not
a direct result of) the NEP.[122] This resulted in a series of bitter contests between
1981 and 1987, culminating in the leadership challenge and open party split in
1987.[123]

These changes in social relations help explain the seemingly dramatic policy
shift from direct state intervention under the NEP to privatisation (and the
accompanying shift from EOI to ISI). While this shift was, in part, motivated
by economic considerations related to NEP inefficiencies, it was largely politically driven by social changes related to the growth of, and subsequent differentiation within, the Malay middle class under the NEP. In particular, was the
emergence of an influential group of Malay businessmen linked to key NEP
institutions and closely associated with key political leaders in UMNO, whose
support enabled Prime Minister Mahathir Mohamad to centralise authority and
introduce privatisation.[124] Privatisation was thus an extension of the NEP and
part of ongoing state policies aimed at creating Malay capitalists through the
transfer of resources, this time favouring an emerging group of big businessmen
that stood to benefit from the sale of state assets at the expense of those who
continued to rely on NEP-style assistance and handouts.

However, this process remained constrained by the lack of domestic entrepreneurial capacity and preference for non-productive sectors as opposed to manufacturing, with privatisation focusing largely on sectors where Malay enterprises were most concentrated, namely in "construction" (the largest privatised sector), "government services", and "wholesale and retail trade, hotels and restaurants", all of which primarily benefited the emerging group of Malay businessmen closely associated with the key political leaders in UMNO.[125] More crucially, the state's capacity to create a dynamic industrial capitalist class was constrained by the growing political contestation and factionalisation within the party that led to increasingly personalised patron–client relationships. This compromised policy choice and undermined the political leadership's ability and/or willingness to discipline those whose support it relied on.[126] State capacity to direct domestic capital into strategic manufacturing industries, and to ensure that efficiency gains through learning took place, was thus constrained by the nature of social relations in Malaysia. This, in turn, adversely affected industrialisation, preventing the emergence of an efficient, "deepening" industrial policy.

CONCLUSION

This chapter has sought to explain the performance of Malaysia's industrialisation in terms of the East Asian developmental state model. Our discussion has focused on the issue of the state's capacity to promote late industrialisation by: (1) transferring resources to productive groups and specific industries; (2) managing opposition to this process by losers; and (3) promoting learning. The state's capacity to undertake these tasks in East Asia were the outcome of specific social conditions that favoured the state, reducing its need to accommodate competing political interests and at the same time enabling it to transfer resources to an existing capitalist class and enforce discipline to ensure that learning, and hence technological catching-up, took place. Malaysia's industrialisation strategy closely followed the East Asian model, but was notably poorer in design and implementation because of different social conditions that constrained the state's capacity to design and implement effective industrial policy and, most critically, its disciplinary capacity to promote learning.

The absence of an established industrial capitalist class, and the political demands from a Malay middle and business class, meant that the transfer of resources was not necessarily to productive groups. Demands by the Malay middle class coincided with wider Malay dissatisfaction with growing inter-ethnic inequality. The NEP aimed to create a Malay industrial capitalist class through preferential treatment, but failed to promote learning or technological catching-up because subsidies and protection were not conditional on performance. Furthermore, a reliance on FDI (to bypass Chinese capital) weakened domestic industrial and technological capacity. The government sought to address these problems and at the same time transfer resources to an emerging group of large Malay capitalists through privatisation and a second round of state-led ISI based on heavy industries. However, this process was also politically driven by the differentiation within the Malay middle class that altered the balance of power in the ruling Malay party. Growing competition, conflict and factionalisation led to increasingly personalised patron–client networks that made it difficult for the state to discipline Malay capitalists.

Malaysia's industrialisation suggests that the transferability of the East Asian developmental state will depend not just on the state's institutional capacity to design the appropriate policies but, crucially, on its political capacity to enforce discipline. This will be contingent on political factors specific to a country, in particular the nature of social relations that determine the balance of power between the state and groups it engages with. These specific social conditions can help explain why similar institutions and policies can have very different outcomes. The East Asian developmental state remains central to successful late industrialisation. Whether this can be replicated will depend on the extent to which the appropriate institutional and political capacities can be strengthened.

NOTES

1. See, for example, A. Amsden, *Asia's Next Giant: South Korea and Late Industrialization*, New York: Oxford University Press, 1989; R. Wade, *Governing the Market: Economic Theory and Role of Governance in East Asian Industrialisation*, Princeton, NJ: Princeton University Press, 1990; Chang H. J., "The Economic Theory of the Developmental State", in M. Woo-Cummings (ed.), *The Developmental State*, London: Cornell University Press, 1999.

2. See, for example, R. Brenner, "Agrarian Class Structure and Economic Development in Pre-Industrial Europe", *Past and Present*, no. 70, February 1976, pp. 30–75; P. Bardhan, "Corruption and Development: A Review of Issues", *Journal of Economic Literature*, September (XXXV), 1997, pp. 1320–46.

3. See for example Chang, H. J., *The Political Economy of Industrial Policy*, London: Macmillan, 1994; D. Rodrik, "Industrial Policy for the Twenty-First Century", John F. Kennedy School of Government, Harvard University, 2004.

4. See A. Gerschenkron, *Economic Backwardness in Historical Perspective*, London: Oxford University Press, 1962.

5. See, for example, F. List, *The National System of Political Economy*, Philadelphia: J. B. Lippincott and Co., 1856.

6. Koo H. and Kim E. M., "The Developmental State and Capital Accumulation in South Korea", in R. Applebaum and J. Henderson (eds), *States and Development in the Asian Pacific Rim*, London: Sage Publications, 1992.

7. T. J. Pempel, "The Development Regime in a Changing World Economy", in M. Woo-Cummings (ed.), *The Developmental State*, London: Cornell University Press, 1999; R. Jenkins, "The Political Economy of Industrialization: A Comparison of

Latin American and East Asian Newly Industrializing Countries", *Development and Change*, no. 22, 1991, pp. 197–231.

8. Jenkins, "The Political Economy of Industrialization", p. 202.

9. M. Castells, "Four Asian Tigers with a Dragon Head: A Comparative Analysis of the State, Economy and Society in the Asia Pacific Rim", in R. Applebaum and J. Henderson (eds), *States and Development in the Asian Pacific Rim*, London: Sage Publications, 1992, pp. 56–7.

10. C. Johnson, *MITI and the Japanese Miracle*, California: Stanford University Press, 1982.

11. P. Evans, "The State as Problem and Solution: Predatory Developmental, and Other Apparatuses: A Comparative Political Economy Perspective on the Third World State", in A. Kincaid and A. Pates (eds), *Comparative National Development, Society and Economy in the New Global Order*, Chapel Hill, NC: University of North Carolina Press, 1994, p. 96.

12. P. Evans, *Embedded Autonomy*, Cambridge: Policy Press, 1995.

13. See, for example, C. Kay, "Why East Asia overtook Latin America: Agrarian Reform, Industrialisation and Development", *Third World Quarterly*, vol. 23, no. 6, 2002, pp. 1073–1102.

14. Jenkins, "The Political Economy of Industrialization".

15. See, for example, ibid.

16. See, for example, R. Wade, "What Can Economics Learn From East Asian Success?", *The Annals of the American Academy of Political and Social Sciences*, no. 505, September 1989, pp. 68–79; J. Macomber, "East Asia's Lessons for Latin American Resurgence", *The World Economy*, vol. 10, no. 4, 1987, pp. 469–82.

17. Jenkins, "The Political Economy of Industrialization".

18. Ibid., p. 214.

19. Jenkins, "The Political Economy of Industrialization".

20. Ibid.; Kay, "Why East Asia overtook Latin America".

21. Jenkins, "The Political Economy of Industrialization".

22. A. O. Hirschman, "The Political Economy of Import-Substituting Industrialisation in Latin America", *Quarterly Journal of Economics*, vol. 82, no. 1, 1968, pp. 1–32; Jenkins, "The Political Economy of Industrialization".

23. See, for example, S. Seguino, "Gender Inequality and Economic Growth: A Cross-Country Analysis", *World Development*, vol. 28, no. 7, 2000.

24. C. Hamilton, "Capitalist Industrialization in the Four Little Tigers of East Asia", in P. Limqueco and B. McFarlane (eds), *Neo-Marxist Theories of Development*, London: St. Martin's Press, 1983, p. 143.

25. Jenkins, "The Political Economy of Industrialization"; Kay, "Why East Asia overtook Latin America".

26. P. Evans, "Class, State and Dependence in East Aisa: Lessons for Latin Americanists", in F. Deyo (ed.), *The Political Economy of the New Asian Industrialism*, Ithaca, NY: Cornell University Press, 1987, p. 210.

27. Barzelay 1986, cited in Choi B. S., "Financial Policy and Big Business in Korea: The Perils of Financial Regulation", in S. Haggard, C. H. Lee and S. Maxfield (eds), *The Politics of Finance in Developing Countries*, London: Cornell University Press, 1993,

pp. 23–4; L. Weiss, *The Myth of the Powerless State*, Ithaca, NY: Cornell University Press, 1998.

28. J. Vartiainen, "The Economics of Successful State Intervention in Industrial Transformation", in M. Woo-Cummings (ed.), *The Developmental State*, London: Cornell University Press, 1999; Koo and Kim, "The Developmental State".

29. Pempel, "The Development Regime", p. 164.

30. J. Campos and H. Esfahani, "Why and When Do Governments Initiate Public Enterprise Reform?", *Public Administration and Development*, vol. 10, no. 1, 1996, p. 3–18.

31. See, for example, Hirschman, "The Political Economy of Import-Substituting".

32. M. H. Khan, "Patron–Client Networks and the Economic Effects of Corruption in Asia", *European Journal of Development Research*, vol. 10, no. 1, 1998, pp. 15–39.

33. See, for example, World Bank, *The East Asian Miracle: Economic Growth and Public Policy*, New York: Oxford University Press, 1993.

34. Pempel, "The Development Regime", p. 169–70.

35. Khan, "Patron–Client Networks", p. 19.

36. H. Alavi, "State and Class Under Peripheral Capitalism", in H. Alavi and T. Shanin (eds), *Introduction to the Sociology of "Developing Countries"*, London: Macmillan Press, 1982, p. 299; Khan, "Patron–Client Networks", p. 19.

37. See, for example, Evans, "The State as Problem and Solution".

38. Khan, "Patron–Client Networks", pp. 23–6.

39. M. H. Khan, "State Failure in Developing Countries and Strategies of Institutional Reform", in B. Tungodden, N. Stern and I. Kolstad (eds), *Toward Pro-Poor Policies: Aid Institutions and Globalization*, Proceedings of Annual World Bank Conference on Development Economics, Oxford: Oxford University Press and World Bank, 2004, p. 178.

40. P. Bardhan, "Corruption and Development"; A. Shleifer and R. Vishny, "Corruption", *Quarterly Journal of Economics*, vol.108, no. 3, 1993, pp. 599–617.

41. See, for example, Khan, "Patron–Client Networks".

42. Ibid.; M. H. Khan, "The New Political Economy of Corruption", Department of Economics SOAS (undated).

43. For example, as argued by D. K. Crone, "State, Social Elites and Government Capacity in Southeast Asia", in J. Ravenhill (ed.), *Singapore, Indonesia, Malaysia, The Philippines and Thailand: Volume I*, Aldershot: Edward Elgar Publishing, 1995.

44. Khan, "State Failure in Developing Countries".

45. See, for example, S. Neuman, "The Malay Political Elite: An Analysis of 134 Malay Legislators, Their Social Backgrounds and Attitudes", PhD dissertation, New York University, 1971; M. Puthucheary, "The Political Economy of Public Enterprise in Malaysia", in Lim L. L. and Chee P. L. (eds), *The Malaysian Economy at the Crossroads: Policy Adjustment or Structural Transformation*, Kuala Lumpur: Malaysian Economic Association and Organisational Resources, 1984; Lim M. H., "Contradictions in the Development of Malay Capital: State, Accumulation and Legitimation", *Journal of Contemporary Asia*, vol. 15, no. 1, 1985; Ho K. L., "Indigenizing the State: The NEP and the Bumiputra State in Peninsular Malaysia", PhD dissertation, Ohio State University, 1988; J. Jesudason, *Ethnicity and the Economy: The*

State, Chinese Business, and Multinationals in Malaysia, Singapore: Oxford University Press, 1989.

46. Jomo K. S., "Manufacturing Growth and Employment", in Jomo K. S. (ed.), *Malaysia's Economy in the Nineties*, Petaling Jaya: Pelanduk Publications, 1994.

47. See Jomo K. S., "Prospects for Malaysian Industrialisation in Light of East Asian NIC Experiences", in Jomo K. S. (ed.), *Industrializing Malaysia: Policy, Performance, Prospects*, London: Routledge, 1993; Anuwar Ali, "Technology Transfer", in Jomo K. S. (ed.), *Malaysia's Economy in the Nineties*, Petaling Jaya: Pelanduk Publications, 1994.

48. See Jomo, "Manufacturing Growth and Employment".

49. See Jomo K. S. and C. Edwards, "Malaysian Industrialisation in Historical Perspective", in Jomo K. S. (ed.), *Industrializing Malaysia: Policy, Performance, Prospects*, London: Routledge, 1993; R. Rasiah, "Lessons From Penang's Industrialization", in Jomo K. S. and Ng S. K. (eds), *Malaysia's Economic Development: Policy and Reform*, Petaling Jaya: Pelanduk Publications, 1996.

50. Malaysia 1969, p. 6 (cited in Rasiah, "Lessons From Penang's Industrialization", p. 191).

51. See Anuwar Ali, "Technology Transfer".

52. Anuwar Ali, "Technology Transfer in the Malaysian Manufacturing Sector", in Jomo K. S. (ed.), *Industrializing Malaysia: Policy, Performance, Prospects*, London: Routledge, 1993; Anuwar Ali, "Industrial Technology Capacity", in Jomo K. S. and Ng S. K. (eds), *Malaysia's Economic Development: Policy and Reform*, Petaling Jaya: Pelanduk Publications, 1996.

53. Anuwar Ali, "Technology Transfer".

54. Ibid.

55. Ibid.; R. Rasiah, "Pre-Crisis Economic Weaknesses and Vulnerability", in Jomo K. S. (ed.), *Malaysian Eclipse: Economic Crisis and Recovery*, London: Zed Books, 2001.

56. Jomo, "Manufacturing Growth and Employment"; Mohamed Ariff, "External Trade", in Jomo K. S. (ed.), *Malaysia's Economy in the Nineties*, Petaling Jaya: Pelanduk Publications, 1994.

57. Mohamed Ariff, "External Trade".

58. S. Lall, "Malaysia: Industrial Success and the Role of the Government", in H. Hill (ed.), *The Economic Development of Southeast Asia: Volume IV*, Cheltenham: Edward Elgar Publishing, 2002.

59. See, for example, P. M. Lubeck, "Malaysian Industrialisation, Ethnic Division and the NIC Model: The Limits of Replication", in R. Applebaum and J. Henderson (eds), *States and Development in the Asian Pacific Rim*, London: Sage Publications, 1992; J. Henderson and R. Applebaum, "Situating the State in the East Asian Development Process", in R. Applebaum and J. Henderson (eds), *States and Development in the Asian Pacific Rim*, London: Sage Publications, 1992; Jomo, "Prospects for Malaysian Industrialisation"; Jomo K. S., "East Asian Comparisons", in Jomo K. S. (ed.), *Malaysian Eclipse: Economic Crisis and Recovery*, London: Zed Books, 2001.

60. Jomo K. S., "From Currency Crisis to Recession", in Jomo K. S. (ed.), *Malaysian Eclipse: Economic Crisis and Recovery*, London: Zed Books, 2001; Ghazali Atan, "Foreign Investment", in Jomo K. S. (ed.), *Malaysia's Economy in the Nineties*,

Petaling Jaya: Pelanduk Publications, 1994; Anuwar Ali and Wong P. K., "Direct Foreign Investment in the Malaysian Industrial Sector", in Jomo K. S. (ed.), *Industrializing Malaysia: Policy, Performance, Prospects*, London: Routledge, 1993; Lall, "Malaysia: Industrial Success".

61. G. Felker, "Political Economy and Malaysian Technology Policy", in Ishak Yussof and Abdul Ghafar Ismail (eds), *Malaysian Industrialisation: Governance and the Technical Change*, Bangi: Penerbit Universiti Kebangsaan Malaysia, 1998; G. Felker, "Malaysia's Innovation System", in Jomo K. S. and G. Felker (eds), *Technology, Competitiveness and The State: Malaysia's Industrial Technology Policies*, London: Routledge, 1999; R. Rasiah and Ishak Shari, "Market, Government and Malaysia's New Economic Policy", *Cambridge Journal of Economics*, no. 25, 2001, pp. 57–78.

62. Cited in Jomo, "Manufacturing Growth and Employment", p. 120.

63. See, for example, Jomo and Edwards, "Malaysian Industrialisation"; Jomo, "Manufacturing Growth and Employment".

64. Mohamed Ariff, "External Trade"; Mohamed Aslam and Jomo K. S., "Implications of the GATT Uruguay Round for Development: the Malaysian Case", in Jomo K. S. and S. Nagaraj (eds), *Globalization Versus Development*, Basingstoke: Palgrave, 2001.

65. Jomo and Edwards, "Malaysian Industrialisation"; Mohamed Ariff, "External Trade"; Anuwar Ali, "Technology Transfer".

66. Anuwar Ali and Wong, "Direct Foreign Investment", Anuwar Ali, "Technology Transfer"; Felker "Malaysia's Innovation System".

67. MIDA 1986 (cited in Jomo, "Manufacturing Growth and Employment", p. 121).

68. See, for example, Anuwar Ali, "Technology Transfer"; Felker, "Political Economy".

69. Anuwar Ali, "Technology Transfer".

70. See, for example, Felker, "Political Economy"; Rasiah, "Pre-Crisis Economic Weaknesses".

71. M. Bell, B. Rosa-Larson and L. Westphal, "Assessing the Performance of Infant Industries", *Journal of Development Economics*, no. 16, 1984, pp. 101–28; S. Jacobsson, "The Length of the Infant Industry Period: Evidence from the Engineering Industry in South Korea", *World Development*, vol. 21, no. 3, 1993, pp. 407–19; H. Bruton, "A Reconsideration of Import Substitution", *Journal of Economic Literature*, no. 36, June 1998; L. Kim, "The Multi-faceted Evolution of Korean Technological Capabilities and its Implications for Contemporary Policy", *Oxford Development Studies*, vol. 32, no. 3, 2004 pp. 341–63.

72. See, for example, Jomo, "Prospects for Malaysian Industrialisation"; *Malaysian Eclipse*.

73. Jesudason, *Ethnicity and the Economy*.

74. Anuwar Ali, "Technology Transfer".

75. See, for example, Jomo K. S. and N. Hamilton-Hart, "Financial Regulation, Crisis and Policy Response", in Jomo K. S. (ed.), *Malaysian Eclipse: Economic Crisis and Recovery*, London: Zed Books, 2001.

76. Jesudason, *Ethnicity and the Economy*; E. T. Gomez and Jomo K. S., *Malaysia's Political Economy: Politics, Patronage and Profits*, Cambridge: Cambridge University Press, 1997.

77. Jomo and Edwards, "Malaysian Industrialisation"; R. Alavi, "Management of Protection Policy: Lessons from Malaysian Experience", in Ishak Yussof and Abdul

Ghafar Ismail (eds), *Malaysian Industrialisation: Governance and the Technical Change*, Bangi: Penerbit Universiti Kebangsaan Malaysia, 1998; Rasiah and Ishak Shari, "Market, Government and Malaysia's New Economic Policy".

78. H. Bruton, *Sri Lanka and Malaysia*, Washington, DC: Oxford University Press, 1992; R. Alavi, *Industrialisation in Malaysia: Import Substitution and Infant Industry Performance*, London: Routledge, 1996; Alavi, "Management of Protection Policy"; Jomo K. S. and Tan K. W., *Industrial Policy in East Asia: Lessons for Malaysia*, Kuala Lumpur: University of Malaya Press, 1999; Rasiah, "Pre-Crisis Economic Weaknesses"; Rasiah and Ishak Shari, "Market, Government and Malaysia's New Economic Policy".

79. B. Gale, *Politics and Public Enterprise in Malaysia*, Singapore: Eastern Universities Press, 1981; Jesudason, *Ethnicity and the Economy*; A. Bowie, *Crossing the Industrial Divide (State, Society and the Politics of Economic Transformation in Malaysia)*, New York: Columbia University Press, 1991; Kamal Salih, "The Malaysian Economy in the 1990s: The Alternative Scenarios", *MIER [Malaysia Institute of Economic Research] Discussion Paper*, 27 August 1989; Khoo B. T., *Paradoxes of Mahathirism*, Kuala Lumpur: Oxford University Press, 1989; H. Crouch, *Government and Society in Malaysia*, New York: Cornell University Press, 1996; Gomez and Jomo, *Malaysia's Political Economy*.

80. Jomo K. S., *A Question of Class: Capital, the State and Uneven Development in Malaya*, Singapore: Oxford University Press, 1986; O. Mehmet, *Development in Malaysia: Poverty, Wealth and Trusteeship*, Kuala Lumpur: Insan, 1988; Bowie, *Crossing the Industrial Divide*; Bruton, *Sri Lanka and Malaysia*; Jomo and Tan, *Industrial Policy in East Asia*.

81. See, for example, Anuwar Ali, "Technology Transfer".

82. Rasiah, "Pre-Crisis Economic Weaknesses"; Ghazali Atan, "Foreign Investment".

83. See, for example, Jomo and Hamilton-Hart "Financial Regulation, Crisis and Policy Response".

84. Chin K. F. and Jomo K. S, "Financial Intermediation and Restraint", in Jomo K. S. and S. Nagaraj (eds), *Globalization Versus Development*, Basingstoke: Palgrave, 2001.

85. Ibid., p. 98.

86. Chin and Jomo, "Financial Intermediation and Restraint".

87. Lall, "Malaysia: Industrial Success", p. 767.

88. Bruton, *Sri Lanka and Malaysia*.

89. Lall, "Malaysia: Industrial Success"; Felker "Political Economy".

90. Felker, "Political Economy".

91. Jomo and Edwards, "Malaysian Industrialisation"; Jomo, "Manufacturing Growth and Employment"; Lall, "Malaysia: Industrial Success".

92. Jomo and Tan, *Industrial Policy in East Asia*; Lall, "Malaysia: Industrial Success".

93. Felker, "Political Economy".

94. Lall, "Malaysia: Industrial Success"; Rasiah and Ishak Shari, "Market, Government and Malaysia's New Economic Policy".

95. Ghazali Atan "Foreign Investment"; Anuwar Ali and Wong, "Direct Foreign Investment"; Jomo, "From Currency Crisis to Recession".

96. Lall, "Malaysia: Industrial Success", pp. 769–70; Jomo, "From Currency Crisis to Recession".

97. See, for example, Lall, "Malaysia: Industrial Success".

98. See J. Tan, *Privatization in Malaysia: Regulation, Rent-Seeking and Policy Failure*, London: Routledge, 2008.

99. Malaysia, *Seventh Malaysia Plan*, 1996–2000, Kuala Lumpur: Government Printers, 1996; Malaysia, *Eight Malaysia Plan*, 2001–2005, Kuala Lumpur: Government Printers, 2001.

100. See Tan, *Privatization in Malaysia*.

101. Lall, "Malaysia: Industrial Success".

102. Jomo and Tan, *Industrial Policy in East Asia*.

103. See, for example, Alavi, "Management of Protection Policy".

104. Rasiah, "Pre-Crisis Economic Weaknesses"; Jomo, "East Asian Comparisons".

105. Leong 1991 (cited in Felker, "Political Economy", p. 90).

106. Jesudason, *Ethnicity and the Economy*; H. Crouch, "Malaysia: Neither Authoritarian Nor Democratic", in K. Hewison, R. Robison and G. Rodan (eds), *Southeast Asia in the 1990s: Authoritarianism, Democracy and Capitalism*, Sydney: Allen and Unwin, 1993; Khoo K. J., "The Grand Vision: Mahathir and Modernisation", in J. Kahn and F. Loh (eds), *Fragmented Vision: Culture and Politics in Contemporary Malaysia*, Sydney: Allen and Unwin, 1992; Felker, "Political Economy".

107. Felker, "Political Economy"; Leong 1991 (cited in Felker, "Political Economy", p. 90).

108. Jomo, *A Question of Class*; O. Mehmet, *Development in Malaysia: Poverty, Wealth and Trusteeship*, Kuala Lumpur: Insan, 1988; Bowie, *Crossing the Industrial Divide*; Bruton, *Sri Lanka and Malaysia*; Jomo and Tan, *Industrial Policy in East Asia*.

109. Jesudason, *Ethnicity and the Economy*.

110. M. Leigh, "Politics, Bureaucracy, and Business in Malaysia: Realigning the Eternal Triangle", in A. McIntyre and J. Kanishka (eds), *The Dynamics of Economic Policy Reform in Southeast Asia and South West Pacific*, Singapore: Oxford University Press, 1992.

111. Ho, "Indigenizing the State".

112. Jesudason, *Ethnicity and the Economy*.

113. Lim, "Contradictions in the Development of Malay Capital".

114. P. Searle, *The Riddle of Malaysian Capitalism*, Honolulu: Allen and Unwin and University of Hawai'i Press, 1999.

115. Crouch, "Malaysia: Neither Authoritarian Nor Democratic"; Searle, *The Riddle of Malaysian Capitalism*.

116. Jomo K. S., "A Malaysian Middle Class?: Some Preliminary Analytical Considerations", in Jomo K. S. (ed.), *Rethinking Malaysia*, Hong Kong: Asia, 2000.

117. See, for example, R. Milne and D. Mauzy, *Malaysian Politics Under Mahathir*, London: Routledge, 1999.

118. Shamsul A. B., *From British to Bumiputra Rule*, Singapore: ISEAS, 1986.

119. Khoo, "The Grand Vision"; Crouch, "Malaysia: Neither Authoritarian Nor Democratic"; Aziz Zariza Ahmad, *Mahathir's Paradigm Shift*, Taiping: Firma, 1997.

120. Shamsul, *From British to Bumiputra Rule*.

121. Ahmad Atory Hussain, *Pembentukan Dasar Awam Malaysia* [Malaysia's Public Policy Formation], Kuala Lumpur: Utusan Publications, 1985.

122. Shamsul, *From British to Bumiputra Rule*.

123. Khoo, "The Grand Vision"; Crouch, "Malaysia: Neither Authoritarian Nor Democratic".
124. Leigh, "Politics, Bureaucracy, and Business in Malaysia"; Felker, "Political Economy".
125. E. T. Gomez, "Introduction: Political Business in East Asia", in E. T. Gomez (ed.), *Political Business in East Asia*, London: Routledge, 2002; Tan, *Privatization in Malaysia*.
126. See Tan, *Privatization in Malaysia*.

CHAPTER 8

Governance and Development: A Case Study of Pakistan

ISHRAT HUSAIN

Theoretical and empirical evidence from the past two decades shows that socio-economic development is affected by the quality of governance and its institutions. Traditional factors of production (capital, skilled and unskilled labour, and intellectual human capital) obviously contribute to the growth process, but the residual or total factor productivity incorporates not only technical change, but also organisational and institutional change. Well-functioning and healthy institutions not only affect the rate of economic growth but, moreover, the distribution. If governance structures and supporting institutions are healthy, then the distribution of benefits of growth will be equitable. This chapter will argue that the process by which good economic policies and aggregate economic outcomes are translated into an equitable distribution of wealth and benefits involves the institutions of governance. It addresses the following three questions, and then explores the case of governance and development in Pakistan in some detail:

1. Why is good governance crucial for development?
2. What are the critical success factors essential for achieving development and good governance?
3. What are the channels by which governance affects development?

GOOD GOVERNANCE AND DEVELOPMENT

While it may be difficult to agree on a clear definition of governance, there is a wide consensus that good governance enables the state, civil society and private sector to enhance the well-being of a large segment of the population.

According to the World Bank, governance refers to the manner in which public officials and institutions acquire and exercise the authority to shape public policy, and provide public goods and services.[1] Corruption is one outcome of poor governance involving the abuse of public office for private gain. The Asian Development Bank considers the essence of governance to be sound development management. The key dimensions of governance are: public-sector management; accountability; the legal framework for development; information; and transparency.[2] The six core principles identified by Hyden et al. related to good governance are: participation, fairness, decency, accountability, transparency, and efficiency.[3]

Through its research work, the Overseas Development Institute (ODI) has developed a framework for analysing governance and development.[4] According to this framework, the main determinants of governance and development are: historical context, previous regime, socio-cultural context, economic system, and international environment. Under the governance realm falls: civil society, political society, government, bureaucracy, economic society, and judiciary; and under development, outcomes are: political freedoms and rights, human security and welfare, economic growth, human capital, trust, and social cohesion.

Each nation's path to good governance is different and depends on many factors (including culture, geography, political and administrative traditions, and economic conditions). The scope of activities allocated to the public and private sector diverges markedly, but all government share similar responsibilities: they need to establish a basic policy framework, provide critical goods and services, protect and administer the rule of law, and advance social equity. The importance of good governance was highlighted in the 1980s, when developing countries began to feel the adverse effects associated with the over-extension of the state to functions beyond its capacity and capabilities. The concept of "modernisation" that was propagated in the 1950s and 1960s had become synonymous with state-led development. It was argued that where market institutions and local entrepreneurs were weak, only state-owned enterprises (SOEs) were capable of investing in and expanding the economy. The import-substitution industrialisation (ISI) strategy provided the intellectual underpinning of this argument. State intervention took place in the choice of industries and production technologies, monitoring the level of employment, and the determination of input and output prices became a widely accepted policy instrument. Protection against imports – through high tariffs – insulated the SOEs from the competitive pressures of the market, and also generated substantial revenues for the governments themselves. This "inward"-looking strategy was pursued vigorously by a large number of countries in Asia, Latin America and Africa from the 1950s to the 1970s.

Empirical research evaluating the experience of these countries during this period presents persuasive evidence that the "statist" model has done more harm than good to developing countries. "Government failure", rather than "market failure", was pervasive in the developing world. Public bureaucracies were driven by narrow and parochial interests rather than by larger developmental goals. The "soft state" syndrome articulated by Myrdal for Asia, and the "weak state" phenomenon applicable to sub-Saharan Africa, both debunk the myth of a neutral, competent and legitimate state capable of enforcing policy *and* managing enterprises to maximise the collective good of the society.[5] By the end of the 1970s, a serious debt crisis plagued Latin America, dictatorial regimes were mismanaging the economies in Africa, and economic stagnation took root in India, the "statist" model pioneer.

Meanwhile, the success of newly industrialising countries (NICs) – Korea, Taiwan, Singapore and Hong Kong – was demonstrating that opening up a state's economy to the rest of world, and an "outward", export-oriented strategy, could bring about rapid, sustained and shared growth for a majority of people. Interpretations of the success of NICs and East Asia in the 1980s remain highly controversial, even today. Although the state played a pro-active role in these countries, intervening selectively, it avoided the mistakes committed by "statist" model governments whose political leaders and bureaucracy acted haphazardly in their pursuit to control the "commanding heights" of the economy.

The "heavy and over-extended state" model was gradually replaced by a new model in which the state, while continuing to provide infrastructure and promote human development, acted more as a strategist, guide or facilitator for market competition. The domestic private sector was allowed to compete with industrial export markets – protection was avoided. One should note, as Wade points out, that the East Asian economies should be described as "governed markets", rather than either free markets or command economies.[6]

The governance structure in East Asia that led to impressive outcomes was characterised by a public bureaucracy that was, by and large, meritocratic, performance-oriented, hierarchic, and free from political interference. Evans uses the phrase "embedded autonomy" to describe these states.[7] While keeping strong contacts with civil society organisations engaged in social sectors that are crucial to development, these bureaucracies held sufficient authority to maintain a distance from social pressures. Public–private consultations, networks and partnerships were their modes of functioning.[8]

There is now – almost – a consensus that high rates of economic growth can take place without benefiting large segments of the population. Such growth is to be shunned, however, for its inimical effects on social cohesion and political unity of the sub-groups of population living in a country. In addition, spurts of growth that do not leave enduring benefits to a country's population are not of interest. Therefore, the two characteristics we are looking for in a development model are inclusive growth and sustained growth. The combination of these two characteristics would spread the benefits of high economic growth to a vast majority of the population over an extended period of time. Governance is the glue that binds these two characteristics with economic growth, and is critical in producing sustained and inclusive development. How, then, can this development be achieved? This question can be addressed by first identifying critical successful factors that have been associated with sustained and inclusive growth.

CRITICAL SUCCESS FACTORS

A large body of evidence accumulated over the last five decades can be used to arrive at a list of those factors that contribute to a developing country's success in achieving inclusive and sustained growth. Although there is some variation, like a recipe modified for different tastes, there are essential ingredients. These have been summarised by the Commission on Growth and Development (2007) as follows:

1. Participation in the global economy can leverage limited domestic demand and knowledge spillovers can enhance productivity.
2. Decentralised decision-making and market incentives improve efficiency.
3. High levels of savings and investment are needed to sustain growth.
4. Rapid diversification, particularly in the export sector, can provide incremental productive[9] employment.
5. Structural transformation from an agriculture-based economy to a services or industry-based economy is an inevitable part of the development process.
6. Factors of production, particularly labour and skills, should be mobile across sectors and across regions.
7. Rapid urbanisation is an expected outcome of development.
8. A stable and enabling environment is required to attract private investment.
9. Strong political leadership that is effective and pragmatic makes a difference in activist interventions.
10. Development is a long process and takes several decades.
11. The strategies, priorities and role of the government evolve over time and do not remain static.
12. A government that is pragmatic and flexible raises its chances of successfully implementing policies and projects.
13. A focus on inclusive growth combined with persistence and determination can produce desired results.
14. Governments that act in the interests of all the citizens can promote inclusive growth.

In light of these success factors, it is crucial to develop capable and accountable state institutions that can devise and implement sound policies, provide public services, set the rules for regulating the markets, and combat corruption. Although the role of government in a developing nation evolves over time, it is essential to continue demanding better – not less – government. While there is no conclusive evidence that links the size of government with desired development outcomes, there is broad agreement about the key responsibilities of a government:

1. Devise the right strategy from the beginning, but allow for changes and modifications in the course of execution.
2. Stabilise the economy, liberalise trade and prices, and privatise state-owned enterprises.
3. Help create an environment that ensures private firms, farms and businesses thrive.
4. Ensure public investment has a long-term horizon that deals with bottlenecks, removes constraints, and is directed towards infrastructure and education.
5. Develop and strengthen institutions in the judiciary, executive and legislative branches of the government, as well as those involved in supporting markets.
6. Engage leadership in building consensus and practising pro-active communication.

The above listed responsibilities of government are tied to questions about the effectiveness of governance structures in a particular country. Institutions of governance are important: differences in the quality of institutions helps to explain the gap in economic performance between rich and poor nations, and, in the South Asian context, between rich and poor states. In addition, there is some association between institutional quality and the distribution of income – an unequal distribution of income often relates to a lower quality of institutional development.

CHANNELS OF TRANSMISSION

One channel through which governance affects development is the civil service – that is, the quality of civil servants, the incentives facing them, and their accountability for results. The key to achieving high performance lies in attracting, retaining and motivating civil servants of a professional calibre. Also, civil servants should have the authority and power to act on public interest, and be held accountable for wrongdoing such as nepotism, favouritism, corruption, and so on. An effective civil service can be achieved by introducing a merit-based recruitment system, providing opportunities for continuous training and the upgrading of skills, and ensuring equal opportunity in career progression, adequate compensation, proper performance evaluation, financial account-ability and last of all, rule-based compliance.

Another important channel is responsiveness to public demands. The World Bank asserts that governments are more effective when they listen to busi-nesses and citizens, and work in partnerships to decide and implement policy.[10] Where governments lack mechanisms to listen, they are not responsive to people's interests. Decentralisation and the devolution of authority to local tiers of government facilitate the representation of local business and citizens' interests. The visibility of results in a specific locality, made possible by a careful deployment of resources, provides evidence to those living in the area of the government's capacity to address local issues, and, in so doing, will encourage citizens to maintain pressure on government functionaries to act on the relevant local issues. Public–private partnerships, including NGO–public partnerships, have proved effective tools for fostering good governance.

The reality of globalisation in the twenty-first century highlights another channel: governance reforms affect participation in the larger world economy, and thus increase the pace of development. Countries can bring about an improvement in the well-being of their population by successfully competing in the larger world economy through markets, trade, investment and exchange. The state plays an important role in nurturing markets that foster this compe-tition. It should provide information about opportunities to all participants, act against collusion and monopolistic practices, build the capabilities and skills of people engaging in productive activities, set the rules of "the game" in a transparent manner, and last of all, adjudicate and resolve disputes in a fair and equitable manner. For the state to perform these functions, the capacity, competencies and responsiveness of relevant institutions have to be upgraded along with the rules, enforcement mechanisms, organisational structures and incentives.

Is there any evidence that shows a particular form of government to be best-suited to successfully maximise the benefits of governance for its people? In Pakistan, as elsewhere, it has been demonstrated that the nature of the government – whether military, democratically elected, nominated, or selected – has not mattered much. As long as the underlying institutions are working, the form of government remains irrelevant. The challenge of reforming these institutions so that they work as they should is formidable, as vested interests wishing to perpetuate the status quo are politically powerful. Alliances between the political leadership and the beneficiaries of the existing system are very strong. Elected governments, with an eye on electoral cycles, often think in the short-term, and are not in positions to incur the immediate pains from institutional reforms because they are afraid that future gains may be credited to other political parties. Authoritarian governments are not effective because their reforms do not enjoy legitimacy, and, as a result, are not often sustained. Changing institutions is a slow and difficult process requiring, in addition to significant political will, fundamental measures to reduce the opportunity and incentives for particular groups to capture economic rents.

According to Acemoglu and Johnson (2003) good institutions ensure two desirable outcomes: that there is relatively equal access to economic opportunity (a level playing field), and that those who provide labour or capital are appropriately rewarded and their property rights protected.[11]

The above analysis clearly points out that institutions play a critical role in bettering economic performance and ensuring that the distribution of wealth is equitable. I would now like to present case study of Pakistan, to illustrate the relationship between institutions of governance and development.

CASE STUDY OF PAKISTAN

The case of Pakistan makes for an interesting study. Pakistan is one of the few countries that have recorded an impressive growth rate of more than 5 per cent per annum between 1947 and 2007. Only a few developing countries, mainly in Asia, have been able to achieve such high rates of growth over an extended period of time. Pakistan overthrew the "statist" model of development and has pursued an outward-oriented strategy (for the most part) since its independence (except for the 1970s). Despite its stellar record, almost a quarter of the population still lives below the poverty line, and social indicators are among the worst in the developing world. Pakistan ranks 134th among 177 countries on the Human Development Index. Income inequalities, regional disparities and gender differentials have worsened over time. How, then, can this paradoxical situation be explained?

The intermediation process through which good economic policies and economic growth get translated into equitable distribution of benefits involves the institutions of governance. It is the quality, robustness and responsiveness of the institutions of governance that can transmit social and economic policies. The main institutions of governance consist of: (a) the judiciary to protect property rights, and enforce contracts; (b) the legislature to prescribe laws and create a regulatory framework; and (c) the executive to make policies, and supply public goods and services. If access to the institutions of governance is difficult, time-consuming and costly for common citizens, then benefits from economic growth become distributed unevenly, as only those who enjoy preferential access to institutions can gain from them. The 1999 and 2005 Human Development reports on South Asia provide ample evidence to show that unequal access is attributed to poor governance:

> South Asia presents a fascinating combination of many contradictions. It has governments that are high on governing and low on serving; it has parliaments that are elected by the poor but aid the rich; and society that asserts the rights of some but perpetuates exclusion for others. Despite a marked improvement in the lives of a few, there are many in South Asia who have been forgotten by formal institutions of governance. These are the poor, the downtrodden and the most vulnerable of the society, suffering from acute deprivation on account of their income, caste, creed, gender or religion. Their fortunes have not moved with those of the privileged few and this in itself is a deprivation of a depressing nature.[12]

> Governance constitutes (for ordinary people) a due struggle for survival and dignity. Ordinary people are too often humiliated at the hands of public institutions. For them, lack of good governance means police brutality, corruption in accessing basic public services, ghost schools, teachers' absenteeism, missing medicines, high cost of and low access to justice, criminalisation of politics and lack of social justice. These are just few manifestations of the crisis of governance.[13]

Access to justice is a major problem for the poor. In the convention on "The Judiciary and the Poor", organised by the Campaign for Judicial Accountability and Reforms in India, but also apt in the case of Pakistan, a telling description is presented:

> The judiciary of the country is not functioning as an instrument to provide justice to the vast majority of the people in the country. On the other hand, most of the judiciary appears to be working in the interest of wealthy corporate interests, which are today controlling the entire ruling establishment of the country. Thus, more often than not, its orders today have the effect of depriving the poor of their rights, [rather] than restoring their rights, which are being rampantly violated by the powerful and the State. [The judicial system] cannot be accessed without lawyers ... And the poor cannot afford lawyers. In fact, a poor person accused of an offence has no hope of defending himself in the present judicial system and is condemned to its mercy.[14]

Why have these institutions – judiciary, legislature and executive – deteriorated and failed to deliver to the poor? A history of governance in Pakistan will shed some light on this question.

HISTORY OF GOVERNANCE IN PAKISTAN

At the time of its independence, Pakistan inherited a well-functioning judiciary, civil service and military, but a relatively weak legislature. Over time, the affairs of the state became dominated by the civil service and military, disrupting the evolution of democratic political processes and further weakening the legislative organ of the state. The judiciary, with few exceptions, plodded along, sanctifying the dominant role of the military and the civil service.

The institutions inherited from British rule were relevant during the time before independence; however, they failed to adapt themselves to meet the new challenges of development and social change of a newly independent country. The "business as usual" mode of functioning was the approach used by incumbents holding top- and middle-level positions in the bureaucracy, and this did not endear them to political leaders or the general public. Several commissions and committees were consequently formed during the twenty-five years following independence, in an attempt to reform administrative structures and civil services. Some changes to improve the efficiency of the secretariats were introduced during by the regime of Ayub Khan, president of Pakistan during the 1960s; however, at the same time, personalised decision-making and a favouring of centralised controls also occurred. The reluctance to grant provincial autonomy to East Pakistan – the most populous province of the country yet physically remote from the hub of decision-making (Islamabad) – led to a serious political backlash and eventual break-up of the country into two independent nations.

In 1973, a populist government headed by Zulfikar Ali Bhutto took the first step to breaking the steel frame of the civil services by taking away the constitutional guarantee of job security. Furthermore, he demolished the exclusive and privileged role of the civil service of Pakistan (CSP) within the overall structure of the public service.

However, the next twenty-five years witnessed a significant decline in the quality of new recruits to the civil services, as the trade-off between job security and low compensation ceased to operate and the private sector – including multinational corporations – expanded, offering more attractive career opportunities. The erosion of real wages in the public-sector led to low morale, little motivation, inefficiency, and a resorting to corrupt practices among civil servants at all levels. In real terms, the compensation paid to higher civil servants was only a half that of the 1994 package. The abuse of discretionary powers, bureaucratic obstruction and delay tactics became commonplace for government functionaries as a means to supplement their pay. Low wages also meant that the civil service no longer attracted the most talented young men and women. To maintain their positions and associated higher status, some long-serving members of the civil services became identified with a political party, and thus integrated into corrupt political regimes that rewarded them as per Pakistan's political culture of patronage. During the 1990s, each time one political party replaced another, changes in the top bureaucracy usually followed. The informal political affiliations of those in the bureaucracy resulted in a civil service that was no longer impartial, neutral, competent and responsive to the needs of the common man. Loyalty to the ministers, chief ministers and prime minister took priority over accountability to the general public. The frequent take-overs by military regimes, and the consequent screening of hundreds of civil servants, led to a bureaucracy subservient to military rulers, the erosion of the authority of traditional institutions of governance, and a loss in initiative among the higher bureaucracy.

The devolution plan, outlining a strategy of devolution and decentralisation combined with the creation of a local government system, was unveiled by President Pervez Musharraf's military regime in 2001, dealing the civil service another major blow as the commissioners, deputy commissioners (DC) and assistant commissioners (AC) were abolished, and the authority of the district administration was transferred to elected *Nazims*, (co-ordinators of cities that are similar to mayors but more powerful). To ordinary citizens, the government was most tangibly embodied in these commissioners; it was the DC and AC that they approached on a daily basis for the redress of their grievances against government departments and their functionaries. The substitution of the civil servant by an elected head of administration is quite a new phenomenon and it will take some time before the effectiveness of this change can be judged. While this transition takes place, the checks and balances implicit in the previous administrative set-up have become redundant as the DC and AC controlled the excesses committed by the police. Now, the police have assumed greater clout and, consequently, the opportunities for collusion with the *nazims* have multiplied, and in many instances, alienated common citizens and diluted the impartiality of the administration at the grassroots levels. The sanctity of private property rights has been threatened in several cases when the *nazims* have given orders to make unauthorised changes in the land ownership records, usually in rural areas, in collusion with government functionaries, often to benefit them-selves and their cronies. The district administration has yet to grow as an auton-omous institution, as it is challenged by the central administration and suffers from inequitable resource distribution.

Instead of becoming stronger and more responsive over time, the institu-tional infrastructure of Pakistan's governance has outlived its usefulness. Human resource intake and motivation is poor; career progression does not depend on competence and performance, but on keeping the political bosses satisfied; pay and compensation packages are out of sync with the rising cost of living; business processes are outdated; performance appraisal is perfunctory; and use of modern technology is limited. Furthermore, the courts are congested with a backlog of cases stretching back several decades, while police investigations and prosecutions are often corrupt. Simultaneously, the legislature has been suspended several times before completing its due tenure, with many members heavily indulging in their social privileges. Laws passed by the legislature, devised to help the poor, have not been fully implemented.

Transparency and accountability mechanisms have grown weak since Pakistan's independence. Excessive discretionary powers, the violation of established rules and a diversion of public resources for private profits are the norm. Accountability mechanisms are used selectively to win over the opponents of the ruling parties or the military regimes; alternatively, they are used to coerce them in the event that they refuse to support certain projects.

The culprits of corruption, whether in the bureaucracy or political office, have, by and large, remained unscathed. The use of accountability for political manoeuvring has brought the very idea into disrepute in public eyes – even serious and genuine attempts to bring the corrupt to justice are met with scepticism, scorn and ridicule.

The ruling elites, still under the influence of patron-lineage dating back to the feudal landowning systems which resisted modern mechanisms of governance and notions of civil society out of a preference for traditional systems of tribal loyalty, have used public offices for their personal and familial enrichment. In the absence of transparency and accountability, these elites appoint their cronies and confidantes to key departments, and often divert resources away from the general public and towards themselves and their benefactors. As a result of these practices, on a daily basis, poor people are unable to access health clinics, schools or other essential services because they cannot pay bribes and do not have the connections or influence to demand access to these basic public goods and services. Complaints and grievances to higher-ups remain unattended because it is they who are the direct beneficiaries of this system. Corruption and weak governance often mean that public resources that should have created opportunities for poor families to escape poverty, enrich corrupt elites.

How, then, can these institutions be revitalised? The government of former President Pervez Musharraf, realising the gravity of the situation and unsatisfied with the slow trickledown effect of economic growth, appointed a National Commission on Government Reforms (NCGR) in May 2006, with a mandate to develop a governance reform agenda for Pakistan.

REFORM AGENDA FOR PAKISTAN

A governance reform agenda should be designed to restructure government and revitalise institutions so that the state actualises some of its most important functions: the provision of basic services – education, health, water sanitation and security – to citizens in an effective and efficient manner, and to promote inclusive markets in which all citizens have an equal opportunity to participate. A restructuring process should minimise corruption, ensure public order, guarantee security of life and property, lower transaction costs, and provide market access without frictions by curtailing the arbitrary exercising of discretionary powers and reducing over-taxation.

A competitive private sector has to be nurtured and relied upon to achieve sustained economic growth. Therefore, one of the major reforms in Pakistan has focused on creating space for the growth of new entrants in the private sector; this has usually been done by removing existing constraints created by the state and then ensuring the smooth operation of new entrants. Pakistan is one of the few South Asian countries that ranks highly on World Bank indicators for ease of doing business. The pursuit of policies of liberalisation, deregulation, de-licensing and disinvestment during the last fifteen years has brought about significant improvements for economic agents, domestic as well as foreign.

Despite this, the overbearing burden of government intervention at lower levels in the business life-cycle continues to loom large. Numerous difficulties face new businesses: acquiring, titling, pricing, transferring and possessing of land transactions; obtaining no-objection certificates from various agencies; getting water and gas connections, sewerage facilities, reliable electricity supply and access to roads; securing finances for greenfield projects; and using emerging technologies. The powers of inspectors from various departments and agencies are vast, and they can often determine the success of a business. The growing trend towards "informalisation" of the economy, particularly by small and medium enterprises, is best explained by the still dominant nature of the government at the local tiers: small and medium enterprises are reluctant to participate in a formal economy subject to government rules that are restrictive. More than 96 per cent of businesses documented in the Economic Census of 2005 fall into the "informal" category. While national policies are quite investor-friendly, the attitude of middle and lower functionaries of the government (in the provinces and districts) towards private business remains unwelcoming. Functionaries harass businesses in order to extract pecuniary and non-pecuniary benefits for themselves, and are distrustful, hesitant or even hostile towards private entrepreneurs. As a result, new entrant businesses must deal with multiple agencies, pass a high number of clearances and avoid delays, resulting in high costs. Unless the powers of officials working with small- and medium-scale businesses are curbed, competitive forces will not improve. Additionally, reforms to upgrade the quality and level of these officials should be implemented.

Another major area of reform is accountability. There is both too much and too little accountability of those involved in public affairs in Pakistan. On the one hand, too much emphasis on the ritualistic compliance with procedures and rules has taken the place of substantive concerns about the results and outcomes for welfare and justice. Also, a plethora of laws and institutions, such as the Anti-Corruption Bureaus, National Accountability Bureau, Auditor General's reports, Public Accounts Committees of the legislature, and the Ombudsman system, have created an atmosphere of fear, causing a lack of decision-making among civil servants. In addition, instances of rampant corruption, malpractice, nepotism, favouritism, waste and inefficiency have become common in the administrative culture of the country.

Transparency can be introduced by simplifying codification of laws, updating rules and regulations, and making use of e-governance tools. Dynamic websites and information kiosks would ensure wide dissemination of information about government activities. Creating online access to government functionaries aids citizens in carrying out hassle-free transactions. Further online access helps to publicise government activities and, in so doing, encourages the government to adhere to its own accountability standards. Strong pressure from advocacy groups, organised by civil society, can be applied to the media, political parties and private sector, and think tanks can also compel government departments and ministries to become more accountable for results.

A final area of reform must tackle the size, structure and scope of the federal, provincial and local governments. The division of responsibilities between different tiers of the government must be clarified and better delineated. The elongated hierarchy within ministries needs to be trimmed, and the relationship between a ministry, executive departments and autonomous bodies must be redefined. This area of reform includes reviewing the skills, incentives and competencies of civil servants. Entire human-resource policy, from recruitment to compensation, requires review and redesign.

The governance reform agenda outlined above cannot be implemented as if it were a technical exercise, because it is political, taking into account the existing power relationships in which the polity is rooted. Balancing the diverse interests of various stakeholders involves many politically difficult choices. The sustainability of reforms requires broad consultation, consensus-building and the effective communication of a long-term vision. Concerns, criticism and scepticism of citizens should be addressed. There will undoubtedly be adverse effects from the scope, phasing, timing, implementation strategies and mitigation measures of the reforms, and these effects should be widely discussed and debated. If events do not proceed the way they were conceptualised, corrective actions should be taken in the light of feedback received. Instruments that may be used for receiving regular feedback about the impact of reforms on society include citizens' charters, citizens' surveys and report cards, citizens' panels and focus groups.

Care should also be taken to ensure that governance reforms are not perceived by citizens to be driven by external donors. Resistance towards governance reforms by internal constituencies is quite strong to begin with; and as the argument that externally motivated reforms ignore context (and are therefore unsuitable) quickly gains currency and stiffens resistance, any indication that reforms are being carried out under external pressure will lead to their failure. There should be no harm, however, in looking at the successful experiences of other countries, gaining insights and learning lessons that can be tailored and applied to Pakistan.

CONCLUSION

This chapter has tried to address questions concerning governance and development, and has demonstrated that the Pakistan paradox – rapid economic growth combined with poor social indicators, poverty and inequality – can be explained by looking at the institutions of governance. The overall governance structure through which social and economic policies are intermediated has become corroded and dysfunctional, blocking the transmission of benefits of growth to a significant segment of the population. Starting with fairly sound institutions following its independence, there has been a gradual deterioration in the capacity of Pakistani institutions to deliver public goods and services equitably. Waste and corruption induced by patronage, and privileges exercised by the ruling elites, have created a large wedge in the distribution of economic gains; there is differential growth between different classes and regions. The manner in which the ruling elite continue to control institutions leaves the poor without adequate access to institutions whose very purpose is to serve them. A reform agenda has, therefore, been developed to strengthen these institutions of governance, and to ensure that rapid economic growth is enjoyed by all peoples of Pakistan.

FURTHER READING

J. E. Campos and H. L. Root, *The Key to the Asian Miracle*, Washington, DC: Brookings Institution Press, 1996.

W. Cline, "Can the East Asian Model of Development be Generalised?", *World Development*, vol. 10, no. 2, 1982, pp. 81–90.

International Monetary Fund, "Chapter III. Building Institutions", *World Economic Outlook: Building Institutions*, Washington, DC: IMF, 2005.

R. Islam and C. Montenegro, "What Determines the Quality of Institutions?", *World Bank Policy Research Working Paper No. 2764*, Washington, DC, 2002.

D. Kaufmann, A. Kraay and P. Zoid-Lobaton, "Governance Matters", *World Bank Policy Research Working Paper No. 2196*, Washington DC, 1999.

S. Knack and B. Keefer, "Why Don't Poor Countries Catch-up? A Cross-National Test of Institutional Explanation", *Economic Inquiry*, vol. 35, no. 3, 1997, pp. 590–602.

D. Rodrik, A. Subramian and F. Trebbiu, "Institutions Rule: The Primacy of Institutions Over Geography and Integration in Economic Development", *Journal of Economic Growth*, vol. 9, no. 2, 2004, pp. 131–65.

World Bank, "The East Asia Miracle: Economic Growth and Public Policy", *World Bank Policy Research Report*, New York: Oxford University Press, 1993.

World Bank, "Building Institutions for Markets", *World Development Report*, New York: Oxford University Press, 2002.

NOTES

1. The World Bank, *Governance and Development*, Washington, DC: World Bank, 1992.
2. Asian Development Bank, *Governance: Promoting Sound Development Management*, Manila: A.D.B., 1997.
3. G. Hyden, J. Court and K. Mease, *Making Sense of Governance*, Boulder, CO: Lynne Rienner Publishers, 2004.
4. ODI, *Governance, Development and Effectiveness: ODI Briefing Paper*, London: ODI, March, 2006.
5. G. Mydal, *Asian Drama, An Inquiry into the Poverty of Nations*, New York: Pantheon, 1968.
6. R. Wade, *Governing the Market: Economic Theory and the Role of Government in East Asian Industrialisation*, Princeton, NJ: Princeton University Press, 1990.
7. P. Evans, P., *Embedded Autonomy: States and Industrial Transformation*, Princeton, NJ: Princeton University Press, 1995.
8. Public–Private partnerships are a common formal way of doing business, while networks and partnerships are informal.
9. Employment that raises productivity in the economy.
10. The World Bank, *World Development Report: The State in a Changing World*, Washington, DC: World Bank, 1997.
11. D. Acemoglu and S. Johnson, "Unbundling Institutions", NBER Working Paper 9934 , Cambridge, MA: NBER, 2002.
12. *Human Development in South Asia Report*, Karachi: Oxford University Press, 1999.
13. *Human Development in South Asia Report*, Karachi: Oxford University Press, 2005.
14. J. Naqvi, "Time to judge the Judiciary?", *Dawn*, Karachi, 28 February 2008.

CHAPTER 9

Is "Good Governance" an Appropriate Model for Governance Reforms? The Relevance of East Asia for Developing Muslim Countries

MUSHTAQ KHAN

INTRODUCTION

Governance is what states do, and since states play a vital role in the development process, almost all economists can agree that governance must be important for development. The growing recognition within mainstream economics that governance is important, is simply a belated recognition within economic orthodoxy that the state plays a critical role even in a market-oriented society. The controversy and debate is about what the feasible governance capabilities are of a poor country attempting to develop in a global market with an essentially market-oriented economy. The answer to this is not as obvious as it may seem. The answer provided by the good-governance approach is based on a theoretical understanding of a market economy that is contested by many economists supporting the construction of a market-oriented economy. But most significantly, the good-governance approach ignores the feasibility of achieving these governance capabilities in poor countries, and therefore overlooks alternative methods of overcoming the obstacles and constraints that are preventing many developing countries from fully participating in and benefiting from the global economy.

Markets are simply mechanisms for private contracting. The good-governance reform agenda is based on the presumption that efficient markets are achievable in developing countries, and are sufficient for achieving sustained growth and development. These presumptions are derived from a specific reading of institutional economics that is plausible in theoretical terms, even though many of the theoretical links that it asserts can be strongly challenged in terms of alternative readings of orthodox economic theory. The specific claim of good-governance theory is that while market failures in developing countries can be serious, the best way to address these failures is by improving the efficiency of the market through good-governance reforms. The experience of intervention to correct market failures in most developing countries after they became independent from colonial powers left a lot to be desired. Even though most of these countries did better after independence than they had under colonial rule, many eventually began to run into fiscal and banking-sector problems by the 1970s. These problems were often the result of inadequate governance capabilities to manage their interventions properly, resulting, for instance, in attempts to accelerate industrialisation with subsidies for infant industries without adequate performance standards being enforced.

A perception developed within mainstream economics through the 1980s that while there were indeed market failures, the cost of government failures when states attempted to correct market failures in these ways was likely to be greater than the cost of the initial market failure itself.[1] Initially, the policy consensus was that the role of the government should be reduced, but it eventually became clear that even this was inadequate because the market failures remained significant. The good-governance reform agenda emerged to address this problem from a different angle. Instead of trying to improve the governance capabilities that would enable developing countries to directly correct market failures, the good-governance agenda argued that if the government could create the conditions for markets to work efficiently, then market failure would be indirectly reduced and, with it, would the need for specific interventions to address these market failures.

The argument that was now developed was that market failure happens primarily because developing countries do not have well-defined property rights, a rule of law to adjudicate conflicts, and a state that is restrained from expropriation and rent creation. All of these features of developing country markets raise the "transaction costs" of trying to agree on and enforce contracts in markets, and this is the ultimate source of the market failure that developing countries suffer from. So if governance reforms could reduce these transaction costs by, for instance, improving the definition of property rights and the rule of law, and reducing corruption and expropriation in the economy, then market failures would be significantly reduced, and private contracting would be able to allocate resources efficiently and drive growth and poverty-reduction in these countries.

This is why the good-governance reform agenda can be described as an agenda for market-enhancing governance.[2] It is certainly theoretically plausible. The question is whether it is a practical route to governance reform in developing countries. Can these reforms be implemented to an extent that will significantly increase market efficiency, and will this improvement in market efficiency be sufficient to drive economic growth and broad-based development? One way to answer these questions is to look for any historical evidence of countries that followed good-governance reforms and achieved *as a result* sustained growth and development. Despite the strong correlation between high per capita incomes and market-enhancing governance, the evidence is much shakier when we begin to look for countries that first undertook good-governance reforms *and then* achieved growth and development. The absence of any significant evidence of such a trajectory should raise doubts about the plausibility of the underlying theory, even if it appears plausible a priori.

In fact, the weakness of the available evidence leads us to suggest that the theory underpinning good-governance theory is not actually plausible because these reforms are difficult to implement in the absence of a significant social surplus and therefore the prior existence of a sufficiently productive economy, for reasons that we will briefly explain later. In contrast, the empirical evidence, such as it is, strongly suggests that actual developing countries did not follow such a route on their way to prosperity. Instead, they had a variety of other governance capabilities that allowed them to sustain growth by addressing specific market failures, and we describe these capacities as growth-enhancing governance capabilities. The contemporary reform agenda is, therefore, in real danger of setting vulnerable developing countries unachievable tasks and inadvertently furthering the frustration and despair that often already exists. In many Muslim countries, frustration with reform agendas that create social disruption and pain without leading to any observable improvements in developmental prospects has already contributed to disillusionment with many governments, and this process can only deepen if these strategies continue to be followed without any critical interrogation of their empirical and theoretical roots.

Market-enhancing versus Growth-enhancing Governance

The contemporary consensus about the governance requirements for development is based on the underlying assumption that efficient markets are the most important requirement for achieving development. The governance agenda underpinning this is a strategy of developing market-enhancing conditions.[3] The common feature of these governance reforms is to make markets more efficient by reducing market transaction costs. In theory, all market failures are ultimately due to transaction costs that prevent potentially beneficial private contracts from being executed. And therefore, again in theory, if transaction costs across-the-board could really be significantly reduced, then specific interventions to correct market failures would become unnecessary.

These arguments build on a number of selectively chosen links established by New Institutional Economics and the New Political Economy. The major links are summarised in Figure 1. It is important to note that these are by no means uncontested links, even in terms of mainstream institutional theories,

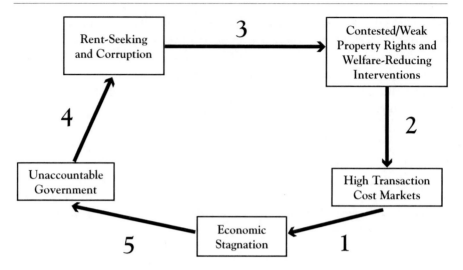

Figure 1. Theoretical Links in the Good-governance Agenda

but these are nevertheless the links that are emphasised in the new consensus. Link 1 is the claim that economic stagnation is ultimately due to high-transaction-cost markets, or, in other words, market failures.[4] This link can be a tautology, however, because all missed opportunities for development can be defined as market failures. The debate is, in fact, between two very different approaches to dealing with market failures. The first, and more conventional, approach is to identify specific market failures that are particularly important in specific contexts, and to address these with appropriate solutions, as well as, where necessary, the development of specific governance capabilities for their implementation. The second approach implicitly adopted by good-governance theory is to argue that piecemeal corrections of market failures are unnecessary if generic improvements in market efficiency through good-governance reforms can be achieved.

Link 2 shows the innovation of the new good-governance agenda, which argues that instead of addressing these market failures individually, the recommendation is to try and make markets across-the-board more efficient by addressing the underlying causes of market failure, namely weak property rights, weak rule of law and arbitrary interventions.[5] The theory here is that markets are essentially systems of contracts and that, if the absence of clear expectations and rights prevent contracting, then market failure will follow by definition. But why do high-transaction-cost markets characterise every developing country? Instead of looking at the full range of possible explanations, in particular the cost of establishing efficient markets even to the extent that we find them in advanced countries, Link 3 asserts that unstable property rights, poor rule of law and expropriation by states are primarily the result of small groups engaging in rent-seeking and corruption.[6]

Finally, the good-governance approach has to explain why corruption and rent-seeking appear to be widespread in every developing country, particularly given the significant negative effects attributed to them. Once again, the good-governance approach identifies a selective set of reasons, not the full range that contemporary theory has identified. In particular, as Link 4 shows, the approach asserts that small corrupt groups can profit from rent-seeking and corruption at the expense of the majority because government accountability is weak or non-existent.[7] In fact, rent-seeking is widespread in all societies, including advanced ones. As Stiglitz and others have pointed out, rents are an essential part of the normal operation of market economies, as well as being the subject of redistributive politics without which societies would not survive politically.[8] It follows, therefore, that rent-seeking is an essential element in all societies.

The good-governance approach does not ask the important questions: namely, why some rent-seeking creates rents that are particularly damaging, while other countries appear to have rent-seeking that sustains growth-enhancing rents. It also does not ask why poor countries appear to have significantly greater illegal rent-seeking which is an important component of corruption, while rich countries appear to be able to legalise and regulate a greater part of rent-seeking.[9] Link 5 completes the cycle for the good-governance approach because economic stagnation, in turn, prevents the poor from mobilising and enables autocracy to continue.

On the basis of these theoretical links, the good-governance agenda argues that it is necessary to complement liberalisation and other market reforms with a simultaneous set of governance reforms that include improvements in the rule of law, defining and protecting property rights better, fighting corruption and rent-seeking, and embedding democracy and decentralisation. As we have already argued, the power of the good-governance agenda has been that many of these reforms are perceived by many civil society groups in developing countries as goals that are desirable in themselves. The issue of concern for us is not whether these goals should be abandoned, but rather whether they are achievable in developing countries to an extent that they can form the basis of a poverty-reduction and development agenda.

The problem for the good-governance agenda is that these are not the only theoretical links that can explain the persistence of patron–client politics, autocracy, corruption, weak rule of law and contested property rights in developing countries. We will not, here, review the alternative theoretical arguments explaining these phenomena in poor countries, as this has already been done elsewhere.[10] The pertinent issue for us now is that even if the theoretical links asserted in the good-governance argument are partially relevant, there is little evidence that good-governance sets *achievable* governance goals for poor countries. Indeed, no poor country appears to achieve high scores in these governance capabilities, regardless of their economic performance and development strategies.

It is important to reiterate that the importance of markets in fostering and enabling economic development is not in question. Economic development is likely to be more rapid if markets mediating resource allocation (in any country) become more efficient. The development debate is, instead, about the extent to which markets can be made efficient in developing countries, and whether maximising the efficiency of markets (to the degree that is achievable) is sufficient to maximise the pace of development. The alternative approach to governance argues not that markets should be supplanted, but rather that they will remain inherently inefficient in developing countries in the foreseeable future due to certain limitations in the structural characteristics of the economy that will always remain until a substantial degree of development is achieved.

Given the possibility that there are structural factors preventing markets achieving significant efficiency, it follows that successful development requires critical governance capacities to address specific market failures. This is a very different reform agenda compared to the good-governance one that presumes that effective, across-the-board market efficiency can be achieved through this route. In fact, the historical evidence strongly suggests that successful developing countries did not achieve across-the-board market efficiency through good-governance reforms, but rather had governance capabilities to correct market failures that were specific to their development strategies and social requirements.

In particular, the evidence of successful East Asian developers of the last five decades shows that the governance capacities that mattered were very different from the good-governance capabilities. In terms of the market-enhancing conditions prioritised by the good-governance approach, East Asian states often performed rather poorly. Democratic accountability was typically low, corruption was high and property rights were typically not well-defined.[11] Instead, these states had effective institutions that could accelerate growth in conditions of technological backwardness and high transaction costs. To distinguish these governance capabilities from the good-governance ones, we define these developmental governance capabilities as growth-enhancing governance.

Growth is clearly not sufficient for broad-based development, but sustaining growth is a necessary part of achieving sustainable development. Without growth, broad-based development is arithmetically impossible unless the country is already very rich in per capita terms and the only thing required is redistribution. On the other hand, if broad-based development cannot be achieved in line with growth, a growth strategy can become politically unsustainable. The capacity to correct critical market failures constraining development, therefore, to a large extent, requires governance capabilities to sustain growth, and these capacities are a necessary component of developmental capabilities. The broader political and redistributive institutions that sustain growth and ensure that it is broad-based can differ from country to country, but no country has achieved broad-based development without sustaining relatively high growth for long periods of time.[12]

Box 1 (overleaf) summarises the main characteristics of governance emphasised in these two contrasting approaches. Market-enhancing governance is about setting up effective institutions that can achieve across-the-board enforcement of property rights, enforce a rule of law, limit corruption and rent-seeking and achieve political accountability. This is essentially the "good governance" agenda. In theory, these capabilities would allow the developing country to achieve rapid growth and development, but we will see that this expectation is unlikely to be borne out because the implementation of these governance goals is virtually impossible to any significant effect in poor countries. If progress on immediately achieving market-enhancing governance is likely to be very limited, growth and development may depend on the achievement of a much more targeted set of governance capabilities that enable the overcoming of specific market failures and constraints that stand in the way of growth. Therefore, what we describe as a growth-enhancing governance agenda would try to identify and set up institutional capabilities that are effective in addressing critical market failures that are relevant for a particular developing country at a particular stage of its development. The range of capabilities here are clearly much broader, and the relevant market failures that need to be addressed – and which can feasibly *be* addressed – may be different in different countries.

Depending on the initial conditions, it may only be feasible to develop effective growth-enhancing governance capabilities to a much more limited extent in some countries compared with others. But given that it is most unlikely that across-the-board enforcement of property rights and a rule of law can be effective enough to achieve low transaction costs and efficient markets (which the market-enhancing governance agenda wants to achieve), it is important to have some institutions that can assist investors and developers to acquire land and other resources in a context of otherwise high transaction costs. Similarly, institutions that can address failures in labour markets by providing or financing labour upskilling in an effective way, backed by appropriate governance capabilities to ensure that the country achieves and maintains global competitiveness in at least some sectors, can be critical for sustaining its growth rate. The same applies to institutions that address some of the critical capital market failures in developing countries, given that across-the-board improvements in capital

Box 1 Market-enhancing versus Growth-enhancing Governance Capabilities

The dominant "good governance" reforms aim to promote governance capabilities that are **market-enhancing:** *they aim to make markets more efficient by reducing transaction costs. To the extent that these reforms can be implemented, they are likely to improve market outcomes in developing countries. Transaction costs are the costs of using markets to allocate resources. A fundamental requirement of efficient (low-transaction-cost) markets is that property rights should be well-defined and well-protected, and for there to be a good rule of law so that contracts can be easily and cheaply enforced.*

The key market-enhancing governance goals are to set up institutions that:

- Protect and maintain stable property rights
- Enforce a rule of law and effective contract enforcement
- Minimise rent seeking and corruption
- Achieve a transparent and accountable provision of public goods in line with democratically expressed preferences

However, there are structural problems that prevent a significant implementation of such a strategy in poor countries. Given these constraints, growth can require more targeted strategies whose implementation requires specific governance capabilities that we describe as growth-enhancing governance capabilities.

Growth-enhancing *governance capabilities are capabilities that allow developing countries to cope with the property-right instability of early development, manage technological catching-up, and maintain political stability in a context of endemic and structural reliance on patron–client politics.*
Key growth-enhancing governance goals are to set up institutions that can:

- Organise transfers of land and resources to productive sectors in a context where land and asset markets are generally inefficient
- Address labour market failures that result in inadequate training and investment in human capital
- Address failures in capital markets that result in inadequate savings and investment, and inadequate investment in learning and adopting new technologies
- Maintain political stability and acceptable redistributive justice in a context of rapid social transformation

market efficiency can take decades to achieve. If narrowly focused financing institutions can provide financing and risk-sharing for critical growth sectors and social sectors in a context of generally high transaction costs, and provided (growth-enhancing) governance capabilities can be developed to effectively operate these financing institutions, the effects for sustaining growth and development can be significant.

This is why identifying the necessary growth-enhancing governance capabilities and selecting the ones that can be feasibly and effectively developed in a particular country is extremely important to sustain growth and development at the highest feasible level. The growth-enhancing institutions that will be most appropriate, and the optimal scale on which they can operate, will be different in different countries because of differences in their initial conditions. Clearly, the total absence of such institutions, or the attempt to construct institutions that cannot effectively implement the growth strategies they are trying to implement, will result in lost growth opportunities.

The two sets of governance capabilities are not necessarily mutually exclusive, but the distinction between them is important, particularly if an exclusive focus on achieving market-enhancing governance capabilities diminishes the capacity of states to develop growth-enhancing governance capabilities. In particular, if structural economic and political factors prevent the achievement of market-enhancing governance capabilities to a significant extent, a focus on trying to achieve these will be particularly frustrating for poor countries because the effort will not pay off in terms of higher or more sustainable growth and is likely, eventually, to be abandoned, with significant economic and political consequences.

Market failures in land, labour and capital markets that constrain growth in developing countries are, of course, widely acknowledged in economic theory. In the period up to the 1980s, the consensus within economics was that states in developing countries needed to intervene to correct these market failures to promote development. Indeed, the interventionist policies of many developing countries in industrial policy, trade policy, and so on, were often justified in terms of addressing these market failures. However, it was not recognised at the time that the correction of market failures required specific governance capabilities for managing these interventions. These are the capabilities that we have described as growth-enhancing governance capabilities. The absence of effective growth-enhancing governance capabilities in many countries trying to overcome market failures during this period led to significant government failures because the short-term benefits of subsidies and interventions were captured by powerful interests who then failed to deliver productivity growth or new investments. Dissatisfaction with the results of intervention led to the counter-revolution within economics in the 1980s and the abandonment of intervention to correct market failures in many developing countries.[13]

However, the wholesale abandonment of attempts to correct market failures is increasingly recognised as an over-reaction and a mistake (Stiglitz 2007).[14] A more appropriate response may have been to focus on a less ambitious set of corrections for market failures and the development of appropriate governance capabilities for managing these corrections. Instead, the consensus in the 1980s and 1990s abandoned piecemeal corrections to market failures and shifted to a much more ambitious strategy of fixing market failures across the board through market-enhancing (good-governance) reforms. Initially, the policy shift was in the direction of the structural adjustment strategies of the 1980s, where the aim was primarily to reduce the scope of the state, but by the 1990s the consensus had shifted to the good-governance agenda summarised in Figure 1.

Unfortunately, the case-study evidence shows that developmental success in poor and emerging countries has always been based on very specific governance capabilities to address critical market failures. A significant part of the asset and resource reallocations necessary for accelerating development in developing countries have taken place through non-market processes, or market processes assisted by administrative and political measures, precisely because markets remain essentially inefficient in early stages of development regardless of attempts to make them otherwise. Examples of non-market asset transfers that were significant in underpinning growth processes include the English Enclosures from the sixteenth to the eighteenth centuries; the creation of the *chaebol* in South Korea in the 1960s, using public resources; the creation of the Chinese TVEs using public resources in the 1980s and their privatisation in the 1990s; and the allocation and appropriation of public land and resources for development in Thailand. Successful developers have displayed a range of institutional and political capacities that enabled semi-market and non-market asset and property-right reallocations that were growth-enhancing, thereby indirectly addressing failures in land and capital markets. In contrast, in less successful developers, the absence of necessary governance capabilities meant that non-market transfers descended more frequently into predatory expropriation that impeded development. In these countries, government failures prevented the resolution of critical market failures.

Labour market failures that prevent adequate investment in training and skills acquisition are also well known, and these are also unlikely to be adequately addressed through improvements in good-governance. In fact, successful developing countries did not wait to solve their skills and training problems while attempting to achieve good-governance. Yet they were able to finance public investments in skill-acquisition significantly. Even more importantly, they had the governance capabilities to ensure that these investments would not be wasted on training of indifferent quality that would fail to raise productivity and global competitiveness. The lesson for developing countries that are trying to improve their developmental performance should have been to learn the governance capabilities in more successful countries that ensured the success of specific strategies to deal with critical labour market failures.

In addition, we know that the most successful developers also had strategies for addressing market failures in capital markets that keep savings rates low and prevent investment in many sectors because of inadequate arrangements for risk-sharing. Institutional failures, poor contracting and weak state enforcement capacities combine to keep savings rates very low in most developing countries. More seriously, the absence of effective institutions to share risk constrains technology adoption and learning in poor countries.[15] Attempting to construct efficient capital markets through good-governance is, at best, a very partial solution because improvements are unlikely to be sufficient or have a significant impact through this route. Moreover, private investors absorbing large amounts of risk are not likely to be interested in investing in the types of simple low-return technologies where learning primarily needs to be financed to achieve broad-based development in poor countries. This is why the historical evidence also shows that countries that were good at catching up had governance capabilities to address these market failures directly in order to raise savings and investments rates, and to incubate and support learning industries alongside effective conditions and exit strategies.[16]

There is no question that interventions to correct market failures in many developing countries achieved disappointing results in the past. However, if the wholesale improvement of market efficiency through good-governance reforms is an unachievable chimera, then the only realistic option for developing countries is to revisit their own experiences and ask what went wrong. In general, poorly performing developing countries in the 1960s had poor growth-enhancing governance capabilities. Compared to their actual capabilities, they adopted massively ambitious strategies of intervention that could not be properly managed. Here, the link between governance capabilities and political constraints within specific countries comes to the fore. Political realities mean that interventionist strategies that worked in one country are not necessarily enforceable in another. This is also why, when we look at strategies for correcting market failures and the governance capabilities that allowed this, we find significant differences even between successful countries.

The diversity of the experience of successful catching-up in Asia tells us that it is important that strategies for correcting market failure have to be backed by effective governance capabilities that enable the particular mechanisms through which market failures are being addressed to be effectively implemented. Where political conditions and initial institutional capabilities are strong, governance capabilities for effectively managing significant corrections of market failure are feasible. But in countries where the initial institutional and political conditions are not appropriate for extensive growth-enhancing interventions, the feasible range of interventions will have to be narrower. Moreover, success even in a narrow range of interventions may require developing specific growth-enhancing governance capabilities.[17]

At the very least, we can assert that the successful East Asian countries did not demonstrate the achievement of good-governance defined as market-enhancing governance *before* their growth take-offs. Moreover, in no case was there even a commitment to good-governance as it is currently defined, as a precondition for achieving sustainable development. In the next section we will examine some of the evidence, including the cross-section data used by the World Bank and many mainstream economists to argue that good-governance reforms are associated with more rapid and sustained development in contemporary developing countries.

THE EMPIRICAL EVIDENCE

The market-enhancing view of governance aims to explain the observation of poor performance in many developing countries. Superficially, many poorly performing countries appear to conform to the analysis of the good-governance model because they have high levels of corruption, low accountability of political leaders, poor rule of law and plenty of evidence of predatory behaviour. But superficial evidence can be misleading. *All* developing countries have poor governance scores, as measured by the good-governance or market-enhancing characteristics. So if we plot country scores for good-governance (these measures are discussed later) against their per capita incomes, we get an almost perfect fit. However, the test that is required is to see if poor countries that scored higher in terms of market-enhancing governance characteristics actually did better in terms of convergence or catching up with advanced countries. When we conduct such a test we find that the evidence supporting the market-enhancing view of governance is very weak indeed. While poorly performing developing countries fail to meet good-governance conditions, so do high-growth developing countries. This observation suggests that it is difficult for *any* developing country, regardless of its growth performance, to achieve the governance conditions required for efficient markets. This does not mean that market-enhancing conditions are irrelevant, but it does mean that we need to qualify some of the arguments made for prioritising market-enhancing governance reforms in developing countries, if the evidence is that these are not possible to achieve.

Evidence: Market-enhancing Governance and Economic Growth

An extensive academic literature has tested the relationship between what we have described as market-enhancing governance conditions and economic performance. This literature typically reports a positive relationship between the two, appearing to support the hypothesis that an improvement in market-enhancing governance conditions will promote growth and accelerate convergence with advanced countries. This literature uses a number of indices of market-enhancing governance. In particular, it uses data provided by Stephen Knack and the IRIS Center at Maryland University, as well as more recent data provided by Kaufmann's team and available on the World Bank's website. If market-enhancing governance were relevant for explaining economic growth, we would expect the quality of market-enhancing governance at the beginning of a period (of, say, ten years) to have an effect on the economic growth achieved during that period.

However, the Knack–IRIS data set is only available for most countries from 1984 and the Kaufmann–World Bank data set only from 1996 onwards. We have to make sure that we test the importance of market-enhancing governance by using the score of a country at the beginning of a period of economic performance, in order to see if differences in market-enhancing governance can explain the subsequent differences in performance between countries. This is important, as a correlation between governance indicators at the end of a period and economic performance during that period could be picking up the reverse direction of causality, where rising per capita incomes result in an improvement in market-enhancing governance conditions. There are good theoretical reasons to expect market-enhancing governance to improve as per capita incomes increase (more resources become available in the budget for securing property rights, running democratic systems, policing human rights, and so on). This reverses the direction of causality between growth and governance. Thus, for the Knack–IRIS data, the earliest decade of growth that we can examine would be 1980–90, but even here we have to be careful to remember that the governance data that we have is for a year almost halfway through the growth period. The World Bank data on governance begins in 1996, and therefore can at best be used for examining growth during 1990–2003, keeping in mind once again that these indices are for a year halfway through the period of growth being considered.

Stephen Knack's IRIS team at the University of Maryland compile their indices using country risk assessments based on the responses of relevant constituencies and expert opinion.[18] These provide measures of market-enhancing governance quality for a wide set of countries from the early 1980s onwards. This data set provides indices for a number of key variables that measure the performance of states in providing market-enhancing governance. The five relevant indices in this data set are for "corruption in government", "rule of law", "bureaucratic quality", "repudiation of government contracts", and "expropriation risk". These indices provide a measure of the degree to which governance is capable of reducing the relevant transaction costs that are considered necessary for efficient markets. The IRIS data set then aggregates these indices into a single "property rights index" that ranges from 0 (the poorest conditions for market efficiency) to 50 (the best conditions). This index therefore measures a range of market-enhancing governance conditions and is very useful (within the standard limitations of all subjective data sets) for testing the significance of market-enhancing governance conditions for economic development. Annual data for the index are available from 1984 for most countries.

A second data set that has become very important for testing the role of market-enhancing governance comes from Kaufmann's team[19] and is available on the World Bank's website.[20] This data aggregates a large number of indices available in other data sources into six broad governance indicators. These are:

1. Voice and accountability – measuring political, civil and human rights
2. Political instability and violence – measuring the likelihood of violent threats to, or changes in, government, including terrorism
3. Government effectiveness – measuring the competence of the bureaucracy and the quality of public service delivery
4. Regulatory burden – measuring the incidence of "market-unfriendly" policies
5. Rule of law – measuring the quality of contract enforcement, the police, and the courts, as well as the likelihood of crime and violence
6. Control of corruption – measuring the exercise of public power for private gain, including both petty and grand corruption, and state capture.

We have divided the countries for which data are available into three groups. "Advanced countries" are high-income countries, using the World Bank's classification, with the exception of two small oil economies (Kuwait and the UAE), which we classify as developing countries. This is because although they have high levels of per capita income from oil sales, they have achieved lower levels of industrial and agricultural development than other high-income countries. We also divide the group of developing countries into a group of "diverging developing countries" whose per capita GDP growth is lower than the median growth rate of the advanced country group. There is also a group of "converging developing countries" whose per capita GDP growth rate is higher than the median advanced country rate.

Table 1 summarises the data for the 1980s from the Knack–IRIS data set. For the decade of the 1980s, the earliest property-right index available in this data set for most countries is for 1984.

Table 2 shows the composite data for the 1990s, using an aggregation of the indices available in the Kaufmann–World Bank series. Tables 3 to 8 show the Kaufmann–World Bank data for the 1990s for the six indices separately from the Kaufmann–World Bank data set. Figures 2 to 9 show the same data in graphical form. The tables and plots demonstrate that the role of market-enhancing governance conditions in explaining differences in growth rates in developing countries is, at best, very weak.

Table 1. Market-enhancing Governance: Property Rights and Growth, 1980–90

	Advanced Countries	Diverging Developing Countries	Converging Developing Countries
Number of Countries	21	52	12
Median Property Rights Index 1984	45.1	22.5	27.8
Observed range of Property Rights Index	25.1–49.6	9.4–39.2	16.4–37.0
Median Per Capita GDP Growth Rate 1980–90	2.2	-1.0	3.5

The IRIS property rights index can range from a low of 0 for the worst governance conditions to a high of 50 for the best conditions.
Sources: IRIS-3 (2000), World Bank, World Development Indicators 2005, CD-ROM, Washington, DC: World Bank (2005b).

Table 2. Market-enhancing Governance: Property Rights and Growth, 1990–2003

	Advanced Countries	Diverging Developing Countries	Converging Developing Countries
Number of Countries	24	53	35
Median Property Rights Index 1990	47.0	25.0	23.7
Observed range of Property Rights Index	32.3–50.0	10–38.3	9.5–40.0
Median Per Capita GDP Growth Rate 1990–2003	2.1	0.4	3.0

The property right index here is an aggregate of the corruption, rule of law, bureaucratic quality indices on a 10-point scale, together with the index of repudiation of government contracts and expropriation risk.
Sources: World Bank, Governance Indicators: 1996–2004, Washington, DC: World Bank (2005a), World Bank (2005b).

Table 3. Market-enhancing Governance: Voice/Accountability and Growth, 1990–2003

	Advanced Countries	Diverging Developing Countries	Converging Developing Countries
Number of Countries	24	53	35
Median Voice and Accountability Index 1996	1.5	-0.4	-0.3
Observed range of Voice and Accountability Index	0.4–1.8	-1.5–1.1	-1.7–1.4
Median Per Capita GDP Growth Rate 1990–2003	2.1	0.4	3.0

The Kaufmann–World Bank index has a normal distribution with mean 0 and standard deviation 1.
Sources: World Bank (2005a), World Bank (2005b).

Table 4. Market-enhancing Governance: Political Instability and Growth, 1990–2003

	Advanced Countries	Diverging Developing Countries	Converging Developing Countries
Number of Countries	24	53	35
Median Political Instability and Violence Index 1996	1.2	-0.4	0.0
Observed range of Instability and Violence Index	-0.5–1.6	-2.1–1.1	-2.7–1.0
Median Per Capita GDP Growth Rate 1990–2003	2.1	0.4	3.0

The Kaufmann–World Bank index has a normal distribution with mean 0 and standard deviation 1.
Sources: World Bank (2005a), World Bank (2005b).

First, there is virtually no difference between the median property-rights index for converging and diverging developing countries (particularly given the relative coarseness of this index and that, for our data, the governance indicators are for a year halfway through the growth period). Second, the range of variation of this index for converging and diverging countries almost entirely overlaps. The absence of any clear separation between converging and diverging developing countries in terms of market-enhancing governance conditions casts doubt on the robustness of the econometric results of a large number of studies

Table 5. Market-enhancing Governance: Government Effectiveness and Growth, 1990–2003

	Advanced Countries	Diverging Developing Countries	Converging Developing Countries
Number of Countries	24	53	35
Median Government Effectiveness Index 1996	1.9	-0.5	-0.2
Observed range of Govt Effectiveness Index	0.6–2.5	-2.1–0.8	-2.2–1.8
Median Per Capita GDP Growth Rate 1990–2003	2.1	0.4	3.0

The Kaufmann–World Bank index has a normal distribution with mean 0 and standard deviation 1.
Sources: World Bank (2005a), World Bank (2005b).

Table 6. Market-enhancing Governance: Regulatory Quality and Growth, 1990–2003

	Advanced Countries	Diverging Developing Countries	Converging Developing Countries
Number of Countries	24	53	35
Median Regulatory Quality Index 1996	1.5	-0.1	0.2
Observed range of Regulatory Quality Index	0.8–2.3	-2.4–1.2	-2.9–2.1
Median Per Capita GDP Growth Rate 1990–2003	2.1	0.4	3.0

The Kaufmann–World Bank index has a normal distribution with mean 0 and standard deviation 1.
Sources: World Bank (2005a), World Bank (2005b).

that find market-enhancing governance conditions have a significant effect on economic growth.[21] Third, for all the indices of governance we have available, the data suggest a *very* weak positive relationship between the quality of governance and economic growth. The direction of the relationship is as the market-enhancing governance view predicts, but the weakness of the relationship demands a closer look at the underlying data. Doing so demonstrates that the positive relationship depends to a great extent on a large number of advanced countries having high scores on market-enhancing governance (the countries

Table 7. Market-enhancing Governance: Rule of Law and Growth, 1990–2003

	Advanced Countries	Diverging Developing Countries	Converging Developing Countries
Number of Countries	24	53	35
Median Rule of Law Index 1996	1.9	-0.4	-0.3
Observed range of Rule of Law Index	0.8–2.2	-1.8–1.1	-2.2–1.7
Median Per Capita GDP Growth Rate 1990–2003	2.1	0.4	3.0

The Kaufmann–World Bank index has a normal distribution with mean 0 and standard deviation 1.
Sources: World Bank (2005a), World Bank (2005b).

Table 8. Market-enhancing Governance: Corruption and Growth, 1990–2003

	Advanced Countries	Diverging Developing Countries	Converging Developing Countries
Number of Countries	24	53	35
Median Control of Corruption Index 1996	1.8	-0.4	-0.3
Observed range of Control of Corruption Index	0.4–2.2	-2.0–0.8	-1.7–1.5
Median Per Capita GDP Growth Rate 1990–2003	2.1	0.4	3.0

The Kaufmann–World Bank index has a normal distribution with mean 0 and standard deviation 1.
Sources: World Bank (2005a), World Bank (2005b).

shown as diamond-shaped points in Figures 2 to 9) and the bulk of developing countries being *diverging* low-growth countries which also have low scores on market-enhancing governance (shown as triangular points). However, if we look only at these countries, we are unable to say anything about the direction of causality because we have good theoretical reasons to expect market-enhancing governance to improve in countries with high per capita incomes. The critical countries for establishing the direction of causality are the *converging* developing countries (shown as square points). By and large, converging countries do not have significantly better market-enhancing governance scores than diverging ones. In the 1980s data set, there are relatively very few converging countries, and so the relationship between market-enhancing governance and growth

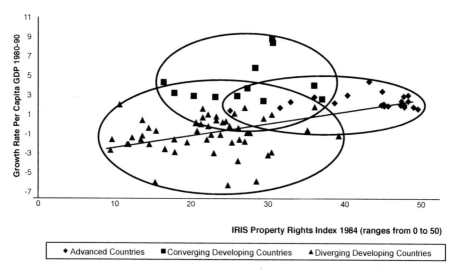

Figure 2. Market-enhancing Governance and Growth, 1980–90

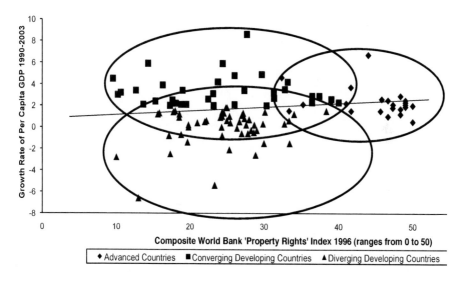

Figure 3. Market-enhancing Governance and Growth, 1990–2003

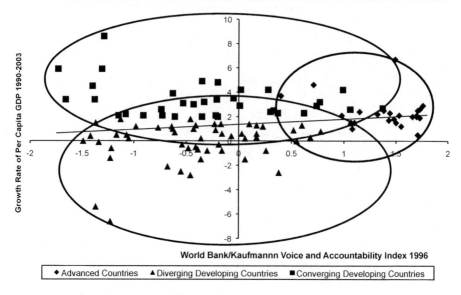

Figure 4. Political Accountability and Growth, 1990–2003

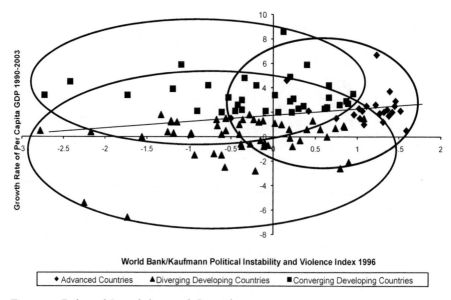

Figure 5. Political Instability and Growth, 1990–2003

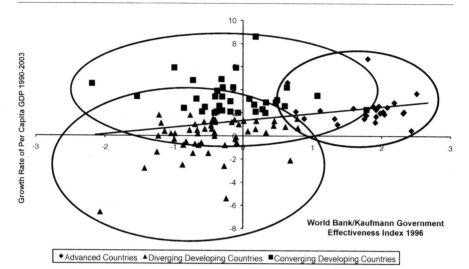

Figure 6. Government Effectiveness and Growth, 1990–2003

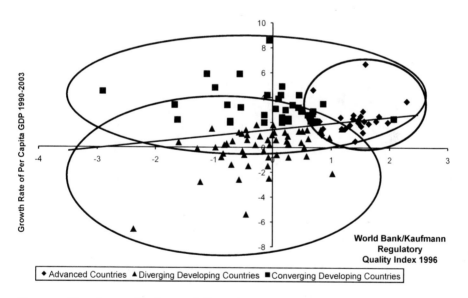

Figure 7. Regulatory Quality and Growth, 1990–2003

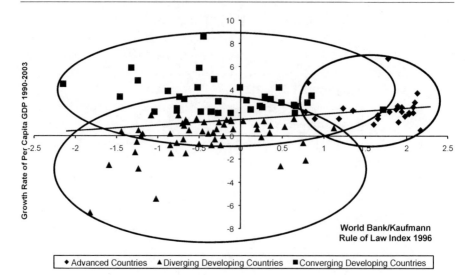

Figure 8. Rule of Law and Growth, 1990–2003

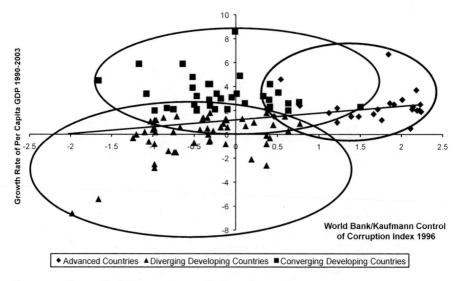

Figure 9. Control of Corruption and Growth, 1990–2003

appears to be relatively strong, using the Knack–IRIS data set. However, in the 1990s data set, the number of converging countries is now greater and the positive relationship becomes much weaker both visually and using measures of goodness-of-fit, despite the bias created by the governance indicators only being available from around 1994 for the Kaufmann–World Bank data set. The data therefore suggests that even the weak positive relationship between market-enhancing governance and growth could be based largely on a reverse direction of causality, with richer countries having better scores in terms of market-enhancing governance.

The policy implications of these observations are rather important. Given the large degree of overlap in the market-enhancing governance scores achieved by converging and diverging developing countries, we need to significantly qualify the claim made in much of the governance literature that an improvement in market-enhancing governance quality in poorly performing countries is necessary and sufficient to achieve a significant improvement in growth. If anything, the data suggests that since differences in market-enhancing governance capabilities are not significant between converging and diverging countries, we need to examine other dimensions of governance capabilities that could explain differences in growth performance.

The many studies that find a significant positive relationship between market-enhancing governance and growth usually do so by pooling advanced and developing countries together, or pooling together developing countries at different levels of development. Our examination of the data suggests that these studies can be misleading because we expect more advanced countries to have better market-governance capabilities. Pooling can thus confuse cause and effect. When developing countries are looked at separately, the relationship is much weaker, if it exists at all, and even in this case, we need to be aware of sample-selection problems if we pool relatively advanced and poorer developing countries. The causality problem here has to be carefully defined. We do not need to reject the hypothesis that *if* market-enhancing governance could be improved, then perhaps growth would be higher. It is quite plausible that an improvement in market-enhancing governance capabilities would have a positive effect on growth. The problem, rather, is the observation that, in fact, market-enhancing governance appears not to be easy to improve in poor countries. In that case, market-enhancing governance is once again not causally responsible for growth, even though in theory an improvement in these conditions may have helped.

These observations suggest that to identify the critical governance capabilities for sustaining growth and development, it is important to look at individual countries that have made a successful transition from under-development to sustained development. This brings us to the Asian high-growth countries of the late twentieth century. Case studies of the governance conditions of these countries demonstrate very strongly that none of them conformed to the expectations of good-governance theory.[22]

Our argument is also supported by the analysis of growth in African countries by Sachs and his collaborators.[23] In their study of African countries, these authors point out that countries with higher per capita incomes are expected to have better market-enhancing governance quality. As a result, higher scores on governance indicators should not be used to explain higher incomes. To correct for this bias, they argue that market-enhancing (good-governance) indicators should not be directly used as explanatory variables. Instead, they use the deviation of the country's governance indicator (in this case, the Kaufmann–World Bank index) from the predicted value of the indicator given the country's per capita income at the beginning of the period. This approach is a sophisticated way of dealing with the two-way causation between governance and growth. If market-enhancing governance matters for growth, we would expect countries that had better governance than expected for their per capita incomes to do better in subsequent periods compared to countries that achieved only average or below-average governance for their per capita incomes. The Sachs study finds that, when adjusted in this way, market-enhancing governance has no effect on the growth performance of African countries. This result is entirely consistent with our observations.

However, we do not entirely agree with the Sachs study when they conclude that these results show that governance reforms are not an immediate priority for African countries. They argue that to trigger growth in Africa, what is required instead is a big push in the form of a massive injection of investment in infrastructure and disease control. While the case for a big push in Africa is strong, this does not mean that African countries have the minimum necessary governance conditions to ensure that a viable economic and social transformation will be unleashed by such an investment push. The evidence of big-push experiments in many countries has demonstrated that growth is only sustainable if resources are used to enhance productive capacity and new producers are able to achieve rapid productivity growth. These outcomes are not likely in the presence of significant market failures and the absence of support and regulation from state structures possessing the appropriate governance capabilities to overcome these market failures.

The econometric results reported by Sachs et al.[24] do not actually show that *all* types of governance were irrelevant for growth, only that the market-enhancing governance measured by available governance indicators clearly has less significance in explaining differences in performance between developing countries. Other forms of governance may be very important, but indices measuring these governance capacities are not readily available. In our next section we look at the evidence suggesting the importance of growth-enhancing governance capabilities.

Our interpretation of the evidence appears to be contradicted by the influential paper by Acemoglu et al.[25] who argue that the achievement of stable property rights decades, or even longer ago, enabled some countries to become prosperous while others who failed to achieve these conditions did not. This argument uses instrumental variables to measure the stability of property rights a century or more ago. Their now-famous indicator is the relative frequency of deaths of white settlers in different parts of Africa that determined whether or not Europeans set up settler colonies with stable property rights. Where malaria deaths were high, white settlers did not come, but they set up extractive colonies within which property rights were then destabilised by the extractive policies of the colonial powers. This analysis is seductive in its use of innovative statistical techniques, but suffers from serious historical problems. Most significantly, the underlying historical processes that the instrumental variables are capturing do not actually support the interpretation of the authors. *The countries where settlers went and settled did not enjoy stable property rights while the settlers were taking over these societies.* Indeed, they suffered from precipitous collapses of traditional property rights as large tracts of land were expropriated by colonial settlers. In some cases, the expropriation was so severe and rapid that indigenous populations collapsed entirely, sometimes in genocidal proportions. To describe the growth that happened as being due to the *prior* establishment of stable property rights does violence to the historical facts.

It is more accurate to say that where the transformation of property rights to capitalist ones happened very rapidly through the use of exceptional amounts of violence, capitalist economies emerged earlier. In these countries, which are the ones white settlers went to, the transition to productive economies allowed the establishment of good-governance. The rapid emergence of viable capitalist economies subsequently allowed property rights to be protected and become stable in the way we would expect. In other developing countries, the process of transformation is still going on. In one sense, we could even argue that property rights were *more* stable in the non-settler countries, because a precipitous historical rupture did not occur there. The problem for these countries is that similar property right-transitions have to be organised today in a context where markets remain inefficient and subject to high transaction costs.

The reform challenge is to organise transitions in these countries with less violence and more justice than the processes through which the apparently good-governance countries with white-settler histories emerged. Of course, once a viable capitalism becomes established, property rights are likely to become well protected because the new owners of rights will be willing to spend resources to protect them. In settler colonies this happened quite a long time ago, but the stability of property rights across-the-board in these societies did not pre-date the establishment of a productive capitalism. In other words, Acemoglu et al.'s argument suffers from exactly the type of causality problem as the other good-governance arguments we discussed earlier, despite their use of more sophisticated econometrics and proxy variables.

Our empirical interpretation is strongly supported by recent work being done at the French development agency, the AFD, by Nicolas Meisel and Jacques Aoudia,[26] whose work replicates our findings using their own data set. They borrow our classification of developing countries into converging and diverging groups and find exactly the same pattern that we have described. The replication of our findings using an independent data set suggests that our argument is robust.

The task of further research is to distinguish between different types of developing countries within the converging and diverging groups. We know that these groups include countries of quite different prospects and, of course, levels of development. For instance, converging countries include some countries that are growing rapidly because of mineral resources, countries that are growing because they possess comparative advantage in some low-technology manufacturing exports, and yet others that are on sustainable growth paths with strong technology acquisition strategies and productivity growth. Clearly, the last subset is the most interesting one, and is the subset that others within the converging set should attempt to emulate, if they are to sustain their growth rates. Similarly, within the diverging group there are various types of countries, including some middle-income countries, that have run into serious problems of sustaining productivity growth, as well as some very poor countries that have not yet achieved a take-off. Further research into these different subsets will enhance our understanding of the governance challenges that different types of countries face in attempting to either trigger or sustain growth and development. In each case, the answer may be to develop specific governance capabilities to enhance growth that are quite different from the general good-governance reforms suggested by the market-enhancing governance approach.

Evidence: Growth-enhancing Governance and Economic Growth

The case for growth-enhancing governance argues that markets in developing countries will be relatively inefficient because of high transaction costs. As a result, developing countries are likely to face significant market failures in transferring assets and resources to growth sectors, in attracting the best and most appropriate technologies requiring prolonged periods of learning, and in providing the right mix of training and incentives for skills enhancement. In consequence, growth through the expansion of new productive capacity and systematically moving up the value chain is likely to be heavily constrained in most developing countries. Not surprisingly, successful developing countries demonstrate a variety of institutions and governance capabilities to address these major areas of market failure, together with institutional and political capacities to achieve sufficient inclusion to manage political stability during transitions that are bound to involve periods of conflict, strife and tension.[27]

The case-study evidence strongly supports our analysis. Not surprisingly, a significant part of the asset and resource reallocations necessary for accelerating growth and development in developing countries have taken place through semi-market or entirely non-market processes. These processes have been very diverse. Examples include the English Enclosures from the sixteenth to the eighteenth centuries, which transferred common lands in rural England to emerging capitalist sheep farmers and led to the agrarian revolution that was the basis of the subsequent industrial revolution in England. The creation of the *chaebol* in South Korea in the 1960s, using transfers of public resources to the *chaebol*, is also an example of effective growth-enhancing governance capabilities on the part of the South Korean state to make valuable resources available to potentially productive new industrial activities and firms. The creation of the Chinese TVEs using public resources in the 1980s, and their gradual transfer to private hands in the 1990s, and the allocation and appropriation of public land and resources for development in Thailand, are further examples of effective growth-enhancing governance capabilities in these countries.

As for failures in labour and capital markets that slow down technological upgrading and the upskilling of labour, the empirical evidence, particularly from East Asia and China, also strongly supports the importance of growth-enhancing governance capabilities for implementing targeted corrections to these market failures. In successful countries, incentives for technology acquisition were created through many different mechanisms, including tariff protection (in virtually every case, but to varying extents), direct subsidies to large firms investing in new technologies (in particular, in South Korea), subsidised and prioritised infrastructure for priority sectors (in China and Malaysia), subsidising the licensing of advanced foreign technologies (in Taiwan), and managing the foreign exchange value of the currency (in many early developers, and recently in China). The governance capabilities of countries to manage these incentives played a critical part in determining the relative success of countries in moving up the value chain. In successful countries, incentives were changed over time in line with changing technological and market conditions. Firms and sectors that did not perform could not expect to receive incentives for ever. In less successful performers, these governance capabilities did not exist, and strategies of moving up the value chain failed in the end.[28]

Thus, one area poor countries need to focus on is national investment

Table 9. Growth-enhancing Governance in Selected Countries, 1960–2000

	Critical Components of Growth-enhancing Strategy	Supportive or Obstructive Governance Capabilities	Economic Outcomes
South Korea 1960s to early 1980s	Non-market asset allocations (consolidations, mergers and restructuring of chaebol). Targeted conditional subsidies for chaebol to accelerate catching-up.	Centralised and effective governance of interventions by agencies with long-term stake in development. Effective power to implement assisted by weakness of political factions so that inefficient subsidy recipients are unable to buy protection from them.	Very rapid growth and capitalist transformation
Malaysia 1980s to 1990s	Public-sector technology acquisition strategies using public enterprises with subcontracting for domestic firms. Targeted infrastructure and incentives for MNCs with conditions on technology transfer.	Moderately effective centralised governance of interventions. Assisted by centralised transfers to intermediate classes, which reduced incentives of political factions to seek rents by protecting inefficient firms.	Rapid growth and capitalist transformation
Indian subcontinent 1960s to 1970s (With some variations, these characteristics describe many developing countries of that period)	Targeted subsidies to accelerate catching-up in critical sectors (using protection, licensing of foreign exchange, price controls and other mechanisms). Public-sector technology acquisition in subsidised public enterprises. Resource transfers to growth sectors using licensing and pricing policy.	Moderate-to-weak governance capacities to discipline non-performing rent recipients. Agencies often have contradictory goals defined by different constituencies. Fragmented political factions help to protect the rents of the inefficient for a share of these rents. State capacities decline as committed and intelligent individuals leave.	Public- and private-sector infant industries often fail to grow up. Rent-seeking costs are often the most visible effects of intervention. Moderate-to-low growth and slow transformation.
Indian subcontinent 1980s to 1990s	Liberalisation primarily in the form of a withdrawal of implicit targeted subsidies, in particular through the relaxation of licensing for capital goods imports. Much more gradual withdrawal of protection across the board for domestic markets.	Moderate-to-weak governance capacities to implement remain, but do less damage as the scope of growth-enhancing policies decline. Fragmented political factions continue to have an effect on market-enhancing governance by restricting tax revenues and making it difficult to construct adequate infrastructure.	Growth led by investments in sectors that already have comparative advantage. Higher growth, but limited to a few sectors.

	Critical Components of Growth-enhancing Strategy	Supportive or Obstructive Governance Capabilities	Economic Outcomes
Latin America 1950s to 1970s	Domestic capacity-building through selective tariffs and selective credit allocation.	Governance effective in directing resources to import-substituting industries, but weak in disciplining poor performers. Weakness linked to "corporatist" alliances that constrained disciplining powerful sectors.	Initial rapid growth slows down. Many infant industries fail to grow up.
Latin America 1980s onwards	Rapid liberalisation across the board.	Focus on market-enhancing governance. Breakdown of corporatist alliances allows rapid liberalisation to be implemented.	Output growth in sectors that already have comparative advantage, in particular in commodities.

and technology policies as a means of achieving technological upgrading.[29] The success of these strategies will, in turn, depend on the development of governance capabilities in these countries to manage the identification and provision of incentives for investment in technological upgrading. These are difficult governance capabilities, but not necessarily more difficult than trying to achieve across-the-board rule of law reforms or anti-corruption reforms in poor countries, and they have at least the support of historical evidence from East Asia as being achievable governance goals for poor countries. Clearly, most poor countries will not be immediately able to emulate China or South Korea in the scale of their ability to encourage new investments. But it is nevertheless very important for developing countries to understand these success stories and why successes in these countries were not necessarily achieved by following a good-governance or market-enhancing strategy. Developing countries, then, need to develop institutional experiments appropriate to their own political and institutional initial conditions in order to address the most significant market failures that are constraining growth in their core economic sectors. The main lesson they should learn from China and East Asia is that appropriate governance capabilities to implement these policies are critical. Clearly, most countries should begin with modest local experiments to upgrade existing sectors and technologies in countries that currently have weak governance capabilities, aiming to gradually build up growth-enhancing governance capabilities.

The importance of these governance capabilities is also indicated by the histories of poorly performing countries because we know that when governments intervene to correct market failure without the governance capabilities to manage and enforce these strategies, the outcome can sometimes be even worse than if the government had done nothing. If the requisite governance capacities are missing, a growth-enhancing strategy may deliver worse outcomes than a market-led strategy, as poorly implemented interventions may worsen resource allocation, as well as inducing high rent-seeking costs.

Paradoxically, the very diversity of strategies for correcting market failures in successful countries can be cause for optimism because it means that a variety of growth-enhancing governance capabilities can play a role in a country's development effort. While a full understanding of this diversity can only be achieved by studying a series of case studies, Table 9 summarises the experiences of a selection of countries, showing the type of growth-enhancing strategies that they followed and the associated governance capabilities that either supported or obstructed the implementation of these strategies. During the 1960s, 1970s and part of the 1980s, most developing countries followed growth-enhancing strategies that had many common elements, even though they often differed quite significantly in their detail. In all countries, two primary goals of developmental interventions were: (a) to accelerate resource allocation to growth sectors and (b) to accelerate technology acquisition and skills acquisition in these sectors through a combination of incentives and compulsions.

To achieve the first, a variety of policy mechanisms were used, including bureaucratic allocation of land (including land reform), the licensing of land use, influencing the allocation and use of foreign exchange, and influencing the allocation of bank credit. In some cases, price controls and fiscal transfers were also used to accelerate the transfer of resources to particular sectors. To achieve the second, incentives for technology acquisition included: targeted tax breaks or subsidies; protection of particular sectors for domestic producers engaged in setting up infant industries; licensing of foreign technologies and subcontracting these to domestic producers; setting up investment zones for high-technology industries and subsidising infrastructure for them; and subsidising higher education and skills acquisition of different types. The critical observation from the perspective of governance strategies is that, for both types of policies, success required the possession or development of growth-enhancing governance capabilities. These included, in particular, the capability to monitor resource-use and withdraw resources or support from sectors, firms or activities that proved to be making inadequate progress.

The growth-enhancing governance challenge for countries is to first identify the most important market failures constraining growth in that country, to identify possible responses to these market failures and, finally, to pick responses that can either be implemented given existing governance capabilities, or that may become viable if critical governance capabilities can be developed. In most countries, sufficient growth-enhancing governance capabilities do not exist to implement very significant responses to critical market failures. At the same time, an attempt to suddenly achieve a high level of growth-enhancing governance capabilities is also likely to fail. A pragmatic appraisal of what is feasible should guide the development of a growth-enhancing governance-reform agenda for each country.[30]

CONCLUSION

The desirability of many of the objectives of the good-governance agenda is not in question. Many social groups and constituencies in developing countries want to see a deepening of democracy, greater accountability of their governments, a clampdown on corruption and the introduction of a rule of law and stable property rights. Many of these goals should, indeed, be long-term goals of development in their own right. The policy question for developing countries is, rather, about the extent to which these goals are immediately achievable, and the extent to which they should be prioritised as targets, given that reform capabilities are limited and the resources to effectively implement reforms even more so. Here, the theoretical arguments and historical evidence suggest that we should be very careful not to confuse means with ends, goals with preconditions, methods with outcomes. There is no credible evidence of any poor country that has first achieved significant improvements in its democratic accountability, reduced corruption to very low levels in a sustainable way, achieved a recognisably good rule of law and stable property rights and *as a result* achieved significantly high and sustainable growth and development. There are good reasons why such empirical examples cannot be found.

All of the available evidence is that the achievement of conventional good-governance has been through a simultaneous and parallel set of improvements in good governance, in line with the achievement of economic prosperity. This is because significant resources and productive political constituencies are required to achieve the effective implementation of good-governance goals, and these resources and constituencies are themselves the outcome of growth and development. There is no question that the achievement of these conditions can further improve confidence in contracts and markets, and thereby further improve market efficiency, allowing growing economies to enjoy virtuous cycles of improvements in governance and economic performance. However, the precondition for these virtuous cycles to emerge is that there is a sustainable prior strategy of promoting growth and development, and that states have capabilities to sustain these strategies. Unfortunately, largely for ideological reasons, the promotion of state capabilities to sustain growth through addressing critical market failures in poor countries has fallen out of the reform agenda, particularly in the international discourse promoted by rich countries, the international financial institutions and the donor community. Yet the actual evidence of growth and development from the most successful developers of the twentieth century, and in particular from China today, suggests that these growth-enhancing governance capabilities are the most important ones, if growth is to be sustained, and that these are, in turn, the real preconditions for the interactive development of market-enhancing governance capabilities over time.

Fortunately, there is a growing perception in the policy community that the focus on good-governance has been a diversion from the most pressing tasks of governance-capability improvements. Consequently, there are some encouraging signs of a re-adjustment of the reform agenda. These shifts need to be welcomed, and a new agenda of reform has to be developed rapidly as frustration with conventional reform strategies grows in many poorly performing and fragile societies. Nevertheless, we should expect strong resistance from many existing reformers, economists and advisors whose reputations have been based on the old agenda, and who feel threatened by any radical shift in policy. However, the indications on the ground are that these reformers have failed to achieve sustainable improvements in terms of their own reforms (defined as sustainable reductions in corruption, improvements in the rule of law or in perceptible improvements in the accountability of their governments). This is often despite the expenditure of vast amounts of grants and loans in the pursuit of the good-governance agenda. Some of these economies are growing, but any examination of the drivers of growth in these countries shows that their economies are often growing due to niche sectors that are struggling to perform *despite* what the government is doing, rather than benefiting from significant improvements in market efficiency as a result of reforms carried out under the good-governance agenda.

The danger of an exclusive focus on market-enhancing governance is that we may lose opportunities for carrying out critical reforms that are more likely to produce results. We may also create disillusionment with governance reforms, leading to the emergence of a false perception that governance does not matter that much for economic development. The urgency of shifting the focus of reforms to growth-enhancing governance is underlined by the fact that these reforms require a very different set of discussions with stakeholders in order to identify critical market failures. This, in turn, needs to be followed by the careful identification of the most appropriate ways of addressing these critical market failures in the specific context of that country, and depending on the potential of developing appropriate governance capabilities. All of these processes will take time and involve a very different set of procedures than the ones that have been developed to raise awareness of good-governance deficits and promote the development of good-governance capabilities. Given the stark situation in terms of policy space and limited reform capabilities, the only option for most developing countries is to embark on the growth-enhancing governance agenda on a relatively small scale. I have elsewhere described this as a "Hirschmanian" approach to pursuing growth-enhancing governance reforms.[31] Developing countries can expect little help or assistance from international donors and financial institutions, given the dominant ideologies informing the understanding of these players. It is not surprising that the successful developers of East Asia did not develop any of their most important governance capabilities to address market failures as a result of advice or persuasion coming from advanced countries.

It is important to reassert the importance of governance reforms at a time when the failure of much of the good-governance agenda in delivering strong results is leading to reform fatigue and the perception that perhaps governance is not, after all, very important for poor countries. This would be an unfortunate conclusion, given the historical evidence that the absence of governance capabilities has severely constrained poor countries from solving market failures that have limited their growth and development. Rather, the conclusion should be that while the good-governance goals are, in many cases, desirable long-term goals for all countries, many of these goals are not achievable to any significant degree in poor countries. They are certainly not achievable to an extent that market efficiency will improve so much that other governance reform goals become irrelevant. On the contrary, the governance capabilities that need to be prioritised in developing countries must be variants of the growth-enhancing governance capabilities required for dealing with critical market failures that we find in successful and sustained growth experiences in East Asia and elsewhere.

NOTES

1. Anne O. Krueger, "The Political Economy of the Rent-Seeking Society", *American Economic Review*, vol. 64, no. 3, 1974, pp. 291–303; "Government Failures in Development", *Journal of Economic Perspectives*, vol. 4, no. 3, 1990, pp. 9–23.
2. Mushtaq H. Khan, *Governance, Economic Growth and Development since the 1960s*, DESA Working Paper No. 54 (ST/ESA/2007/DWP/54), New York: United Nations Department of Economic and Social Affairs, 2007. Available at http://www.un.org/esa/desa/papers/2007/wp54_2007.pdf; Mushtaq H. Khan, "Governance and Development: The Perspective of Growth-Enhancing Governance", in GRIPS Development Forum (ed.), *Diversity and Complementarity in Development Aid: East Asian Lessons for African Growth*, Tokyo: National Graduate Institute for Policy Studies, 2008.
3. Douglass C. North, *Institutions, Institutional Change and Economic Performance*, Cambridge: Cambridge University Press, 1990; Daniel Kauffman, Aart Kraay and Pablo Zoido-Lobatón, *Governance Matters*, World Bank Policy Working Paper No. 2196, Washington, DC: World Bank, 1999.
4. North, *Institutions, Institutional Change and Economic Performance*.
5. Ibid.; Stephen Knack and Philip Keefer, "Why Don't Poor Countries Catch Up?

A Cross-National Test of an Institutional Explanation", *Economic Inquiry*, vol. 35, no. 3, 1997, pp. 590–602; Kauffman, et al., *Governance Matters*; Daron Acemoglu, Simon Johnson and James A. Robinson, "Institutions as the Fundamental Cause of Long-Run Growth", Working Paper No. 10481, Cambridge, MA: National Bureau of Economic Research, 2004. Available at http://www.nber.org/papers/w10481

6. Krueger, "The Political Economy of the Rent-Seeking Society"; Mancur Olson, *The Rise and Decline of Nations*, London: Yale University Press, 1982; Paolo Mauro, "Corruption and Growth", *Quarterly Journal of Economics*, vol. 110, no. 3, 1995, pp. 681–712. Paolo Mauro, *The Effects of Corruption on Growth, Investment and Government Expenditure*, Working Paper WP/96/98, Washington, DC: Policy Development and Review Department (International Monetary Fund), 1996; "The Effects of Corruption on Growth, Investment and Government Expenditure: A Cross-Country Analysis", in Kimberly A. Elliot (ed.), *Corruption and the Global Economy*, Washington, DC: Institute for International Economics, 1997; "Why Worry about Corruption?", *IMF Economic Issues*, vol. 97, no. 6, 1997, pp. 1–12.

7. North, *Institutions, Institutional Change and Economic Performance*; 7. Mancur Olson, "The New Institutional Economics: The Collective Choice Approach to Economic Development", in Christopher Clague (ed.), *Institutions and Economic Development*, Baltimore, MD: Johns Hopkins University Press, 1997; Mancur Olson, "Dictatorship, Democracy and Development", in Mancur Olson and Satu Kähkönen (eds), *A Not-so-Dismal Science: A Broader View of Economies and Societies*, Oxford: Oxford University Press, 2000.

8. Joseph E. Stiglitz, *Whither Socialism?*, Cambridge, MA: MIT Press, 1996; *Making Globalization Work*, London: Penguin, 2007; Mushtaq H. Khan, "Rents, Efficiency and Growth", in Mushtaq H. Khan and Jomo K. S. (eds), *Rents, Rent-Seeking and Economic Development: Theory and Evidence in Asia*, Cambridge: Cambridge University Press, 2000.

9. Mushtaq H. Khan, "The New Political Economy of Corruption", in Ben Fine, Costas Lapavitsas and Jonathan Pincus (eds), *Development Policy in the Twenty-First Century: Beyond the Post Washington Consensus*, London: Routledge, 2001; "Corruption and Governance in Early Capitalism: World Bank Strategies and their Limitations", in J. Pincus and J. Winters (eds), *Reinventing the World Bank*, Ithaca, NY: Cornell University Press, 2002; "Determinants of Corruption in Developing Countries: the Limits of Conventional Economic Analysis", in Susan Rose-Ackerman (ed.), *International Handbook on the Economics of Corruption*, Cheltenham: Edward Elgar, 2006.

10. Mushtaq H. Khan, "Rent-seeking as Process", in Mushtaq H. Khan and Jomo K. S. (eds), *Rents, Rent-Seeking and Economic Development: Theory and Evidence in Asia*, Cambridge: Cambridge University Press, 2000; "Rents, Efficiency and Growth", in Mushtaq H. Khan and Jomo K. S. (eds), *Rents, Rent-Seeking and Economic Development: Theory and Evidence in Asia*, Cambridge: Cambridge University Press, 2000; "Corruption and Governance in Early Capitalism"; "Markets, States and Democracy: Patron–Client Networks and the Case for Democracy in Developing Countries", *Democratization*, vol. 12, no. 5, 2005, pp. 705–25; "Determinants of Corruption in Developing Countries".

11. Khan, "Rent-seeking as Process".

12. Mushtaq H. Khan, "State Failure in Developing Countries and Strategies of Insti-

tutional Reform", in Bertil Tungodden, Nicholas Stern and Ivar Kolstad (eds), *Annual World Bank Conference on Development Economics Europe (2003): Toward Pro-Poor Policies: Aid Institutions and Globalization*, Proceedings of Annual World Bank Conference on Development Economics, Oxford: Oxford University Press and World Bank, 2004. Available at http://www-wds.worldbank.org/servlet/WDS_IBank_Servlet?pcont=details&eid=000160016_20040518162841

13. John Toye, *Dilemmas of Development: Reflections on the Counter-Revolution in Development Theory and Policy*, Oxford: Basil Blackwell, 1987.

14. Joseph E. Stiglitz, *Making Globalization Work*, London: Penguin, 2007.

15. Mushtaq H. Khan, "Rents, Efficiency and Growth".

16. Ibid.

17. Khan, *Governance, Economic Growth and Development*; "Governance and Development: The Perspective of Growth-Enhancing Governance".

18. IRIS-3, *File of International Country Risk Guide (ICRG) Data*, edited by Stephen Knack and the IRIS Center, College Park: University of Maryland, 2000.

19. Daniel Kaufmann, Aart Kraay and Massimo Mastruzzi, *Governance Matters IV: Governance Indicators for 1996–2004*, 2005. Available at http://www.worldbank.org/wbi/governance/pubs/govmatters4.html

20. World Bank, Governance Indicators: 1996–2004, Washington, DC: World Bank, 2005. Available at http://info.worldbank.org/governance/kkz2004/tables.asp

21. Stephen Knack and Philip Keefer, "Institutions and Economic Performance: Cross-Country Tests Using Alternative Institutional Measures", *Economics and Politics*, vol. 7, no. 3, 1995, pp. 207–27; "Why Don't Poor Countries Catch Up? A Cross-National Test of an Institutional Explanation", *Economic Inquiry*, vol. 35, no. 3, 1997, pp. 590–602; Robert Hall and Charles Jones, "Why Do Some Countries Produce So Much More Output Per Worker Than Others?", *Quarterly Journal of Economics*, vol. 114, no. 1, 1999, pp. 83–116; Kauffman, et al., *Governance Matters*.

22. Masahiko Aoki, Hyung-Ki Kim and Masahiro Okuno-Fujiwara (eds), *The Role of Government in East Asian Economic Development: Comparative Institutional Analysis*, Oxford: Clarendon Press, 1997. Also see, for example, Mushtaq H. Khan and Jomo K. S. (eds), *Rents, Rent-Seeking and Economic Development: Theory and Evidence in Asia*, Cambridge: Cambridge University Press, 2000.

23. Jeffrey D. Sachs, John W. McArthur, Guido Schmidt-Traub, Margaret Kruk, Chandrika Bahadur, Michael Faye and Gordon McCord, "Ending Africa's Poverty Trap", *Brookings Papers on Economic Activity* 1, 2004, pp. 117–240.

24. Ibid.

25. Daron Acemoglu, Simon Johnson and James A. Robinson, "The Colonial Origins of Comparative Development: An Empirical Investigation", *American Economic Review*, vol. 91, no. 5, 2001, pp. 1369–401.

26. Nicolas Meisel and Jacques Ould Aoudia, *Is 'Good Governance' a Good Development Strategy?*, Working Paper No. 58, Paris: Agence Française de Développement (AFD), 2008.

27. Aoki, et al. (eds), *The Role of Government in East Asian Economic Development*; Khan and Jomo, *Rents, Rent-Seeking and Economic Development*.

28. Alice Amsden, *Asia's Next Giant: South Korea and Late Industrialization*, Oxford: Oxford University Press, 1989; Khan, "Rent-seeking as Process".

29. Mushtaq H. Khan, *Investment and Technology*, National Development Strategies Policy Guidance Notes, New York: United Nations Development Programme and United Nations Department of Economic and Social Affairs, 2006. Available at http://esa.un.org/techcoop/documents/PN_InvestmentTechnologyPolicyNote.pdf

30. Ibid.

31. Ibid.; Mushtaq H. Khan, "Building Growth-Promoting Governance Capabilities", background paper for *The Least Developed Countries Report 2008*, Geneva: UNCTAD, 2008.

Conclusion:
Not Washington, Beijing nor Mecca:
The Limitations of Development Models

Robert Springborg

Preceding chapters have provided a wealth of data and analyses on the relevance of development models, especially that of China, for majority Muslim countries, with Latin America and Africa having been included to provide comparative context. The purpose of this conclusion is to draw out of these preceding chapters answers to the key questions about the transportability to Muslim countries of development models generally, and especially the Chinese one. Those questions turn on perceptions of the model at the sending and receiving ends; the viability and sustainability of the model itself; the economic, political and cultural bilateral and regional relations that provide the context within which the model is perceived and acted upon; preconditions for the adoption and success of the model; the role of competitive models; and the type of governance assumed by the model and whether viable functional substitutes for governance institutions can be found. Answers to these questions may, in turn, enable us to assess the relevance of models for development, especially across Muslim majority countries.

PERCEPTIONS OF THE "BEIJING CONSENSUS"

William Hurst is of the view that the Chinese model is an external construct, not a self-conscious blueprint for China's development. China's experimental, pragmatic approach has, according to him, been intellectualised and indeed glorified by outside observers, in the process rendering theoretical coherence to what has been an incremental, "groping for stones while crossing the river" approach to development. Aware of the "Beijing Consensus" largely because Western intellectuals have coined the term and written about it, Chinese decision-makers are essentially pragmatic problem-solvers rather than development theoreticians or ideologues. They are, correspondingly, uninterested in the export of that model, although they are committed to globalising China's economic, diplomatic and possibly military reach.

Other contributors view the Chinese model through the lens of their regional experience and expertise, and, therefore, see it somewhat differently. Their tendency to impart more self-awareness and volition to Chinese decision-makers probably also reflects, in part, China's incredible economic success and the natural assumption that what appears so coherent and purposeful from the outside must, in fact, be so by design. Catherine Boone, for example, drawing on African cases, believes that China has consciously presented its development path as an alternative to that put forward by Western-led international financial institutions (IFIs). She does not address, however, whether this is a tactical manoeuvre intended by the Chinese only to generate support for intensification of economic and political relations, or a strategic goal, whereby the Chinese want to impart their development lessons to Africa so as to re-shape African political economies in the Chinese mould, thereby creating organic solidarities rather than just good trading relations.

What undisputedly is the case is that the Chinese have yet to generate, if indeed they ever will, the intellectual explanations and justifications and insti-tutional underpinnings for the Beijing Consensus in the same manner as has been done for the Washington Consensus. Whether this is due to an inevitable time-lag, disinterest, or the actual absence of a coherent model is impossible to know with certainty. So we are in the curious situation of the world wanting to know more about the Chinese model than the Chinese themselves seem to know, or at least are willing to reveal. Emma Murphy raises the interesting prospect that the current contradiction between China's projection of benign power alongside an increasingly strident nationalism could, if the latter gains the upper hand, lead Beijing to follow the well-trodden path of self-glorification. Such a course would likely include claims for the superiority and universality of the Chinese political economy and its associated ideology. German and Italian fascism, Stalin's Soviet Union, Nasser's Arab socialism and, without too much of a stretch, Washington's neo-liberalism combined with democratisation, all suggest that decision-makers of various persuasions can fall victim to the delusion that their experiences are uniquely relevant and applicable regionally, or even globally. Why should the Chinese, if their success continues, be any different? One answer would be that in our new, globalised and increasingly multi-polar, culturally egalitarian world, claims to superiority and uniqueness are manifestly counter-productive, and that the Chinese, having been on the receiving end of colonialism and neo-imperialism, will resist the temptation, content instead to reap the benefits that their relatively benign projection of power provides.

The contributors suggest that the salience of the Chinese model – or at least desire to know its exact architecture – may well be greater outside than inside China, including even in development-lagging and comparatively poorly globalised sub-Saharan Africa. They also come to similar conclusions regarding the lure of the model. First, it is inextricably bound up in broader perceptions of China (a point that will be further developed below). Suffice it to say here that the economic and, to a lesser extent, political contexts within which relations with China are conducted are of much greater importance in the evaluation of the relevance of the model than is the model itself. So, for example, according to Barbara Stallings, Latin America appeared to be much enamoured of China in the early years of the twenty-first century, when extravagant investment promises were made by Chinese leaders. However, lack of fulfilment of those promises stimulated disenchantment that may have fed into an increasingly widespread belief in Latin America that the absence of democracy in China renders its development model less relevant there than it otherwise might be. Catherine Boone's findings in Africa, based in part on content analyses of the Kenyan, South African and Nigerian press, underscore the salience of trade and investment for perceptions of China and, by implication, evaluations of its development model.[1]

A second, related conclusion regarding normative appraisals of the Chinese model is that they seem inversely related to the degree of democracy that obtains in the respective countries and regions. As just mentioned, Barbara Stallings cites the authoritarianism implicit in the model as its chief deterrent to potential emulators in Latin America. This is less of a concern in Africa and the Middle East. In the latter region, there is indeed much speculation that the appeal of the Chinese model is predominantly to incumbent elites precisely because they are seeking a non-democratic path to development. Nevertheless, even where the various waves of democracy have not washed ashore, the Chinese model's authoritarianism is, at best, a mixed blessing. In Egypt, for example, the President is reported to have discussed with key advisors the relevance of the model, dismissing it with manifest regret on the grounds that Egypt was already too democratic to permit the social, economic and political regimentation he believed the model requires.[2]

A third observation is that interest determines normative views of the Chinese model. Just mentioned has been an apparent divide between rulers and ruled, with the former being keenly interested in the model precisely because it embodies the hope of incumbent-led, non-democratic development. Differing economic interests that are impacted variably by commercial and investment relations with China are probably of greater importance, as suggested by Clement Henry's assessment of reactions to Chinese engagement with Algeria, and by Catherine Boone and Barbara Stallings in their respective regions. Manufacturers of tradable goods who are negatively affected by Chinese imports are, not surprisingly, hostile to such commercial relations, and frequently emphasise elements of the Chinese economy, including low wage rates, that enhance its competitiveness but would not be possible, or maybe even desirable, in their own country.[3] Chinese involvement in the construction industry in Algeria and elsewhere also divides indigenous attitudes, with admiration for quality and timeliness being balanced against hostility towards the presence of Chinese workers or by resentment of the Chinese building prestige projects for unpopular ruling elites.

Finally, there is some evidence to suggest that the appeal of the model might be inversely related to the degree of engagement with China, or at least that initial enthusiasm engendered by interaction with China tends over time to be tempered by more sober assessments of prospects. So in various countries in sub-Saharan Africa, North Africa and Latin America, for example, relations with China have either negatively impacted domestic interests or not met initially high expectations, thus resulting in a more generalised disaffection. In this regard, African perceptions that moved quickly from being highly favourable of China, its path to development and of relations with it, to that of China being a neo-neo-imperial power, are particularly noteworthy. In most countries of the Middle East and North Africa, the degree of engagement has been less than in, say, Sudan, so there has been less cause for such strong reactions. Indeed, this tempering of expectations, or even growing hostility, might account for the relatively favourable interpretations of China in the Middle East and North Africa, as compared to those in sub-Saharan Africa and Latin America.

In sum, the speed with which China has developed, and the extent to which it has extended its global economic reach, has had a disorienting impact on perceptions of what the Chinese model, in fact, is. The Chinese have yet to gear up intellectual and operational capacities to explain and project the model, if indeed they ever will. In the meantime, Chinese leadership continues to extol the virtues of flexibility, discipline, indigenous culture and the leadership of the CCP, but more as mantra than as an integrated, replicable approach to development. Those in the developing world who increasingly are dealing with China, or simply observing its phenomenal growth, are generally favourably impressed, and would like to know more, but with some rather obscure exceptions, such as Angola, none have taken any concrete steps to emulate the Beijing Consensus. In the meantime, the emergence of winners and losers in domestic markets as a result of expanding economic relations with China, combined with the profoundly non-democratic nature of China itself, suggests that the lure of the China model is unlikely to become overwhelming.

VIABILITY AND SUSTAINABILITY OF THE BEIJING CONSENSUS

This volume's China expert, William Hurst, raises fundamental questions about the viability and sustainability of China's headlong drive to develop. The China model – which, according to him, is the typical East Asian developmental state "plus two" (massive foreign direct investment and authoritarianism) – is vulnerable not just because of potential threats to FDI, but because the rigid, authoritarian system is incapable of responding to emerging challenges, including rising labour costs, fiscal problems at local levels and general weakness of the financial sector, as well as environmental degradation and associated public health problems. The model in his view, then, is fundamentally flawed and has been oversold as a success story.[4]

Emma Murphy shares much of Hurst's scepticism, and for more or less the same reasons. Weak financial markets and the lack of rule of law will, in her view, impede innovation as corruption eats away at the system's performance and legitimacy. Rising inequality and the emergence of a sub-stratum of working poor will increase political pressures. Rapid rates of growth will slow because China has been living off the accumulated social capital of the previous era, suggesting that the present model is flawed and unsustainable. Although she does not predict it, her analysis suggests that China could go the way of the USSR. In the meantime, however, China will seek to restructure global relations to enhance its standing and relative position, which, if effective, would presumably cushion downward pressures resultant from its development model's shortcomings.

Other contributors to the volume who take up the issue are less inclined to see broad systemic failures in – and an inevitable, cataclysmic decline of – the Beijing Consensus. Instead, they concur that the primary shortcoming is the lack of democracy, which may or may not be addressed over the long haul. One view is that China will emulate other East Asian developmental states, such as South Korea and Taiwan, with headlong development preceding democratisation, which will, in turn, enable the system to address internal pressures and contradictions. Mushtaq Khan's broader argument, which is that good governance results from rather than contributes to economic development, is consistent with such a prognosis. Emma Murphy concludes her chapter with the wry observation that what Arabs should learn from the China model is that the absence of democracy inevitably limits economic growth, however positive initial results are.

In sum, the glass is either broken, half empty or half full. The Chinese model, in other words, is either doomed to failure as a result of inevitable inability to meet growing challenges; may be able to save itself through a transition to democracy; or is, in fact, likely to do so precisely because democratisation is a probable outcome. Clearly absolute, irrevocable systemic breakdown would render irrelevant the Chinese model, much as communism was dealt what seems to have been a fatal blow by the collapse of the USSR. However, the prognosis of collapse is as premature as that of its transition to democracy, and the yet grander hope that such a transition would stimulate a fifth wave of global democratisation that would finally reach the distant shores of the Middle East and Africa. Both the collapse and transformation outcomes are unlikely in the short term at least, so we are left with the more ambiguous present state of affairs in which the appeal of the Chinese model rests heavily on the rapid growth rates it has achieved, with its lack of democratisation tarnishing its appeal in greater or lesser measure for different audiences and its apparently mounting problems causing concerns for those who are sympathetic to the model and might even want to emulate at least parts of it. Whether the Beijing Consensus is truly viable and sustainable is an issue for the future and is unlikely to play a major role in its possible present emulation.

The Context of Bilateral Economic, Political and Cultural Relations

A strictly theoretical development model unassociated with direct relations with the progenitor or emulators of that model is unlikely to gain much traction in a potential emulating country. Arab socialism, for example, would not have taken root in Egypt without the support and engagement of the USSR. As Catherine Boone notes in Africa, the Washington Consensus, which she prefers to term the IFI model, is intimately associated with the guiding role played by the IMF, World Bank and other components of the global political economic architecture associated with the West and especially the US. On the other hand, extensive economic, political and cultural relationships between potential exporters and importers of development models are likely to complicate the process of adoption. They may undermine the appeal of the model. British economic imperialism, for example, undercut support in the empire for Westminster democracy. The Ugly American of the Cold War had his counterpart in the overbearing Russian.

Contributors have noted that bilateral economic relations with China generate winners and losers in host countries, and that the gains and losses tend to be substantial. While trade and investment necessarily have differing effects on various national economic interests, what is especially noteworthy about economic relations with China is their sheer magnitude, hence profound impacts on winners and losers. Whether it is the entry into hitherto largely protected markets for consumer goods in Africa, Latin America and the Middle East, or virtual monopolisation of raw material exports and its associated infrastructure, such as in Sudan, the Chinese presence can be overwhelming.[5] That the backlash against that presence is not stronger than it apparently is, results from at least three factors. First, the balance between winners and losers tilts towards the former. There are far more consumers than producers of consumer goods, for example. Markets flooded with cheap Chinese imports in Africa, Latin America and the Middle East have not yet stimulated strong protectionist, or more generally anti-Chinese, responses. Second, concern with neo-neo-imperialism is probably limited to intellectual and associated circles, rather than being a profound concern with significant sectors of populations who are more likely to see material benefits resulting from mineral and commodity exports. Finally, the Chinese are benefiting from the unfavourable legacy and contemporary nature in many countries of relations with the West, especially those in Africa. Leaving the broad history of colonialism and imperialism aside, the recent history of "tough love" imposed by the West in the form of the Washington Consensus, combined with inadequate investment in development in general, and in public infrastructure in particular, stands in stark negative contrast to China's economic engagement with developing countries. It has been comparatively generous with investments, many have been in needed infrastructure, and it has not wrapped its economic and political relationships in implicit or explicit conditionality intended to improve governance, restrict consumption, open markets, and so on. The West, in short, opened the door to a competitor able and keen to do business and carrying neither historical nor contemporary political baggage. So, despite growing concerns and disappointments with some aspects of economic relations with China, those negative reactions are a long way from creating sufficient pressure on decision-makers to rein in their embrace of Chinese goods and services.

It should be noted, however, that experiences of trade and commerce with China typically differ from those with investment. Criticism of the latter, largely because promises exceed actual delivery, is widespread in Latin America and Africa, as our contributors indicate. The same holds true in the Middle East and North Africa, especially in the Gulf, where extravagant statements about and high hopes for inward investment from China have clearly exceeded reality.[6] It is also the case that outward investment from the Gulf in China has similarly failed to realise the high expectations that arose during the peak of the oil boom. That investments flowing in both directions have yet to reach what was anticipated may reflect not only human exuberance and lack of real financial knowledge on the part of prognosticators caught up in the frenzy of the Chinese and Gulf miracles, but also the shortcomings of financial sectors on both sides, including inadequate regulation, depth and transparency. These obstacles may assume greater significance because of the newness of these relationships, hence absence of investment channels that can bypass structural obstacles, although even established, major players confront difficulties investing in China.[7] The nature of Chinese investment may also lead to disappointments in some sectors of economies, for it is more state-centric than is the case with Western investment. The nexus that binds private-sector actors between developing countries and Western investors is much less well developed in China's case, implying that the base of support for engagement with China may be more fragile.

The overselling of the Chinese investment boom has not, however, seriously damaged trade relations between China and the world's developing regions and countries. Despite growing reservations among losers about the benefits of that trade, it looks set to continue to expand. Strengthening trade relations are, in turn, likely to stimulate yet greater interest in China as its trading partners seek to learn more about this amazing success story. Increasing curiosity aside, expanding trade relations will also stimulate growing human contacts, and their institutionalisation, thus providing linkages through which Chinese experiences and approaches can be learned and copied.

Just as expanding economic relations with China provide an underpinning for interest in, knowledge of and engagement with the Chinese model, political relationships have at a minimum not discouraged potential emulators of the Chinese model. Beijing's benign power projection creates a broadly favourable context within which it pursues its interests. It has skilfully steered away from risky engagements in regional and sub-regional issues, maintaining extensive economic relations with Venezuela and Iran, for example, while avoiding being dragged by these ally-seeking, status quo-challenging regional actors into disputes with their neighbours or with Uncle Sam.[8]

Having skilfully avoided entanglement in regional issues, China nevertheless does confront a growing political issue in its relations with developing countries. Eschewing efforts to induce them to reform their political economies, and winning considerable kudos for demonstrating "respect for sovereignty", China has, as our contributors indicate, nevertheless come in for increased criticism for ignoring egregious abuses of human rights and embracing dictators. Condemnation of their engagement with Mugabe's regime, brought to a head by the embarrassing incident of a shipload of Chinese arms destined for Zimbabwe's government being denied dockage facilities in South Africa, is but one example of the downsides of the policy of "respect for sovereignty". On balance, however, the upsides of the policy have greater weight, if only because non-interference seems to be preferred to democracy promotion in the nationalist-inclined, imperialism-scarred developing world. At an operational level, the policy removes obstacles to effective state–state relationships that ardent democracy promotion, or even active support for the ten commandments of the Washington Consensus, erect.

On reasonably solid ground with its many bilateral economic and political relations, China does not substantially undermine its appeal with its cultural contacts. Indeed, at an intellectual level, the Beijing Consensus, by elevating respect for indigenous culture and emphasising the positive roles it can play in development, provides a welcome antidote to the Washington Consensus's apparent disdain for non-Western cultures. The curious paradox that the system emerging out of communist materialism should emphasise respect for culture, combined with the success of this apparent culture-based development model, captivates many in the developing and especially Muslim world, and instills a desire to learn more about Chinese culture and how it has been drawn upon for the creation of a successful development model. At the operational level, the Chinese are beginning to think and act like preceding superpowers in that they have come to appreciate the need to project their language and culture into the world, one manifestation of which is governmental support for Chinese schools that cater to non-Chinese in countries deemed to be strategically or economically vital.[9] On the negative side, the large and growing number of Chinese living in the developing world, whether as workers on infrastructure mega-projects or as merchants, inevitably results in some irritations with local populations, but there are no cases of such irritations becoming a significant factor in bilateral relations.

On balance, then, China's bilateral economic, political and even cultural relations with countries in the developing world serve to intensify engagement with and interest in this rapidly developing country from which many would like to learn and see as providing an alternative model for their own development. Whether this is a passing phase, to be succeeded by a cooling of interest as a result of disappointments with inadequate investment, flooding of local markets and the presence of too many Chinese in local neighbourhoods, remains to be seen. If the experience of preceding global powers is any guide, there are downsides to the intensification of bilateral relations, but without such relations the chances of that power's path to development inspiring others are very limited.

PREREQUISITES FOR ADOPTION OF THE BEIJING CONSENSUS

A defining feature of the Chinese model as a variant of the Asian developmental state is that the state is, to use Peter Evans" much-quoted term, "embedded" in the political economy. Capable of designing long-term development strategies and inducing the private sector to implement them by rewarding high performers and punishing laggards, the embedded state is both autonomous from society – or at least not a captive of a particular social force – and capable of resolving socio-political conflicts. Over time the embedded, developmental state stimulates the growth and consolidation of class-based political interests. This, in turn, paves the way for democratisation, which is itself an effective mechanism for resolving socio-political conflicts, thereby ensuring the longevity of the developmental state.

Interestingly, Yasheng Huang argues that the Chinese variant is fatally flawed in that an urban-based elite, rooted in state enterprises, aborted China's bottom-up capitalist revolution of the 1980s, replacing it with an exploitative, urban based, top-down, state capitalism linked to multinational enterprises.[10] Its behaviour is generating, according to him, an inevitable political backlash stimulated by developmental failures, including environmental degradation and impoverishment of rural areas. Whether an accurate assessment and prognosis of the Chinese case or not, Huang's analysis, and the broader literature on developmental states, emphasises both the inherent nature of the state – it must be able to both direct the economy and to resolve socio-political conflicts – and its relations with society – they must strike a balance between autonomy and "embeddedness".

Alas, these two preconditions seem rarely to be met in the real developing world outside of the classic success stories in East Asia. Indeed, even there the preconditions are not ubiquitous, as Jeff Tan's assessment of Malaysia indicates. There, the state failed to mediate Chinese–Malay relations, ultimately becoming ensnared in social and economic relations with the rising Malay business class it had spawned. The fine line between a state that is embedded and one that is engaged in rent-seeking relations with favoured clienteles was crossed, with predictable, negative results for Malaysian development and socio-political stability. Similarly, Barbara Stallings points to Latin American states' lack of autonomy from entrenched, typically landowning classes as a major impediment to their emulation of the Asian developmental state model.

Obstacles to replication of that model are yet greater in virtually all Muslim-majority nations. In the first instance, Muslim states confront a much more challenging task than say South Korea or Taiwan, in managing socio-political conflicts. Their populations are divided vertically by more ethnic, religious, kinship and other solidarities, and horizontally by greater inequality. Managing socio-political tensions in Iraq, for example, makes the same task for Korean politicians look like child's play. In these settings, control of the state is the strategic objective of contending social forces. Far more common, then, is the Muslim state that is the captive of such interests, rather than an impartial mediator between them. Hence adjectives such as "brittle" and "authoritarian" are commonly and correctly applied to them, for they are the instruments of domination by one or a coalition of social forces against others.

Nonetheless, in those settings where social forces are more homogeneous, such as in Tunisia, post-colonial, predatory states with roots in the military and security services are also the norm. Thus, state inadequacies in the Muslim world are not simply the product of fragmented societies, although that fragmentation clearly exacerbates them. Shortcomings in the administrative and political management capacities of Muslim states are due also to historical factors, such as: a tradition of military rule and the impacts of colonialism; high levels of regional conflict in the Muslim heartland of West Asia and North Africa; possible resource endowments that tend to be either limited or over-abundant; and no doubt, too, other causes.

Whatever the causal factors at work, though, the inherent capacities of most Muslim states and their relations with society do not meet the require-ments of successful developmental states, and there is no indication that these fundamental deficiencies will be corrected any time soon. As Clement Henry observes, Tunisia and Syria are superficially the MENA's most devout emulators of the Chinese model, but they are much closer to being parodies than successful imitators of the Beijing Consensus. The former, enjoying the benefits of a homo-geneous, comparatively well developed population, reasonable resource endow-ments and an excellent location, has been ruled since independence by two successive dictators, their families and entourages, so the capitalism that has developed has been of a crony, rather than developmental, nature. Syria, with similar endowments other than having a much more heterogeneous population, is under the iron grip of a schismatic Muslim minority that uses the state to impose its will and sustain its economic and political pre-eminence, depending in part on Alawi solidarities induced by fear of the payback if its grip were to loosen.

Curiously, the Muslim states of the MENA that might most closely resemble Asia's developmental states are the Gulf monarchies. Indeed, a recent study of Saudi Arabia by a noted expert concludes that its rentier state is in the process of being transformed into a developmental one.[11] A possible expla-nation of the paradox of "developmental Muslim monarchies" might lie in the role played by their ruling families, which conceivably is closer to that of the Chinese Communist Party than the role that is played by the dominant parties of the republics, such as Egypt's National Democratic Party or Syria's Ba'th. Increasingly these monarchies, largely forsaking other appeals, seek their legit-imacy through economic governance and the benefits it brings. Embedded in their societies by virtue of carefully nurtured tribal ties, and in their economies through direct participation, they are better positioned to mediate socio-political conflicts, formulate development strategies and possibly even to create effective reward schedules for private economic actors than are the MENA republics. These monarchies also more closely resemble China than either South Korea or Taiwan in that the vanguard role of their monarchical political elites has, for the most part, yet to be tempered by democratisation, if indeed it ever will be, although there are considerably more trappings of democracy in Kuwait and Bahrain, for example, than there are in China. So in both the Gulf monar-chies, and in China, the prospects for developmentalism are clouded by the uncertainty surrounding the political intentions of ruling elites. Will they be willing and able to democratise, or will they become yet more self-indulgent, corrupt and contemptuous of those not in the Party or family? Whatever the outcome, it is a curious paradox that the most traditional form of governance in the Muslim world seems more closely to meet the preconditions for having effective, developmental states than do those forms of government which, at least superficially, more closely resemble those of East Asia.

This paradox seems also to hold when considering a set of what might be thought of as tactical preconditions for developmentalism, as opposed to the broad strategic ones just discussed. These preconditions are, in their essence, the ability to develop and harness human resources. At the practical level, they include the integration of education with utilisation and, subsequently, creation of new technologies.[12] In his description of the Beijing Consensus, for example, Ramo includes as a defining characteristic the rejection of dated, labour-intensive technologies in favour of contemporary ones. The essence of this approach, which depends on closely articulating education with industry, has been referred to as the creation of "knowledge economies". Interestingly,that has become a catchphrase in the Gulf monarchies, whereas it is hardly referred to elsewhere in the region. Actions, moreover, are matching words, as reflected in the massive investments in education in the Gulf and in cutting-edge technologies in at least hydrocarbon and hydrocarbon related production processes, although other economic sectors, even including agriculture, are characterised by greater utilisation of modern technology than are their equivalents elsewhere in the region. The role of multinationals in the transfer of that technology was vital in the case of the original developmental states, with much of it coming from Japan. China has followed this path. In the Arab world, it is only the Gulf states, and in limited sectors therein, in which multinational-led technology transfer, supported by investments in human resource development, is occurring on a sizeable scale.

Another human resource precondition for developmentalism is that of an appropriate mindset, characterised by Emma Murphy as being open to new and different experiences and risk-taking. In the Chinese case, overseas Chinese communities played a vital role in modelling and propagating this orientation. Interestingly, Noland and Pack, in their study of Arab economies, focused on the ability to attract émigrés back to their country of origin as a key cause and indicator of development. They find, unfortunately, that in comparison with the rapidly developing countries of Asia, the Arab world performs very poorly in this regard.[13] Again, the Gulf countries stand out as at least partial exceptions to the general Arab rule. In their case, the presence of expatriate workers from virtually all corners of the globe provide a functional substitute. However, regardless of interaction with émigrés or expatriates, the mindset of many Gulf Arabs may traditionally and now be more open to the outside world than that of, say, Egyptians or Moroccans. The mercantile traditions of Kuwait, Bahrain, Dubai and Oman stand out in this regard. Evidence marshaled by Noland and Pack does indeed indicate that citizens of the GCC states are more open to globalisation than are other Arabs. Referencing Pew global attitude surveys, they also note that Egyptians are more inclined to want to protect their existing way of life than are respondents in any other country surveyed.[14] Noland and Pack's evidence and argumentation about Arabs' comparative fear of globalisation and lack of openness to foreign and new experiences is supported by the broader findings of Moataz Fattah, whose survey of almost 40,000 Muslims finds these attitudes to be widely held, especially among Arab Muslims.[15] In sum, to the extent that the development of labour forces capable of utilising up-to-date technologies, combined with a widespread openness to the outside world and willingness to take risks, are prerequisites for rapid development of the sort engineered in East Asia, the Arab world and other Muslim contexts, with the possible exceptions of Turkey and the Gulf, are not well placed to emulate that experience.

As for the broader preconditions of developmentalism based on the nature of states and societies, and their inter-relationships, again it seems that only in the Gulf within the Arab world might they be found, if indeed ruling families can be functional substitutes for Asian political elites, including that of the CCP. This is a pretty tall order, but the emirs, shaykhs and monarchs may at least come noticeably closer to filling it than their republican counterparts. As for Muslim majority countries more generally, the chapters in this volume indicate that Malaysia, Pakistan and Iran all lack the attributes of developmental states, whether of the Chinese or more democratic variants. Their states are captives of particular social forces, hence unable to alleviate socio-political conflicts, or are incapable of providing strategic goal-setting and effective governance, or both.

It is only Turkey in which a quasi-Islamist-led government has over the past few years managed to set strategic objectives and provide reward structures to stimulate private-sector partners and, by so doing, significantly enhance economic performance, including that of exports. This raises the broader question of whether or not a Muslim country may be generating a model that presents an alternative to both the Washington and Beijing Consensuses, a "third path", to use Colonel Qadhafi's term for the erratic course down which he has steered Libya. The lure of an alternative development model, especially one that has cultural resonance in Muslim contexts, is no doubt heightened by the demanding preconditions set by both the Washington and Beijing Consensuses, preconditions that few, if any, Muslim states are likely to meet in the near future. But, as Clement Henry points out, the preconditions for success of a home-grown Muslim model may be just as demanding, even if at this point they are less apparent to potential advocates.

COMPETITIVE MODELS

The very infatuation with China, and the desire to know how it has achieved such remarkable rates of economic growth, suggest that the Washington Consensus is no longer hegemonic in the Gramscian sense, if indeed it ever was. In each global region commitments in varying degrees to the Washington Consensus, and greater or lesser interest in China, is accompanied by some home-grown development theorising and practices. In East Asia, commitment to the developmental state with an admixture of neo-liberalism has survived the Asian crisis. In Latin America, a resurgent nationalism coupled with populism and economic quasi-autarky has captured state power in Venezuela, Bolivia and Ecuador, as well as the imaginations of Argentinians and others. In Africa, resentment of the Washington Consensus has stimulated interest in the Chinese alternative, but the continent remains too diverse politically, and in every other way, for it to have generated a coherent third way that is distinctively African. The Muslim world, stretching from Indonesia across to Morocco, with its heartland in West Asia, is at least as diverse as Africa, but Islam does provide some sort of common denominator, and efforts to construct alternatives to the Washington and Beijing Consensuses on the basis of it are under way. They have yet, however, to approach the status of what might irreverently be termed a Mecca Consensus, even though Islam is suffusing public policy in many Muslim countries.

Chapters in this volume point to the inherent difficulties facing those who would prefer a home-grown model based in Islam to any of the secular competitors. Mohammed Ayoob's comparisons of the political economies of Turkey and Iran suggest just how diverse two not only Islamist-inspired but actually governed countries can be in their approach to fundamental economic and political questions. Products of their own national histories, resource endowments and current political situations, Turkish and Iranian Islamists have constructed profoundly different economies and polities. The former has embraced at least the approach, if not the intellectual, legacy of neo-liberal, export-led growth, led by a democratic government that wants the country's Islamic character to be yet more central to its society, economy and polity, but is very wary of seeking to impose it. Iran, on the other hand, has, under the leadership of its Shia clerics, sought to fashion a uniquely Muslim political system, although in reality it derives more from modern Iranian history than from classical Islam. On the economic front, the Iranian Islamic economy is essentially state capitalism under the control of the clerics, who dress up patronage as inspired by the moral imperatives of being good Muslims while plundering the state's treasury and mismanaging its affairs. Moreover, the clerics have no hesitancy in their efforts to impose what they see to be Islamic practices. In another volume, Mohammed Ayoob has explored the variations in the political economies of several Muslim-majority countries, emphasising that the common denominator of Islam has scant impact on how political economies are structured or function.[16] The widely divergent cases of Pakistan and Malaysia, as described in this volume, underscore the point. In short, in the contemporary real world of states ruled by Muslims, there is little in practice that can be said to be inspired by a common version of Islam, although in each there may be some features that reflect Islam in one way or another.

It is therefore to the extra-state world of Islam that one has to turn to discover thinking and practice that might inform the actual construction of what conceivably could achieve common agreement as being a truly Muslim model of state development. Clement Henry has done just that in this volume, with his investigations of the growth and impacts of Islamic finance and its prospects for re-shaping Muslim political economies more broadly. His conclusions are not as discouraging as Mohammed Ayoob's for those hoping that a real -world, widely-emulated Muslim model of development will be constructed, but they are not very optimistic on those grounds either.

In the first instance, Islamic finance, despite enjoying phenomenal global growth and institutionalisation since its creation in the 1970s, and especially since the recent oil boom that commenced in 2003, is itself not a unified, coherent model. Its most apparent form is the management by financial institutions – some, largely Middle Eastern, claiming to be completely Islamic and others, mainly Western, claiming only to have "Islamic windows" – of funds according to principles their boards of Islamic scholars declare are Sharia compliant. Fuelled by petrodollars, these institutions and their various products have come to occupy a small but significant niche in global finance. However, for the most part this form of Islamic finance is a rich man's game, as the investor base remains limited and the investments themselves driven by the desire to maximise return, hence typically placed in high-yielding markets, including Western ones.[17] This is a far cry from some of the original thinking about what Islamic finance should be, and from the so-called "moral economy of Islam", which Charles Tripp sees as a thread running through modern Islamic history.[18] In these conceptions, finance is meant to serve the interests of Muslim development, both collectively and individually. It should, therefore, be driven not by anticipated financial returns, but by calculations of the capacity to develop society and assist individuals. Some proponents of this conceptualisation of Islamic finance deride the more successful variant, accusing it of having hijacked the original intent and essentially imitating Western financial practices beneath a thin veneer of hastily reconstructed medieval theorising about ostensibly *halal* financial practices.[19] If indeed Islamic finance were to move closer to the core of the political economies of Muslim states, then these competitive views of its very essence would have to be reconciled. Presumably each state would do so in its own particular way, with the net outcome being wide variation in the purposes, means and performances of national Islamic financial systems.

Nevertheless, Clement Henry does not forecast the Islamicisation of national economies any time soon. The primary obstacle is not, in his view, the diversity of theories and practices surrounding it, but the threat it is perceived to pose to incumbent political elites. Facing threats from Islamists, their strategy has been to ensure that established Islamic finance does not bankroll Islamist challengers. Thus, incumbents have utilised their usual strategies of control, including co-optation, isolation and in other ways domesticating Islamic finance. Fearful of retaliation were they to be seen as coalescing with Islamists for the purpose of creating a new, rightly-guided political order, Islamic financiers have, as far as one can detect, thus far turned their backs on political Islamists. It is only in Turkey that democracy, the rule of law and protection of human rights has made it possible for Islamists to both generate material resources and utilise them in the political arena, thereby ultimately achieving power. That Turkey, the sole Muslim democracy in the Middle East, will serve as a model for other states, is unlikely, but not impossible. Furthermore, as Clement Henry speculates, incumbent elites, threatened by Islamists, could pre-empt the challenge by bringing the captains of Islamic finance into ruling coalitions.

In short, syntheses of Islamist and other models, including the Washington Consensus as in Turkey, are by no means inconceivable, and they might provide the popular base that most MENA regimes presently lack. The building blocks of new ruling coalitions in the forms of Islamic finance, Islamist political movements and disillusioned elements within existing regimes are undoubtedly present. But the lack of political freedom in much of the Muslim world renders the task of constructing even theoretical Muslim models of political economies difficult, and the task of actually building one truly formidable. The performance of Iran has hardly helped those tempted to do so. The more favourable Turkish case remains intriguing to many Arabs, but only slightly less distant in terms of real familiarity and ability to meet its preconditions than the Beijing Consensus. For the time being, then, although much of the Muslim world would like to say no to Washington and Beijing, and yes to what they would view as a home-grown model, that alternative, although becoming steadily more fathomable, remains elusive.

The Role of Governance

Governance has assumed a central role in theorising about development and in the international politics surrounding its practice. At the theoretical level, the key questions are what constitutes good governance and how, and in what ways, does it impact development. The absence of definitive answers to these questions has not restrained Western governments and IFIs in their efforts to promote their understanding of good governance in the face of resentment and opposition in much of the developing world. Indeed, it is precisely the desire to avoid having to take the good-governance medicine dispensed by purveyors of the Washington Consensus that underlies much of the appeal of the Beijing Consensus. However, as this volume has demonstrated, both Washington and Beijing have their governance prerequisites for success grounded in their own approaches and experiences. Unless developing nations can come up with some entirely new model shorn of governance – and this was precisely what Muamar Qadhafi attempted with his "third way", and is to some extent the appeal of any putative Islamic model in which the faith of the community of believers substitutes for governance by a state – they have to improve the management of their political economies.

Confusion and disagreement over what constitutes governance stems at least partly from the fact that the Washington Consensus embodies and advocates a broad, inclusive definition of the term, in its most extreme form merging into full-blown democratisation, whereas developmental states, including China, emphasise a much narrower set of criteria that tend also to be more state-focused. The Washington Consensus is predicated on the idea that transparency and other desiderata of good governance depend ultimately on governmental accountability to non-governmental actors, key among whom are citizens expressing choice through elections. As the very term suggests, developmental states, probably reflecting Asian traditions of elite administration bound up in supportive systems of thought, place greater emphasis on voluntaristic state behaviour and less on the need for accountability to society. Indeed, as has already been discussed, the developmental state is one that effectively manages the political and social forces that surround it, not one that responds to them.

In the event, both the IFI model and the developmental-state one have their shortcomings. As Mushtaq Khan has argued in this volume, the former has become too expansive in its claims for the developmental impacts of good governance. Indeed, his correlational analyses lead him to conclude that the causal relationship might well be in the opposite direction, although, as he also suggests, a narrower conception – which he terms "growth-enhancing governance" – and which, incidentally, comes much closer to the key elements of the developmental state – does have direct and profound relevance for development.[20] In his view, the state must meet a minimum set of governance criteria if it is to foster development. At the broad level, it must ensure property rights, manage technological catching-up and maintain political stability. At the more instrumental level, it must transfer resources to productive sectors, address labour and capital market failures, and deliver redistributive justice.[21] However, this begs the question of how states that are not accountable to their citizens can over time continue to deliver these governance goods – precisely the short-coming of developmental states that South Korea and Taiwan have managed to address, but China has not.

Viewed in this light, the differences in prescriptions for governance as handed out by purveyors of the Washington Consensus on the one hand, and advocates of developmental states, even including China, on the other, are not as great as many would have it, although they do differ in their conceptions of the centrality and role of the state. But a "governance-less" path to development in reality does not exist. And, it is precisely such a path that the Chinese model seems to represent to many in the Muslim world. This tempting but mythical path enables them to avoid the prescriptions of the Washington Consensus, pointing with some satisfaction to the fact that China scores lower than the Arab world on many governance measures, as it does vis-à-vis Latin America, but substantially outperforms both in economic development. This dismissal of governance as a prerequisite for development represents a misunderstanding not only of the China model and developmental state more broadly, but it also ignores the needs of the home-grown Islamic financial model, as Clement Henry points out. If it is to prosper, Islamic finance requires even more transparency than its Western equivalents, for prohibition on the taking of interest requires financiers to take stakes rather than just to loan against collateral. They must, therefore, have superior risk-appraisal capacities than purely capitalist bankers, capacities that can only be sustained by quality information guaranteed through institutionalised transparency.

There is, in short, no escape from the need for good governance, whatever the chosen model of development, although precisely what that constitutes and how it is established will vary from country to country. In the Middle East, a governance pattern may, in fact, be in the process of emerging, and its very char-acter suggests the diverse means by which good governance can be achieved. High performers include, paradoxically, democratic Turkey on the one hand, and the small, monarchical states of the GCC and, at least in some measures, Saudi Arabia, on the other. Figures 1 to 5 provide evidence of comparative governance quality between the Gulf Cooperation Council (GCC) states and other Arab states. In the World Bank's measures of regulatory quality – government effectiveness, quality of public administration, control of corruption and political stability – the GCC states as a whole outperform the remainder of the Arab world. Yet, on measures of governance that tap dimensions of citizen participation and are more closely related to democratisation, the GCC under-performs the rest of the Arab world, as suggested in Figures 6 and 7. The former reveals that the civil liberties ratings for the GCC countries as a whole are less favourable than the average for other Arab states. The latter indicates that there is no difference in the performance of GCC and other Arab states on the

Figure 1. Regulatory Quality – 2006

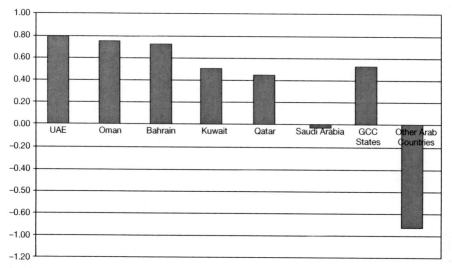

A subjective governance indicator aggregated from a variety of sources and measuring perceptions of the following concepts: incidence of market-unfriendly policies (such as price controls/inadquate bank supervision). Data Source: The World Bank.

Figure 2. Government Effectiveness – 2006

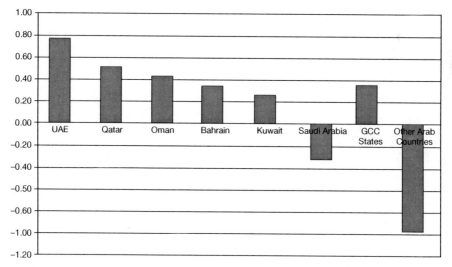

A subjective governance indicator aggregated from a variety of sources and measuring bureaucratic quality, transaction costs, quality of public health care and government stability. Data Source: The World Bank.

Figure 3. Quality of Public Administration in 2006: Current Status (percentile rank)

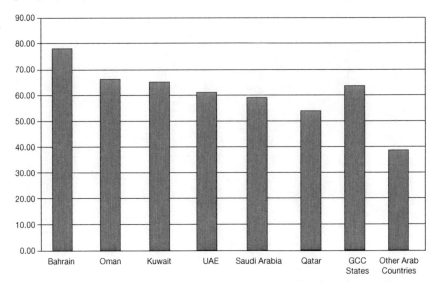

Current status reflects country's current placement in a worldwide ordering of countries, based on a variety of indicators of quality of public administration, expressed as a point in the worldwide cumulative frequency distribution. Data Source: The World Bank.

Figure 4. Control of Corruption – 2006

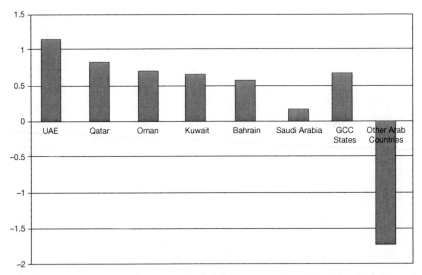

A subjective governance indicator aggregated from a variety of sources and measuring perceptions of certain concepts – for example, corruption among public officials, corruption as an obstacle to business. Data Source: The World Bank.

Figure 5. Political Stability – 2006

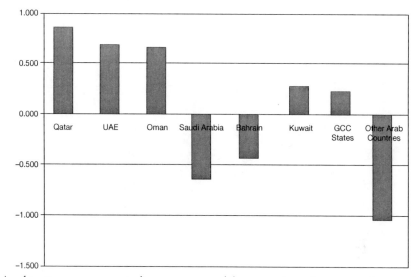

A subjective governance indicator aggregated from a variety of sources and measuring perceptions of the likelihood of destabilisation (ethnic tensions, armed conflict, social unrest, internal conflict, and so on. Data Source: The World Bank.

Figure 6. Civil Liberties Ratings – 2006

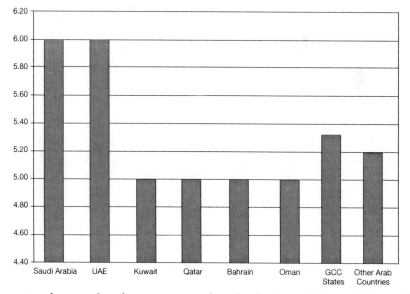

Countries whose combined average ratings for politial rights and for civil liberties fall between 1 and 2.5 are designated as "free", between 3 and 5.5 "partly free", and between 5.5 and 7 "not free". Data Source: Freedom House.

Figure 7. Political Rights Ratings

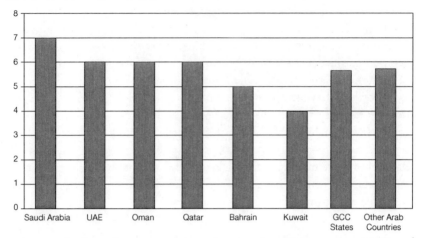

Beginning with ratings for 2003, countries whose combined average ratings fall between 3 and 5 are designated as "partly free", and those between 5.5 and 7 "not free". Data Source: Freedom House.

measure of political rights. In short, while the GCC has comparatively author-itarian politics in which citizens have little chance of holding governments accountable, those governments have seen it to be in their interest to manage economic development effectively. The resemblance to China, as noted above, is striking. The Gulf's ruling families appear to be functional substitutes for the CCP in the sense that they perform the key tasks of governance narrowly conceived, without being structurally accountable to their populations.

Turkey, by contrast, has developed comparatively good governance through a democratic process in which Islamism sought to enhance its legitimacy and elec-toral appeal by providing it. In much of the Arab world, the lack of democracy renders this strategy for Islamists almost irrelevant, although Moroccan, Jordanian, Egyptian and other Islamists do indeed try to broaden their appeal by appearing to both value and to be able to deliver good governance. Alas, incumbent authoritarian Arab governments, although having grudgingly and only marginally improved governance over the past generation, would probably still prefer to think that governance and development are independent, and therein lies the appeal to them of their mistaken conception of the China model.

Given the comparatively good performance of authoritarian GCC states in improving governance, and the fact of entrenched authoritarianism in much of the Muslim world, it is tempting to conclude that a focus on narrowly defined governance as embodied in the developmental state is a more realistic goal than the broader, shading-into-democracy good governance of the Washington Consensus. This, however, may not be the case, if only because most Muslim-majority states are so far from meeting the criteria of being developmental that an approach to good governance that emphasises accountability to political society may offer more hope. Ishrat Husain, for example, laments the failures of the Pakistani bureaucracy, and lays the blame for the country's developmental shortcomings at its doorstep. The same analysis could be offered of many, if not most, Muslim-majority countries. Administrative deficiencies are widespread precisely because they are symptomatic of more fundamental problems in their political economies that virtually guarantee that their states cannot orchestrate economic development as has China and other East Asian countries. Profound deficiencies in state–society relations are less likely to be addressed in the developmental state model than they are through an approach modelled on the Washington Consensus, so it may well be that the task that seems more difficult – namely, seeking to improve governance as broadly rather than narrowly defined – is ultimately easier than trying to gear up versions of developmental states, the traditions underlying which are probably even further from indigenous experiences than are those that gave rise to the Washington Consensus.

CONCLUSION: THE DIVERSITY OF APPROACHES TO DEVELOPMENT

Despite globalisation, the varied reactions of developing countries and regions to alternative development models suggest that emerging political economies are far from being homogenised. They are being informed by the Washington and Beijing Consensuses, as well as by other approaches and experiences, but slavish copying is notable in its absence. The appeal of China, based largely on the country's growth and the belief that its model seems to offer an alternative to the frequently disliked and rather discredited Washington Consensus, is tempered by actual engagement with China and, in many places, a perception that it would be neither possible nor preferable to seek to imitate its party-led, non-democratic political economy. The embrace of the Beijing Consensus has yet anywhere in the countries and regions looked at in this book to be tight enough for those locked into it to appreciate the magnitude of the task of emulating even the governance component of the China model, but if they did try it is unlikely they would find it any easier than implementing the ten commandments of the Washington Consensus. In sum, the globe is unlikely to turn the developmental clock back to the Cold War, when being on one side or the other in the developing world also meant adopting in substantial measure and paying a lot of lip service to the political economy model of that side's champion. Those days, thankfully, are over.

The challenge now is not to slavishly copy the socialist or some other hypothetical but politically endorsed path to development, but to actually fabricate one drawing upon international, regional and national experiences and resources. This is clearly the better way of proceeding, given the diversity of developing countries' histories, cultures, resource endowments, foreign relations and existing political economies. Yet it is no easy task to construct a successful development model, or even to modify a prototype. It is even hard to know where to look for inspiration. Neo-liberalism has been discredited by a global financial meltdown, to say nothing of Washington's political excesses. The China model, as Barbara Stallings put it, generates interest, but scepticism. The European Union likes to present itself as offering a model independent of that served up in Washington and one more appropriate to at least the Mediterranean area. But the cumbersome, bureaucratic approach of the EU, both at home and abroad, does little to endear it to its neighbours and it, in any case, is caught up in trying to address its own growing pains. In Latin America, populists of varying descriptions are trying to turn clocks back to the days of economic nationalism, and even autarky, but they are running up against economic realities and political opposition even at home, so their export potential is also limited.

In the Muslim world, the stirrings of an indigenous approach can be discerned, but it is fragmented between "globalisers" and "moralisers", or those who would emulate the West but in native garb, so to speak, and those who reject the West root and branch and seek to clothe themselves exclusively as locals. Islamic finance is dominated by the former, so is cut off from a potential populist base, thereby unable to convert economic into political resources and really shape Muslim political economies. For its part, populist Islamism has been kept at bay by entrenched regimes and has, in any case, not formulated a coherent model for Muslim political economies. Within the world of Muslim states, there is a great diversity of approaches to structuring economies and polities.

In sum, while the developing world is being transformed into an "emerging" one through globalisation, and its Muslim component is becoming more aware of its shared religion and the potential of that religion to contribute to development, the reality is one of ever greater eclecticism. The emergence of China simply reinforces that trend, in that it has caused almost everyone to re-think how development occurs. Nevertheless, Beijing, whatever its desires and its popularity, is probably even less likely to recognise itself in how states proceed with development than Washington has been. Models, after all, are theoretical constructs, whereas political economies are the product of contestation between political actors. They are bound, therefore, to be messy affairs, owing more to local political calculus than to the appeal of any foreign design, no matter how elegant and coherent.

NOTES

1. At the same time there is a strong desire in at least some of the developing world for China to develop its capacities to counterbalance the US. In the Arab world, a 2006 poll conducted by Zogby International and the Brookings Institution showed that China was second only to France as the country most Arabs would like to see emerge as a superpower. See Chris Zambelis and Brandon Gentry, "China through Arab eyes: American Influence in the Middle East", *Parameters*, US Army War College Quarterly, Spring 2008). Available at http://www.carlisle.army.mil/usawc/Parameters/o8spring/zambelis.htm

2. This conversation was reported to the author by one of the President's advisors in an interview, 20 January 2008.

3. Conversations with various Egyptian textile manufacturers with the author, 2007 and 2008.

4. William Hurst is by no means the only specialist on China to come to this conclusion. For a recent indictment of the Chinese model and its lack of sustainability, see Yasheng Huang, *Capitalism with Chinese Characteristics: Entrepreneurship and the State*, Cambridge: Cambridge University Press, 2008. Minxin Pei of the Carnegie Endowment also views the China model as having fatal flaws, including an inability to control corruption because of the over-large role of the state in the economy and lack of democracy. See, for example, Minxin Pei, "Corruption Threatens China's Future", *Policy Brief*, no. 55, October 2007, Carnegie Endowment for International Peace.

5. Chinese firms invested $15 billion in Sudan between 1996 and 2008, largely in the oil industry, thereby enabling Sudan to evade sanctions and drive its oil production up to some 500,000 barrels a day, of which China takes about 85 per cent. See "A Ravenous Dragon: Special Report on China's Quest for Resources", *The Economist*, 15 March 2008, pp. 3–18.

6. The Chairman of the Dubai International Financial Center, David Eldon, noted in regard to two-way investments between China and the Gulf that "rosy prospects don't necessarily translate into unabated exponential growth". He and others interviewed identified various problems confronting potential investors, one of whom concluded that there ultimately would be more Chinese investment in the Gulf than vice versa. Within days of the appearance of these comments, it was announced that Saudi Basic Industries Corporation (SABIC) would not be carrying through with the planned $5.2 billion petrochemical plant in China. No reasons were given. See Simeon Kerr, "With cash to burn, China and Mideast eye each other's riches", *Financial Times*, 6 September 2007, p. 10; and Reuters, 24 October 2007.

7. The EU Trade Commissioner, Peter Mandelson, for example, lashed out at China in September 2008 for its "unpredictable policy for mergers and acquisitions and barriers to market entry, including capital requirements, licensing and forced joint ventures". This was but one of many warnings by "international business and government leaders that China is becoming less attractive as a place to invest because of the restrictions companies face". Geoff Dyer, "EU hits out at Beijing's economic nationalism", *Financial Times* , 26 September 2008, p. 10.

8. Although both China and Venezuela appear eager to expand oil ties, the former out of resource needs and the latter out of political motives, problems of investment have arisen. See "Maoist Chavez strengthens oil ties with China", *Financial Times*, 25 September 2008, p. 8. A specialist on Chinese – Middle Eastern relations observes

that "For all their increased economic power and enhanced international standing, the Chinese still prefer not to be directly – or even indirectly – involved in regional conflicts so as to avoid alienating any side and undermining their interests". Yitzhak Schichor, "Competence and Incompetence: The Political Economy of China's Relations with the Middle East", *Asian Perspective*, vol. 30, no. 4, 2006, pp. 39–67.

9. In September 2008, for example, the Chinese and Egyptian governments signed a protocol calling for the establishment of the first Chinese school in Egypt financed by a $3.75 million grant from the former. On the occasion of the signing, the Chinese ambassador to Egypt, Wu Sike Hua, said, "When the number of Egyptians speaking Chinese increases, we hope that would boost our economic and cultural co-operation with Cairo and lure more Chinese investors into pumping their money here", *Al Ahram Weekly*, 18 September–1 October 2008.

10. Huang, *Capitalism with Chinese Characteristics*.

11. Tim Niblock with Monica Malik, *The Political Economy of Saudi Arabia*, London: Routledge, 2007.

12. The emphasis, however, should be placed on *subsequently*, for even in China, where spending on R&D is now sixth in the world in absolute terms and 1.34 per cent of GDP, which matches many OECD countries, "genuine technological innovation by Chinese companies remains surprisingly rare". The problem appears to lie in a series of policy deficiencies, including poor links between academia and industry. See Mure Dickie, "Research and development is slow to grow", *Financial Times*, 9 October 2007, p. 6.

13. Marcus Noland and Howard Pack, *The Arab Economies in a Changing World*, Washington, DC: Peterson Institute, 2007.

14. Ibid.

15. Moataz A. Fattah, *Democratic Values in the Muslim World*, London: Lynne Rienner, 2006.

16. Mohammed Ayoob, *The Many Faces of Political Islam: Religion and Politics in the Muslim World*, Ann Arbor, MI: University of Michigan Press, 2008.

17. According to Anour Hassoune, an expert at Moody's involved in rating Islamic financial bonds, or *sukuk*, "Islamic banking is a luxury product". It thrives only where there are established banking systems, so in Africa, for example, it remains a niche market. See "Turning towards Mecca", *The Economist*, 10 May 2008, p. 99.

18. Charles Tripp, *Islam and the Moral Economy: The Challenge of Capitalism*, Cambridge: Cambridge University Press, 2006.

19. See, for example, Mahmoud A. Al-Gamal, *Islamic Finance: Laws, Economics and Practice*, Cambridge: Cambridge University Press, 2006.

20. Interestingly, this narrower definition of governance is reflected in recent World Bank work, in which a more direct focus on government institutions is noticeable. See, for example, "On Governance and Growth", Washington: The World Bank (June 2008). http://web.worldbank.org/wbsite/external/countries/menaext/extmnar.

21. These preconditions for rapid growth can be compared to those identified in the 2008 Growth Report, which reviewed 13 countries that achieved growth rates of 7 per cent a year over at least 25 years. The five points they had in common were: fully exploited opportunities offered by the world economy; maintained macroeconomic stability; sustained high rates of saving and investment; allowing markets to allocate resources; and having committed, capable governments. www.growthcommission. org and Martin Wolf, "Useful dos and do nots for an economy set on growth", *Financial Times*, 4 June 2008, p. 19.

About the Contributors

Mohammed Ayoob is University Distinguished Professor of International Relations, Michigan State University. He holds a joint appointment at James Madison College and the Department of Political Science and is the Coordinator of the Muslim Studies Program. A specialist on issues of conflict and security in the post-colonial world, he has written on security issues relating to South Asia, the Middle East and Southeast Asia, as well as on conceptual and theoretical issues relating to security and conflict in the international system. In addition, he has published books and articles on the intersection of religion and politics in the Muslim world. He has authored and/or edited eleven books and published around ninety research papers in leading academic journals and as book chapters. His books include: *The Politics of Islamic Reassertion* (New York: St. Martin's Press, 1981) and *The Third World Security Predicament: State Making, Regional Conflict, and the International System* (Boulder, CO: Lynne Rienner Publishers, 1995). His latest book, *The Many Faces of Political Islam*, was published in 2007 by the University of Michigan Press. The book challenges other commonly held views that create what he calls "a highly distorted overall perception" of the Muslim world.

Catherine Boone is a professor within the Department of Government at the University of Texas at Austin. She received her PhD in Political Science from MIT. Boone specialises in comparative politics, with an emphasis on theories of political economy and economic development. She has conducted research on industrial, commercial and land-tenure policies in West Africa, where her work has been funded by the Social Science Research Council, Fulbright, the World Bank, and the Harvard Academy for International and Area Studies. Her current research focuses on territorial politics and rural property rights in contemporary Africa. She is author of *Merchant Capital and the Roots of State*

Power in Senegal (Cambridge and New York: Cambridge University Press, 1992), which was a finalist for the African Studies Association's Herskovitz book award, and *Political Topographies of the African State: Territorial Authority and Institutional Choice* (Cambridge and New York: Cambridge University Press, 2003), which won the Mattei Dogan Award from the Society for Comparative Research. She is currently serving as president of the West Africa Research Association, which directs the West African Research Center in Dakar, Senegal. In 2005, she was elected to the executive council of the American Political Science Assocation.

Dhawal Doshi is an undergraduate student on the Bridging the Disciplines program at the University of Texas at Austin.

Clement Henry is a professor within the Department of Government at the University of Texas at Austin. In addition to the politics of international oil, his research interests include banking systems in Muslim Mediterranean countries, Islamic banking, and the development of civil societies in the Arab world. In *The Mediterranean Debt Crescent* (1996, 1997) he examined inter-relationships between financial and political liberalisation in Algeria, Egypt, Morocco, Tunisia and Turkey. He has also co-authored, with Robert Springborg, *Globalization and the Politics of Development in the Middle East* (Cambridge: Cambridge University Press, 2001), and co-edited and contributed to *The Politics of Islamic Finance*(Edinburgh: Edinburgh University Press, 2004) with Rodney Wilson. Current research interests include the impact of political regimes upon economic policy-making and development in the Middle East and North Africa, dilemmas of financial liberalisation and transparency, applications of financial power to the Middle East peace process, and the theoretical implications of financial globalisation for comparative politics. Recent articles by Henry include a contribution to *Oil and Democracy in Iraq* (2007) and "Tunisia's 'Sweet Little Rogue' Regime" (2007) in *Worst of the Worst: Dealing with Repressive and Rogue Nations*.

William Hurst is Assistant Professor within the Department of Government at the University of Texas at Austin. He was previously a post-doctoral fellow at the Institute for Chinese Studies, Oxford University. He received his PhD in Political Science from University of California, Berkeley. His fields of research include Chinese politics and comparative politics. He is the author of *The Chinese Worker after Socialism* (Cambridge University Press), which is scheduled for release in 2009. Hurst's other publications include "Understanding Contentious Collective Action by Chinese Laid-off Workers: The Importance of Regional Political Economy", in *Studies in Comparative International Development* (vol. 39, no. 2, 2004) and "China's Contentious Pensioners", in *The China Quarterly*, co-authored with Kevin J. O'Brien (no. 170, 2002).

Ishrat Husain is chairman of the National Commission for Government Reform in Pakistan. Husain, who obtained his PhD in Economics from Boston University, was the governor of the State Bank of Pakistan for six years. He has previously held the post of Director for Central Asian Republics at the World Bank. This position's primary focus was the management of the World Bank's relations, policies, and programs with countries in Central Asia. Prior to this he was the director of the Poverty and Social Policy Department of the World Bank, where his responsibilities included poverty reduction, gender relations and dynamics, NGOs, and reform within the public sector. Husain served as chief economist for Africa and later became chief economist of the World Bank for the East Asian and Pacific region, with a focus on China from 1991 to 1994. He also assisted in the development of the World Bank's strategic approach to Latin American debt problems, which subsequently resulted in the Bank's support for the Brady Initiative of Debt Reduction. His publications include *Dollars, Debts, and Deficits* (Lahore: Vanguard Books, 2004) and *Pakistan: The Economy of an Elitist State* (Karachi: Oxford University Press, 1999).

Mushtaq Khan is Professor of Economics within the Faculty of Law and Social Sciences at SOAS. He received his PhD in Economics from Cambridge University. Khan's research interests lie in the areas of institutional economics, the economics of rent-seeking, corruption and clientelism, industrial policy, and state intervention in developing countries. Other interests include South and South East Asian economic development with a particular focus on the Indian subcontinent. Khan's teaching interests include microeconomics, the political economy of institutions and South Asian economic development. He is the editor (with Jomo K. S.) of *Rents, Rent-Seeking and Economic Development* (Cambridge: Cambridge University Press, 2000), editor (with George Giacaman and Inge Amundsen) of *State Formation in Palestine: Viability and Governance during a Social Transformation* (London: RoutledgeCurzon, 2004) and is the author of numerous chapters in books, including "Corruption and Governance in Early Capitalism: World Bank Strategies and their Limitations", in Jonathan Pincus and Jeffrey Winters (eds), *Reinventing the World Bank* (Ithaca, NY: Cornell University Press, 2002) and "The Capitalist Transformation", in Jomo K.S. and Erik Reinert (eds), *The Origins of Development Economics: How Schools of Economic Thought Have Addressed Development* (London: Zed Press, 2005). His writings have appeared in *Democratization, Journal of Agrarian Change, New Political Economy, American Economic Review, Economics of Transition, Journal of International Development* and *The European Journal of Development Research*.

Emma Murphy is Professor of Political Economy in the School of Government and International Affairs, University of Durham. She is the author of *Economic and Political Change in Tunisia: From Bourguiba to Ben Ali* (London: Macmillan, 1999) and co-author of *Israel: Challenges to Identity, Democracy and the State* (London: Routledge, 2002) as well as numerous articles on Israel and Palestine, foreign policy, economic liberalisation and political reform in the Arab world. Her current research interests include the impact of contemporary information and communication technologies on the region and the historiography of Mandate Palestine.

Robert Springborg is a professor in the Department of National Security Affairs at the Naval Postgraduate School in Monterey, California. From 2002 to 2008 he held the MBI Al Jaber Chair in Middle East Studies at SOAS and was director of its London Middle East Institute. He was Director of the American Research Centre in Egypt from 2000 to 2002. His publications include *Oil and Democracy in Iraq* (London: Saqi Books, 2007), two monographs on Egypt and another (as co-author) on the role of legislatures in political transactions in the Middle East. He is co-author (with James Bill) of a textbook on the comparative politics of the Middle East and (with Clement Henry) of *Globalization and the Politics of Development in the Middle East* (Cambridge: Cambridge University Press, 2001). He was associated with Macquarie University in Sydney, Australia, for twenty-seven years, where he became a university professor of Middle East Politics. While there, he founded and administered a Middle East Centre and served as president of the Australasian Middle East Studies Association. He has also taught at the University of California at Berkeley, the University of Pennsylvania, the University of Sydney, and Canterbury University.

Barbara Stallings is director of the Watson Institute and is a leading political economist who works on development issues, with a focus on Latin America and East Asia. Stallings is the William R. Rhodes Research Professor at the Institute, co-director of Brown's Graduate Program in Development, co-director of the Brown-Brandeis APEC Studies Center, and editor of *Studies in Comparative International Development*. Stallings has a PhD in Economics from the University of Cambridge and a PhD in Political Science from Stanford University. Her areas of interest range from economic reform and development in Latin America and East Asia to finance for development, development strategy and international political economy. She is author or editor of eleven books and numerous chapters and articles. Most recently, she co-authored: *Finance for Development: Latin America in Comparative Perspective* (Washington, DC: Brookings Institution, 2006). She has served on the editorial boards of several journals, including *Studies in Comparative International Development, Oxford Development Studies, Competition and Change, Oxford Companion to Politics of the World, International Studies Quarterly, American Journal of Political Science* and *Latin American Research Review*.

Jeff Tan is an assistant professor at AKU-ISMC, specialising in issues of development. He completed his PhD in Economics at SOAS, and has taught undergraduate and postgraduate courses in development studies at SOAS and the London School of Economics. His areas of specialisation include corruption, governance, entrepreneurship, industrial policy and urban transportation. He has published on privatisation, including *Privatization in Malaysia* (London: Routledge, 2008), and worked on governance and human rights in Malaysia.

Index

Entries in **bold** indicate tables or figures